Microsoft SharePoint Online for Office 365: Administering and configuring for the cloud

Bill English

PUBLISHED BY
Microsoft Press
A division of Microsoft Corporation
One Microsoft Way
Redmond, Washington 98052-6399

Library of Congress Control Number: 2015934867
ISBN: 978-1-5093-0014-3

Printed and bound in the United States of America.

First Printing

Microsoft Press books are available through booksellers and distributors worldwide. If you need support related to this book, email Microsoft Press Support at mspinput@microsoft.com. Please tell us what you think of this book at http://aka.ms/tellpress.

Acquisitions Editor: Karen Szall
Editorial Production: Christian Holdener, S4Carlisle Publishing Services
Technical Reviewer: Ben Curry; Technical Review services provided by Content Master, a member of CM Group, Ltd.
Copyeditor: Roger LeBlanc
Indexer: Jean Skipp
Cover: Twist Creative • Seattle

Contents at a glance

Contents

What do you think of this book? We want to hear from you!

Microsoft is interested in hearing your feedback so we can continually improve our books and learning resources for you. To participate in a brief online survey, please visit:

microsoft.com/learning/booksurvey

Introduction

Regardless of your title, if you're responsible for designing, configuring, implementing, or managing a SharePoint Online deployment, this book is for you. If you're a member of the team in your organization that is responsible for SharePoint Online in your environment, this book will help you understand what your team needs to think about when it comes to your deployment. If you're responsible for managing a consulting firm that is implementing SharePoint Online on your behalf, you need to read this book.

If you are totally new to SharePoint administration, this book will help you ramp up on how to administrate SharePoint Online—not only because I go through many (but not all) of the core "how to" tasks in which administrators engage, but because I also drop in comments as to "why" you're doing what you're doing and offer ideas to consider relative to that task. In fact, nearly all of Chapter 10, "Site-collection administration," has little to do with *how* to administrate a site collection—it is focused on the business issues that naturally bubble up when SharePoint Online is used.

Solving the core problems of governance, risk, compliance, taxonomies, processes, and training associated with a SharePoint Online deployment is the macro focus of this book and is, in my view, the core of good SharePoint administration. For those who are looking for deep technical drill-downs in the technology, there's a plethora of books, blog posts, podcasts, conferences, magazine articles, online articles, white papers, and websites that will satisfy your curiosities. But don't look to this book to reveal that type of knowledge. I didn't write this book for the highly technical audience.

About the companion content

The companion content for this book can be downloaded from the following page:

http://aka.ms/SPO/files

The companion content includes the following:

- Several processes in Visio form that you can modify to fit your own environment
- A document or artifact file plan in Word that will help you with your taxonomy and information organization planning efforts

Acknowledgments

It's been five years since I wrote my last book. From 2000 through 2010, I authored or co-authored 14 books. Then it turned out that I didn't write for five years. Writing this book reminded me how much I enjoyed the process of writing. I'm one of those nerds who likes to learn and write. It's as much a curse as it is a blessing.

I had also forgotten what a joy it is to work with Karen Szall, the project editor for this book. I've worked with her on several book projects before. As usual, she was not only professional and easy to work with, she didn't pester me when I got behind on the writing schedule. Karen, I'd love to work with you in the future, and, for what it's worth—whatever they're paying you, it isn't enough! You're the best!

My good friend Ben Curry—one of the owners at Summit 7 Systems—stepped up to the technical editor role on this project. He corrected mistakes, found errors, and added significant value to this book. While you won't see his name on the cover, you will see the results of his work on nearly every page. He and I co-authored books in the past, and he is also a highly acclaimed author in the SharePoint space. Any mistakes you find in the book are mine, not his. Thanks, Ben, for being a great friend and for helping out on short notice.

Roger LeBlanc was the copy editor on this book. I continue to be amazed at how good copy editors take average writing and turn it into something that just flows and yet is clear and concise. I don't have that ability, but Roger does. Thanks for your hard work, Roger. Along with me, all the readers of this book deeply appreciate your efforts!

Brett Lonsdale, the owner at Lightning Tools—a company you should become familiar with—stepped up on short notice to write Chapter 3, "Working with Business Connectivity Services." I can't think of anyone who knows the BCS technology better than Brett and his team. Brett wrote a great chapter and added real value to what is included in this book. Thanks, Brett, for your help, your flexibility, and your friendship.

Back here in Minnesota, I want to thank my wife, Kathy, for her continued support of my ever-changing workloads and environments. I can't think of anyone better to have married. Thanks for being my best friend and my wife. I also want to engage in a short contest with my two kids, David and Anna, who are both teenagers now. (Where did the time go?) Whoever reads this acknowledgement first and tells me they read it gets a free Caribou coffee and mug—your choice on both counts. As always: I love you both more than life itself.

Finally, I'd like to thank Jesus Christ, my Lord and Savior, for giving me the talent and the opportunity to write this book and without whom I would be lost forever.

Bill English

May 7, 2015

Maple Grove, Minnesota

Free ebooks from Microsoft Press

From technical overviews to in-depth information on special topics, the free ebooks from Microsoft Press cover a wide range of topics. These ebooks are available in PDF, EPUB, and Mobi for Kindle formats, ready for you to download at:

http://aka.ms/mspressfree

Check back often to see what is new!

Errata, updates, & book support

We've made every effort to ensure the accuracy of this book and its companion content. You can access updates to this book—in the form of a list of submitted errata and their related corrections—at:

http://aka.ms/SPO/errata

If you discover an error that is not already listed, please submit it to us at the same page.

If you need additional support, email Microsoft Press Book Support at *mspinput@microsoft.com*.

Please note that product support for Microsoft software and hardware is not offered through the previous addresses. For help with Microsoft software or hardware, go to *http://support.microsoft.com*.

We want to hear from you

At Microsoft Press, your satisfaction is our top priority, and your feedback our most valuable asset. Please tell us what you think of this book at:

http://aka.ms/tellpress

The survey is short, and we read every one of your comments and ideas. Thanks in advance for your input!

Stay in touch

Let's keep the conversation going! We're on Twitter: *http://twitter.com/MicrosoftPress*.

CHAPTER 1

An overview of the SharePoint Admin Center

Most system administrators who have experience working with Microsoft SharePoint Server 2013 or prior versions are familiar with the Central Administration interface. When Microsoft updated SharePoint Portal Server 2003 to SharePoint Server 2007, it abstracted the tasks performed by system administrators (those who manage the SharePoint servers and the overall SharePoint farm) into a common interface known as *Central Administration*. Site collections were managed by Site Collection Administrators and individual sites were managed by Site Administrators.

The same basic architecture exists today for SharePoint Online. However, the ability to administrate the *back end*—functions you might normally expect to administrate in Central Administration—is greatly diminished. The following administrative actions and configuration abilities that you'll find in Central Administration are missing or hidden in the SharePoint Admin Center in Office 365:

- Service application management
- Web application management
- Content database management
- Alternate access mappings
- Servers in the farm
- Services on the server
- Backup and Restore capabilities
- Claims-based authentication support

- Configuration wizards
- Distributed Cache
- Host-named Site Collections
- Managed accounts
- Patch management
- Quota templates
- Read-only database support
- Remote BLOB storage
- Request management
- Request throttling
- Resource throttling
- SharePoint health analyzer
- State service
- System status notifications
- Timer job management
- Usage reporting and logging

Other abilities to administrate and configure SharePoint 2013 will be limited compared to what you can do with an on-premises deployment, such as a limited use of Windows PowerShell commands, the ability to create external content sources, and the ability to create multiple term stores.

> ***MORE INFO*** **The *term store* is the SharePoint Online name for the Managed Metadata Application Service in SharePoint 2013. You can learn more about the term store by referencing Chapter 5, "Configuring and managing the term store."**

From this author's perspective, the SharePoint Online version that is included in the Office 365 E3 tenant exposes mainly the collaboration and introductory content-management parts of the fuller SharePoint 2013 administration experience. As you go through the interface, we'll note the elements you can administrate as well as go over the risk and governance considerations inherent in the different configuration options that will be available to you.

Comparing the different SharePoint Online versions

The information in Table 1-1—taken from the Microsoft website at *https://products.office.com/en-us/sharepoint/compare-sharepoint-plans*—outlines the SharePoint features and services you'll receive, depending on which tenant your organization selects. At the time of this writing, this table is accurate.

MORE INFO The product team keeps an updated, online spreadsheet that lists the different plan elements. It is kept up to date at *https://onedrive.live.com/view.aspx?cid=41e528b989881d4a&id=documents&resid=41E528B989881D4A!194&app=Excel&authkey=!AJTaHXrAwKrOd68&*.

TABLE 1-1 Comparison of SharePoint on-premises and online features with Office 365 tenant levels

	SharePoint Server		**SharePoint Online**	
	Standard	**Enterprise**	**Plan 1**	**Plan 2**
Apps				
App Catalog and Marketplace	N	N	N	N
Collaboration				
Team Sites	I	I	I	I
Work Management	N	N	N	N
External Sharing			N	N
Search				
Basic Search	I	I	I	I
Standard Search	I	I	I	I
Enterprise Search		I		I
Content Management				
Content Management	I	I	I	I
Records Management	I	I	I	I
E-discovery, ACM, Compliance		N		N
Business Intelligence				
Excel Services, PowerPivot, PowerView		N		N
Scorecards and Dashboards		I		
Business Solutions				
Access Services		I	I	I
Visio Services		I		I
Form-Based Application		I		I
SharePoint 2013 Workflow	N	N	N	N
Business Connectivity Services	I	I		I
N = New I = Included				

Finding the SharePoint Admin Center in Office 365

When you first log in to your Office 365 tenant, you're brought to the home page, which lists the various features and functionalities your organization has purchased (shown in Figure 1-1). If you have administrative privileges, you'll have an Admin button appear as part of this lineup. (See the Admin tile in the lower-right part of the screen in Figure 1-1.) It might appear in a different sequence in your environment, which is not a problem.

FIGURE 1-1 Office 365 home page

When you click the Admin tile, you'll be taken to the Office 365 Admin Center (shown in Figure 1-2) that offers up an Office 365 administration dashboard. Because this book is focused on SharePoint administration in Office 365, I won't take time to cover the balance of the back end. You'll navigate to the SharePoint Admin Center by expanding the Admin link at the bottom of the left pane and then clicking the SharePoint link.

> ***NOTE*** **The Office 365 Admin Center displays the current health of each part of the tenant. Referring to Figure 1-2, you'll notice several different messages for the various services of this tenant. For those that have a notification (such as "Service degraded"), just click the down arrow and you'll be presented with the entire notification and the historical actions Microsoft has or is taking to resolve the issue. At the bottom of the full notification, you'll see a View Details And History link, which will present the full notification in a table format presented in a new webpage, which makes it easier to read and follow the action history to resolve the problem.**

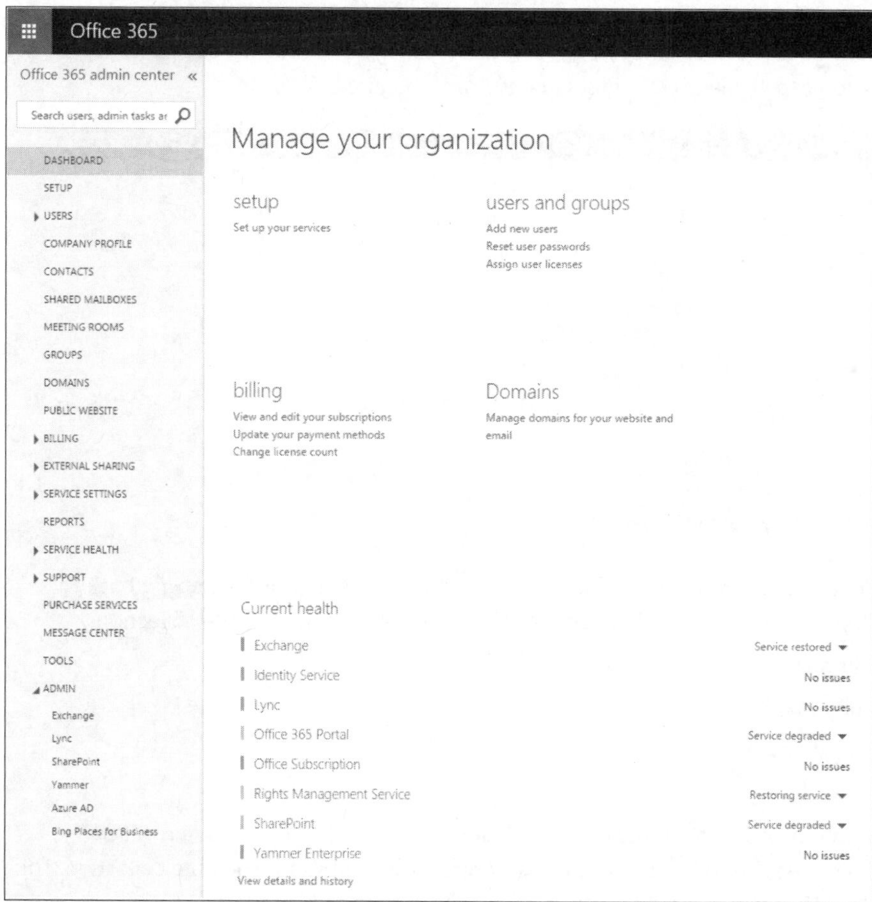

FIGURE 1-2 The Office 365 Admin Center

A brief walkthrough of the SharePoint Admin Center interface

The SharePoint Admin Center will contain a left pane of links to the major administrative areas. The larger, right pane is context sensitive to the various links you can select in the left pane. For example, if you click the BCS link in the left pane, configuration elements specific to Business Connectivity Services (BCS) will appear in the right pane. If you click the Apps link in the left pane, Apps-specific configuration elements will appear in the right pane.

> ***TIP*** **Bear in mind that the options that appear in the right pane might vary from tenant to tenant based on other tenant-level configuration settings, such as the First Release Updates and External Sharing settings that have been selected.**

When you first come to the SharePoint Admin Center, you're automatically focused on the Site Collections link in the left pane, which means you will see the site collection administration capabilities in the right pane (shown in Figure 1-3).

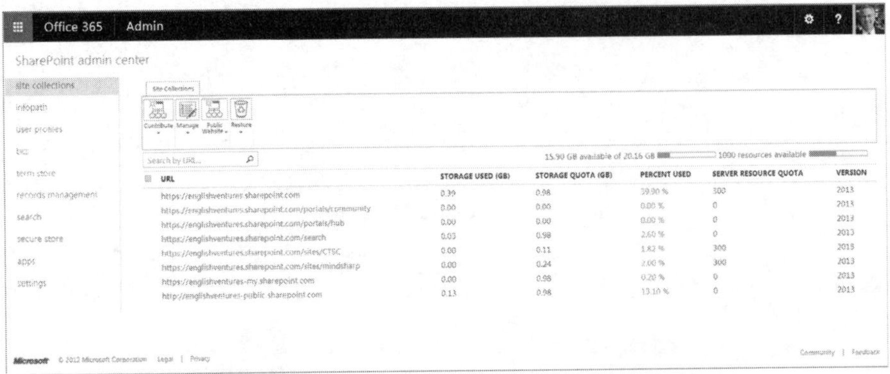

FIGURE 1-3 Default view of the SharePoint Admin Center

SharePoint administration in Office 365 retains the ribbon interface. Referring back to Figure 1-3, you'll note there are four administrative activities related to site collections:

- Contribute
- Manage
- Public Website
- Restore

You'll also notice the URL for each existing site collection appears, including which managed path the site collection is sitting within and the metrics for each site collection. This is actually a different storage model than what you have in the SharePoint 2013 on-premises platform. This model is based on usage, making it easier to manage availability of storage across your SharePoint Online team sites.

Storage is pooled in SharePoint Online. The concept of reserved storage now applies only at the tenant level for SharePoint Online. Site collections (other than Microsoft OneDrive for Business) no longer tie up blocks of reserved storage. Instead, only the actual storage used counts against total pooled storage.

To arrive at the percentages you see in Figure 1-3 in the Percent Used column, you'll divide the Storage Used by the Storage Quota. For example, for the site collection *http://englishventures.sharepoint.com*, you divide the Storage Used number (0.39 GB) by the Storage Quota (0.98 GB) to calculate the 39.9% Percent Used figure.

The Server Resource Quota column lists a site-collection metric calculated by SharePoint Online. The main purpose of resource quotas is to limit the risk that sandboxed custom code can have on available resources on a site collection. Resource usage generally includes performance data (such as processor time and unhandled exceptions) that pertain to the code in sandboxed solutions. When the level exceeds the daily quota, the sandbox is turned off for the site collection. It is not like storage; the server resource quota will not go over the limitation. Your organization is assigned a total Server Resource Pool that is based on the total number of users. By default, when you create a site collection it is assigned a server resource quota of 300. Generally, this an acceptable quota. If you do not want to allow any sandbox solutions to be used within your site collection, you can set this value to zero (0).

> ***NOTE*** **In the lower-right corner of each page is a Community link that will take you to the Office 365 online communities, where you can ask questions and find technical answers. Networking with other Office 365 administrators is something that will help you improve your administrative skills, find support, and advance your career.**

Managing site collections

Four core administrative groups are in the ribbon you can commit when it comes to site collections in Office 365. They are found under the following headings:

- Contribute
- Manage
- Public website
- Restore

Contribute

The first group—Contribute—is where you'll create and delete site collections. (See Figure 1-4.)

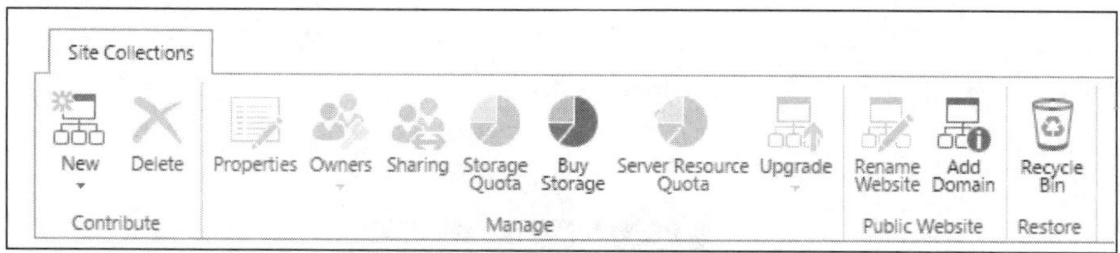

FIGURE 1-4 Site Collections management headings

In the Contribute area, you're given the option to either create a new site collection or delete an existing site collection. (For the latter, you need to already have selected the site collection for this button to be active.) When you create a new site collection, it can be either a private site collection or a public website.

Creating a private site collection

When you choose to create a new private website, you're presented with the New Site Collection dialog box illustrated in Figure 1-5. You'll need to name the site collection; select the managed path underneath which the site collections should be created; select the language, template, time zone, administrator, and storage quota; and set the server resource quota. After you click OK, a new site collection will be provisioned online and will be available within a few minutes.

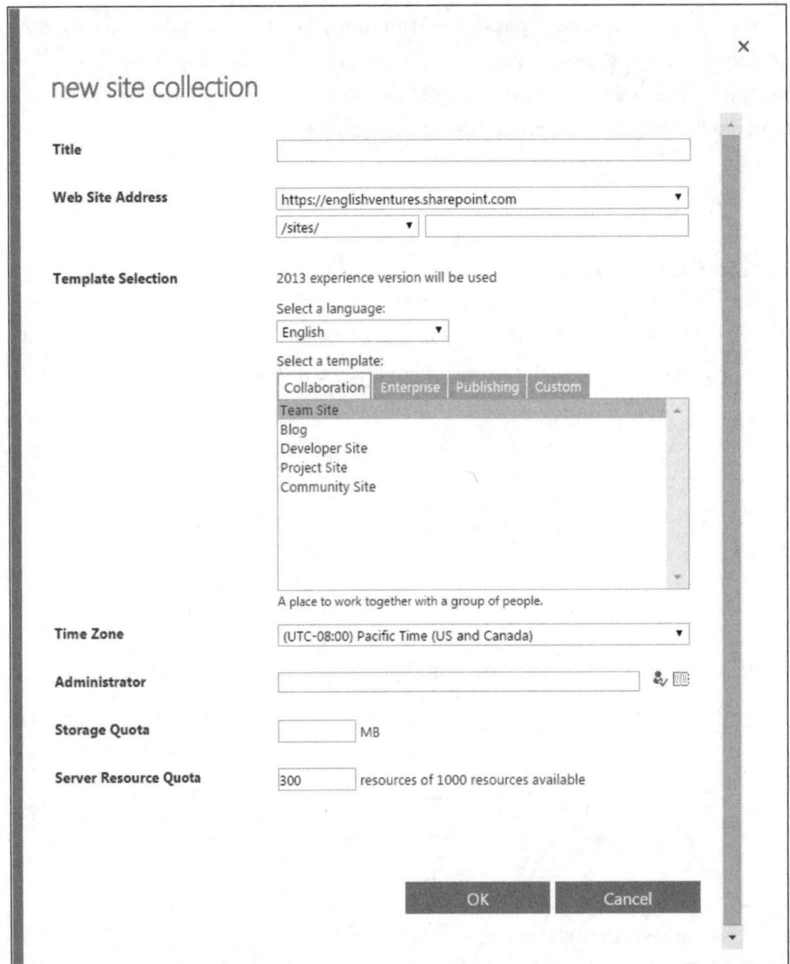

FIGURE 1-5 Creating a New Site Collection dialog box

> ***NOTE*** **Because you cannot create custom managed paths in SharePoint Online, you'll be creating all of your site collections beneath the Sites Managed path. The Portals Managed path was deprecated in January 2015.**

From a governance perspective, if you intend to implement a robust findability solution in SharePoint Online that will ensure content is easily and quickly found, you'll need to focus on two major elements: site-collection names and a robust taxonomy you can develop in the term store. For an on-premises deployment, I recommend spending time developing descriptions and intuitive managed paths that can act as categories for your site collections. In SharePoint Online, custom managed paths cannot be created, so more emphasis is placed on the naming of the site collection (for search purposes) and on a robust taxonomy that will help users find documents via search that discriminates between documents of similar type and content.

> ***NOTE*** **If you want users to be able to create their own sites, navigate to the Settings link in the left pane and then scroll down to the Start A Site configuration options (shown in Figure 1-6). This is the place where you can turn on the creation of new sites inside an existing site collection. This is not the same thing as the on-premises Self Service Site Creation. A New button will appear on the Sites page that lists all the site collections in SharePoint Online.**

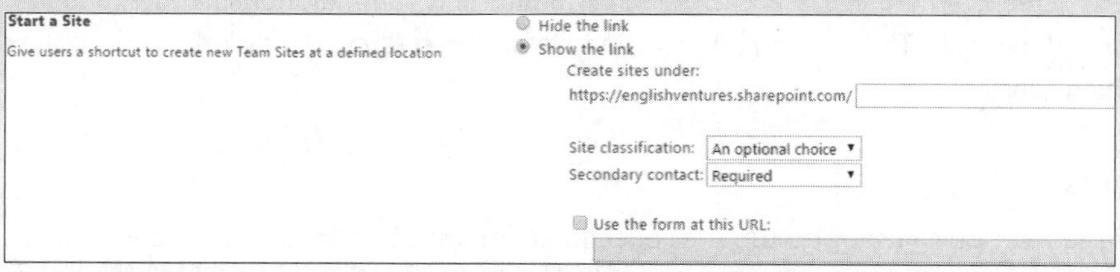

FIGURE 1-6 Start A Site configuration options

Creating a new public website

At the time of this writing, when Office 365 provisions SharePoint Online, it does not automatically create a new public-facing site collection provisioned with the publishing site template. However, if your tenant was created before March 9, 2015, you'll have the ability to create a new public website for two years in your tenant. After this date, this functionality is removed for new customers.

You'll find the new Public Website link is disabled unless you deleted the default public website and you need to create a new one. Each tenant can create only one public website, but other websites can be shared externally. The interface for creating a new public website is similar to creating a new private website. In combination with the Public Website administrative actions, you'll create a new public website here with the domain you want to use and then use the Add Domain functionality to map and expose that domain's public website via your Office 365 environment.

Manage

Under the Manage area, you're able to configure the following for each site collection:

- Properties

- Site collection owners
- Sharing
- Storage quota
- Buying more storage
- Server resource quota
- Upgrade

Let's take a look at each part.

Properties

To see the properties of a site collection, you'll first need to select the site collection by selecting the check box to the left of the site collection. Once you do this, the Properties button will activate. When you click the Properties button, you'll be able to see a number of details about the site collection, such as who the owners are, a clickable link to the site collection, the number of subsites, and storage and resource information. Unlike most property screens, where you're accustomed to committing configuration changes, this screen is informational only. The only action you can take on this screen is to click through to the site collection itself.

Owners

In this section, you can set who the site collection administrators are as well as configure a Support Partner for the site collection. In addition to adding a partner at the tenant level to perform delegated administration, you can also add the Microsoft partner at the SharePoint Site Collection level. They can be configured as either Help Desk Admins or Tenant Admins.

Tenant Admins have full rights to your Office 365 deployment, so be careful to whom you assign this permission. The initial user account used to create your Office 365 deployment will be given this right. Help Desk Admins have read-only permission to all objects within scope and have password reset permissions. However, they cannot reset the password for the Tenant, Billing, or User account administrators.

It's worth noting that the user interface can be confusing. When you click the Owners button, you're just revealing two other links to defined Site Collection Administrators and Support Partner roles. In SharePoint Online, *Owners* really refers to Site Owners, but in this instance, it *doesn't* refer to Site Owners. It's just the name they chose to put on the button in the ribbon.

Sharing

Users have the ability to share content hosted in an Office 365 environment with others who are outside their organization. On a site-collection basis, you can set the sharing abilities of your users. Sharing is enabled by default in the tenant settings. If it is disabled in the tenant admin area, users will receive a "Sharing is disabled in Tenant Settings" message on the configuration screen.

NOTE *Sharing* is the updated term for what we used to call *giving permissions*. In this context, *sharing* should not be confused with *share permissions*, as was done in the NTFS file system. In the old NTFS file system, you would have two levels of permissions: NTFS permissions and, if the folder or file was shared, *shared permissions*. Because you are now in a web-based context, you no longer have NTFS file permissions. So when you *share*, you are giving another user *permissions* to a resource or object. You no longer give or assign permissions, you *share*.

You have three options for sharing at the site-collection level:

- Don't allow sharing at all.
- Allow sharing with external users, and have them authenticate into your directory.
- Allow sharing with external users, and have them authenticate using the Anonymous user account.

Sharing with external users is controlled both at the tenant and site-collection levels. If you don't want users to have the ability to share their sites, turn sharing off at the tenant level. To find where this is, navigate to the tenant administration area and click the External Sharing link. It will reveal four links:

- Sharing Overview
- Sites
- Calendar
- Lync (if purchased as part of your tenant)

If you click the Sharing Overview link, you'll see that you can turn on or off the sharing of SharePoint sites, calendars, Lync, and integrated applications (shown in Figure 1-7). Simply toggle the on-screen sliders to turn on or off sharing as needed by your tenant users and your governance rules. Figure 1-7 shows how easy it is to turn sharing on or off at the tenant level. If you click the Sites link underneath External Sharing (not illustrated), you'll be able to configure sharing on a global basis by first selecting all the site collections and then clearing the Let External People Access Your Site check box. If you want to enable sharing on a site-collection-by-site-collection basis, first select the Let External People Access Your Sites check box, select the site collections for which you want to enable external sharing, and then select one of the two radio buttons beneath the check box:

- No Anonymous Guest Links. Only Allow Sharing With Authenticated Users.
- Allow Sharing With Anonymous Guest Links For Your Sites And Documents.

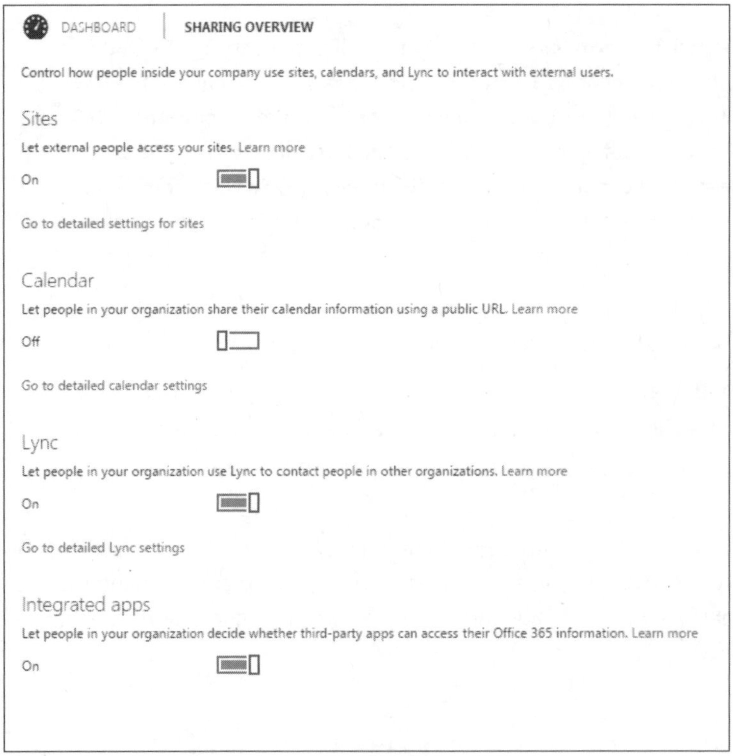

DASHBOARD | SHARING OVERVIEW

Control how people inside your company use sites, calendars, and Lync to interact with external users.

Sites

Let external people access your sites. Learn more

On

Go to detailed settings for sites

Calendar

Let people in your organization share their calendar information using a public URL. Learn more

Off

Go to detailed calendar settings

Lync

Let people in your organization use Lync to contact people in other organizations. Learn more

On

Go to detailed Lync settings

Integrated apps

Let people in your organization decide whether third-party apps can access their Office 365 information. Learn more

On

FIGURE 1-7 The Sharing Overview screen at the tenant level

From a risk-management perspective, it is recommended that you disable external sharing at the tenant level and then enable it selectively at the site-collection level only if needed. The reason I say this is because I assume that your content is valuable and its' dissemination to the wrong parties would be injurious to your organization. So knowing who has logged in to your SharePoint Online, when they logged in, and what resources they accessed would be a minimum risk-and-compliance management effort toward proactively protecting against data loss. This will require turning on auditing within each site collection and reviewing the audit logs from time to time, but these compliance processes should not be overlooked in a world where the hacking of websites and the theft of information is on the rise.

A note about governance

The term *governance* traditionally has been used in the context of a company's board of directors. For our purposes in this book, a good working definition is this: a balanced allocation of control among various stakeholder groups that results in each group experiencing the highest reasonable benefit from their participation in SharePoint Online.

The system of checks and balances inherent within governance is meant to prevent abuse by various players in a SharePoint environment. When organizations ignore good governance—especially in the area of Enterprise Content Management (ECM)—everyone suffers. This is true regardless of the type of organization in question: for-profit, nonprofit, military, social, or government. Hence, it is important to understand the core principles from which effective governance is created:

- Governance is derived, never created. Governance is a result of identifying risk and then enumerating how that risk can be mitigated (or minimized) by compliance actions. If you start with governance instead of risk, you will end up creating a set of rules few will follow and even fewer will understand. But if you start with risk and write up actions (or inactions) that minimize or mitigate the risk, most users will understand and follow the enforcement of those actions. As it pertains to SharePoint Online, the question to ask is "What set of risks does SharePoint Online represent to my organization?"
- Govern what you can enforce; guideline everything else. Because governance is about the enforcement of compliance actions that lower risk, the concept of governance has a strong enforcement flavor. If politics, culture, policies, or other obstacles keep you from enforcing compliance, don't try to govern it. Just put out guidelines and collaborate with others to achieve whatever level of compliance you can achieve while informing the higher powers in your organization of the risks they are assuming through lack of enforcement.
- People enforce the rules, not software. People will figure out ways around software enforcement. Governance is inherently an interpersonal activity.
- Governance requires transparency, cooperation, and consistency. Often, compliance actions are taken within a process that helps move the process forward. Silos of action or information are difficult to govern without visibility and authority in that silo. A lack of cooperation among team members, a lack of transparency in the reporting systems, governance that is not consistently enforced, or all of these will result in a broken system in which the strongest get what they want to the detriment of everyone else. When this occurs, an agency cost has been experienced by the organization.
- Governance is inherently relational. Ultimately, good governance balances competing interests of stakeholder groups within an organization. The assumption here is that each group is willing to give a little for the overall good of the organization and the ongoing goodwill in relationships between the groups. The more political, isolated, or conflictual the relationships are between the stakeholder groups, the less likely it is that good GRC can be implemented within an organization.

Storage and resources

You can change your storage quotas on each site collection by highlighting the site collection in question and then clicking the Storage Quota button on the ribbon. Note that the dialog box will compare the collection's storage to that of the tenant. Note also that the illustration you see in Figure 1-8 will apply only to site collections where you have never set a storage quota. Once a quota is set, if you go back into this dialog box and set the values back to default, you'll receive an error saying that you need to set values within a certain range.

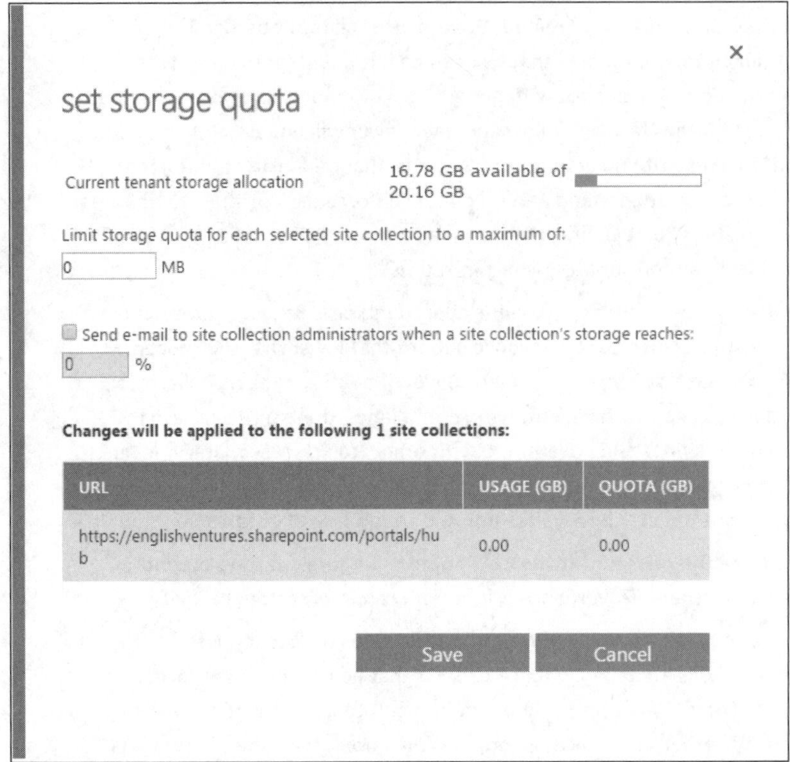

FIGURE 1-8 Default dialog box for setting storage quotas on a site collection

If you need more storage, you can buy it directly from within this interface. The ease with which you can buy storage is well thought out by Microsoft.

You can also manage server resources on a per-site collection basis. As stated, you'll need to do this only if you're working with sandboxed code in a site collection. Otherwise, you can safely leave this setting at zero (0).

Upgrading a site collection

As Office 365 and SharePoint Online mature, future versions of these platforms will be released. As they are applied to your tenant, your site collection administrators may or may not want to manage the upgrade of their site collection to the new version. If you're tasked with managing the upgrades, you'll want to highlight the site collection that needs upgrading, click the Upgrade button, and follow the on-screen prompts.

When compared to the on-premises version, this upgrade path lacks any ability to create a side-by-side comparison of the old and new site collections, the ability to test whether or not the site collection is "ready" for the upgrade, or any rollback features if something goes wrong.

Public website

SharePoint Online has some interesting features when it comes to managing a public website. For example, you can add domains to your tenant for management and then assign those domains to the public website. You can also take an existing public website and rename it, which is to say that you can assign a different domain name to the website and offer up the same site under a new root domain. Microsoft Exchange, Lync, and SharePoint all work with custom domains in Office 365. You need not assign the same custom domain to all three—each can be individually assigned or not be assigned a custom domain name. If done properly, Office 365 will work with multiple domains that you own and manage.

> ***REMINDER*** **If your tenant was created after March 9, 2015, you will not have a public website with which to work.**

You'll want to first manage your domains, so first click Add Domain (which is shown in Figure 1-9). When you do this, you're presented with the Manage Domains page in your Office 365 tenant. Note that when you highlight a domain, you're given the links on the right side to manage DNS, fix issues, or remove the domain from your tenant.

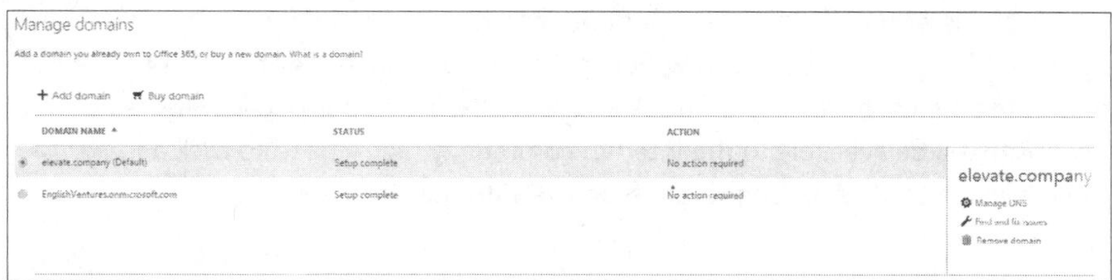

FIGURE 1-9 Manage Domains page in Office 365

If you want to add a domain, click the Add Domain link and then follow the on-screen wizard. If you want to add a new domain and you first need to purchase it, click the Buy Domain link. You'll be working with the *GoDaddy* registrar to register your new domain name.

NOTE Registering multiple domain names isn't just about management of your public-facing website. It also allows you to manage multiple Exchange and Lync domains in a single Office 365 tenant.

The balance of the steps you'll need to perform can be found in this online article: *https://support.office.com/en-US/Article/Use-your-custom-domain-to-rename-your-Public-Website-when-you-have-other-Office-365-services-33b7714c-9f04-4be4-a70b-6ac14c7dfac3?ui=en-US&rs=en-US&ad=US*. Note that when you're ready to associate your domain name with your public website, you'll first highlight your public website and then click the Rename Website button.

When you do this, you'll be presented with the online dialog box shown in Figure 1-10.

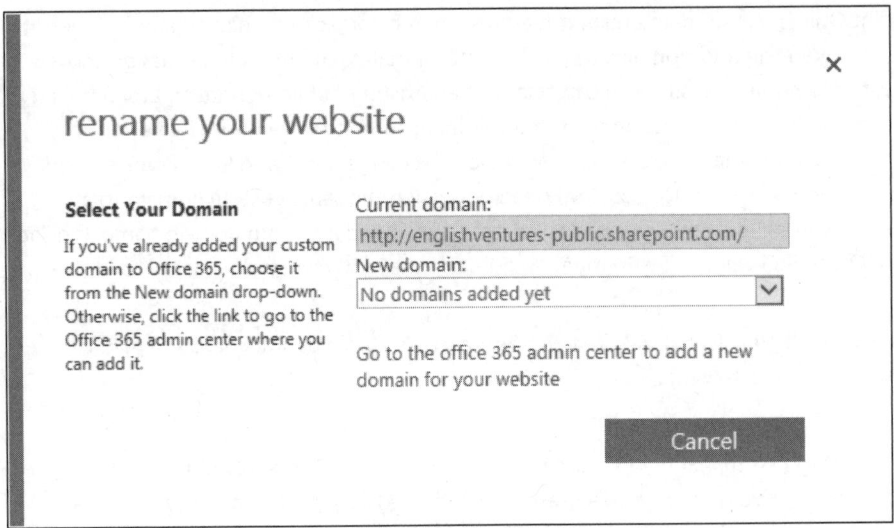

FIGURE 1-10 Rename Your Website dialog box

At the time of this writing, team sites cannot be renamed—only the public-facing website that was created after you clicked the New/Public Website button in the SharePoint Online ribbon. And note that just because you "hook up" your DNS with your public website doesn't mean the website will be available to the Internet community. You'll need to click a *Make Website Online* link in the Site Settings area to go live with the website.

Site Collection Recycle Bin

The Recycle Bin captures deleted content, lists, sites, and site collections in SharePoint Online. You also can restore that content to the location from which it was deleted. The restoration process brings back the data to the same state it was in when it was deleted.

To delete a site collection, select the check box next to the URL you want to delete (not illustrated), and then click the Delete button on the ribbon. The site collection will be moved to the Recycle Bin momentarily.

Once you put something in the Recycle Bin, you have 90 days to restore it. The interface will list the objects that have been moved into the bin and how long you have to restore that object. When it comes to a site collection, deleting the collection also means deleting all sites, lists, libraries, and content items as a single unit. And just as you can delete all those objects as a single unit, you can restore them as a single unit as well (assuming you have enough storage space to do so). Note that restoring My Sites requires a support call to Microsoft.

To restore a site collection, click the Restore Deleted Items button and the collection will be restored to the location and state it was in when it was deleted. (See Figure 1-11.)

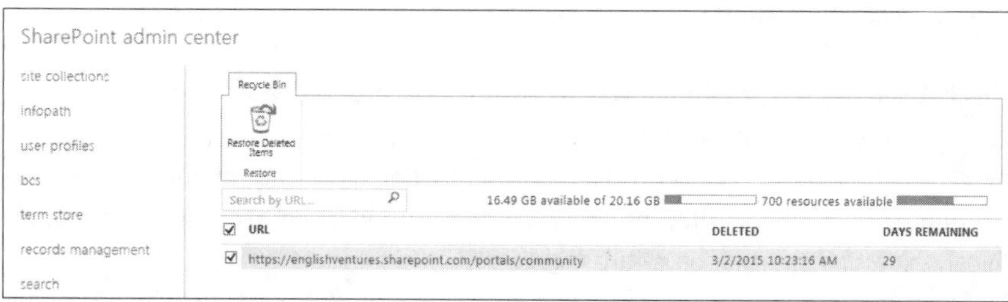

FIGURE 1-11 Getting ready to restore a site collection

Restoring a site collection might take a few minutes or longer, depending on the size of the collection you're restoring.

InfoPath

InfoPath is available for use in the Office 365 tenant. Forms can be presented in the interface as webpages that are built using InfoPath. InfoPath can be utilized using browser-enabled form templates. Form designers can publish user form templates to a list or a form library in a SharePoint Online site collection. Because user form templates can be deployed by many users, a server can potentially host thousands of user form templates.

When an Infopath form is designed, the designer can choose to create a form template that can be opened or filled out in either InfoPath or a Web browser. If the form template can be opened and filled out by using a browser, it is called a *browser-compatible form template.* This type of form template can then be browser enabled when it is published in an Office 365 tenant that has InfoPath Forms Services running. Configuring the forms to be browser enabled gives users who don't have InfoPath installed on their computers the ability to use the form through their browser.

Illustrated in Figure 1-12 are the two selections you can configure:

- Allow users to browser-enable form templates
- Render form templates that are browser-enabled by users

By default, both are selected. Deselect them only if you want to diminish the usability of InfoPath forms in your environment.

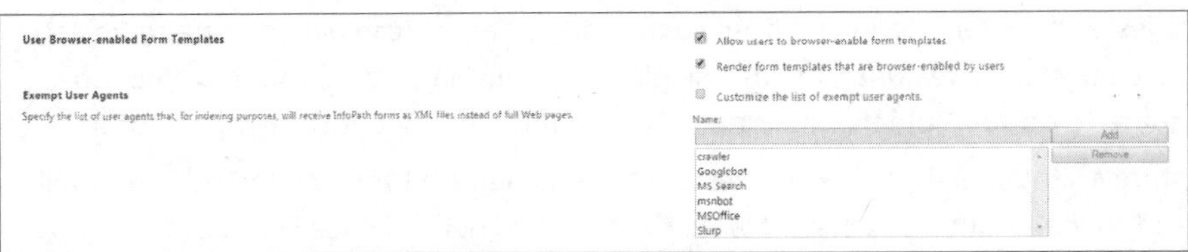

FIGURE 1-12 InfoPath form configurations

Referring back to Figure 1-12, there is a way to ensure search bots see InfoPath forms XML rather than sending the search bot the entire webpage. This configuration is used to make indexing InfoPath forms faster and easier. This means that when a user agent you've specified as exempt encounters an InfoPath form, the form will be returned as an XML file (which looks like a hierarchical text file) instead of an entire webpage.

The existing user agents—Crawler, Googlebot, MS Search, MSNbot, MSOffice, and Slurp—represent search bots that are commonly used in an enterprise environment. If a different search technology is being used and InfoPath files are not being indexed, the user agent for that technology should be added to the collection using an Add method of this collection.

By default, you send XML files to the following bots:

- Crawler
- Googlebot
- MS Search
- MSNbot
- MSOffice
- Slurp

> ***NOTE*** A *bot* is a software application that runs automated tasks over the Internet. Typically, bots perform simple and repetitive tasks that humans could do, but that would take much longer to finish if performed by humans. When indexing content is run by bots, the content is read and then placed into the index. Happily, each server can have a file called robots.txt, containing rules for the restriction of content that should be crawled by a bot. Most bots honor the robots.txt file as a courtesy to the server and content owners.

Summary

In this chapter, I presented an introduction to SharePoint Online and gave you several links to locations that have comparison charts of the features and functionalities available in the online and on-premises versions. I covered how to manage site collections, rename public sites, as well as how to create, delete, and restore them. I explained a bit about governance and why understanding the risks involved in a decision is really the foundation of good governance.

In the next chapter, we'll turn our attention to finding expertise and people by using the User Profiles. Most SharePoint implementations, whether online or on-premises, focus on the management of content and experience. It is to this latter topic—experience and expertise—to which we now turn our attention.

CHAPTER 2

Managing user profiles

In this chapter, we're going to dive into the management of user profiles and I'll explain why user profiles are important to larger organizations that use Microsoft Office 365 and SharePoint Online. User profiles can be the bane of your existence or one of the big wins for your organization. Much of how you and your users experience user profiles in SharePoint Online is directly related to how well you manage this part and then present it to your organization.

As with most software platforms, it doesn't do much good to turn on platform features if they get in the way of how people work, the processes under which they are most comfortable working, and the inputs and outputs of their daily routines. Just because SharePoint Online *can* do something for your organization doesn't mean that it *should*.

Yet I am hard-pressed to explain, except in the smallest of environments, how a robust use of user profiles will cause damage or slow processes down. Indeed, I believe the opposite is the reality. User profiles organize expertise and experience—two elements that reside inside people and that cannot be easily codified. So making your users organize their experience such that their core value to the organization can be found, leveraged, and easily used—it seems to me—makes huge sense.

The SharePoint Online version does not include any of the synchronization administrative activities that you'll find in an on-premises deployment. Compare Figures 2-1 and 2-2 and you'll see that I won't be covering any synchronization topics that you might normally expect to see in a SharePoint administration book, because those tasks have been deprecated in SharePoint Online for the Information Technology professional (IT pro).

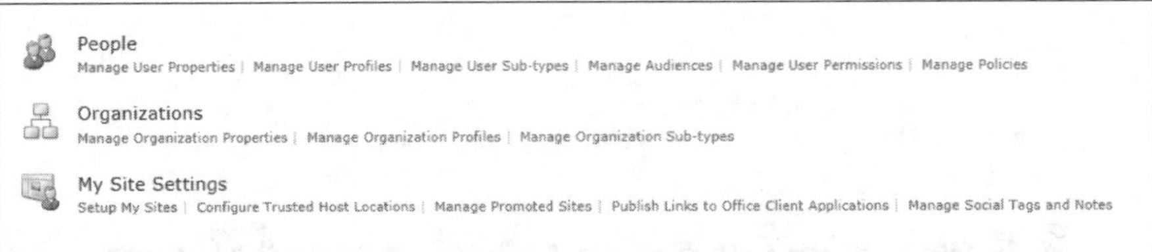

FIGURE 2-1 SharePoint Online User Profiles administration interface

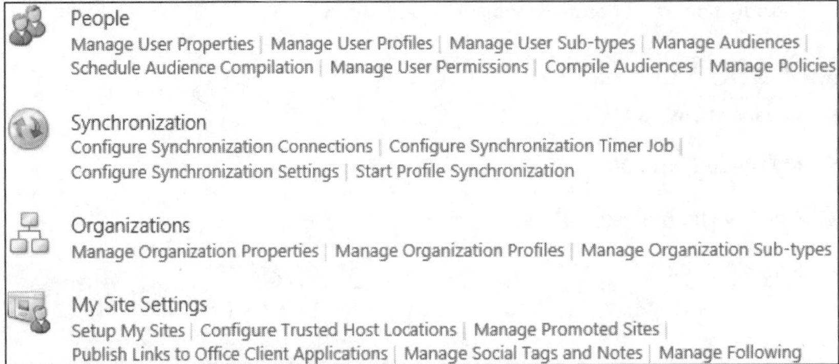

FIGURE 2-2 SharePoint On-Premises User Profile Services administrative interface

Introduction to user profiles, audiences, and My Sites

A user profile is a collection of user properties along with the policies and settings associated with each of those properties. A user profile is a description of a single user—not just that user's account, but the user's skills, experiences, expertise, and other metadata that can be useful in finding that user for particular purposes.

By default, the user-profile properties are populated from the Azure Active Directory service via a one-way synchronization at least once every 24 hours. If your organization manually created user accounts in the Office 365 directory service, users will receive Microsoft Azure Active Directory credentials for signing into the Azure Active Directory service. Similar to SharePoint 2013, Office 365 performs only authorization. It leaves authentication to the Azure Active Directory. These credentials are separate from other desktop or corporate credentials, although in hybrid implementations, there will be a synchronization with your on-premises Active Directory using the Azure Active Directory Connect tool. You'll use the Office 365 Admin Center to make changes to these user accounts.

If your organization is synchronizing Azure Active Directory with an on-premises Active Directory, your user profiles are being synchronized with the Azure Active Directory, which is then synched with SharePoint Online user profiles. Active Directory information goes in only one direction—from the on-premises Active Directory server to Azure Active Directory, which is then synchronized with SharePoint Online. This ensures that user information in SharePoint Online reflects the most current and accurate state of your user data in Active Directory.

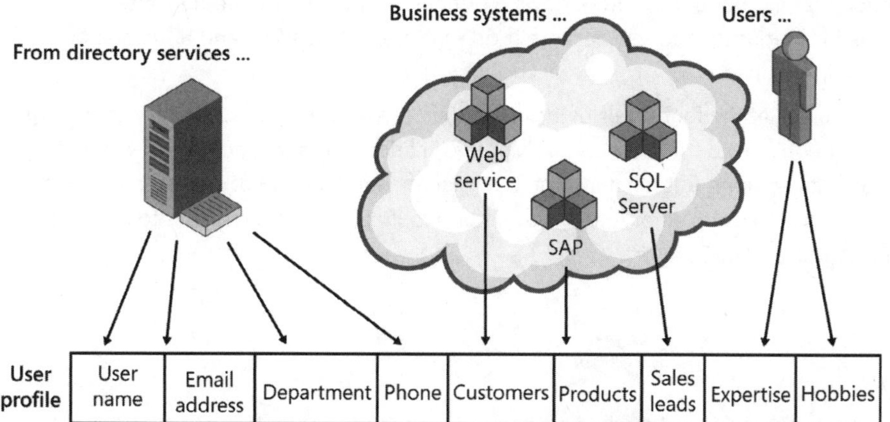

Not all profile information is synchronized from a directory service. Each profile property can be sourced from a different location, such as direct user input, HR systems, directory services, or all of these. New profile properties created within SharePoint Online can pull from various systems, but these custom properties cannot write back to those systems.

Somewhat similar to profiles are *audiences*. Audiences enable organizations to target content to users based on who they are when they come to the page. Audiences are built at the profile layer but applied at the site and web-part layers, depending on how the audience is used. Audiences can be defined by one of the following elements or a combination of them:

- Membership in a distribution list
- Membership in a Microsoft Windows security group
- Location in organizational reporting structure
- Public user-profile properties

Audiences are not a security feature. For example, even if a person is not a member of an audience, if she has permissions to a web part and has the URL of that web part, she will be able to access the content within the web part. So think of audiences as a view-crafting feature—you get to select what people see when they come to the page based on a set of predefined characteristics that are defined within a set of audience rules.

My Site settings and experiences are also affected by user profiles. My Sites are essentially personal portals that give individual users the ability to have a one-to-many collaboration path with the enterprise. My Sites are where the social features of SharePoint Online are consumed (for the most part) and represent a type of personal space that can be individualized directly by the user.

People

People often represent the highest level of information in your organization. *Tacit* knowledge (knowledge that has not been written down) continues to be the most sought-after knowledge in most organizations, because it often represents wisdom and understanding that isn't easily codified.

When you look at the four levels of information in the following illustration, you can swiftly discern that people need the top two levels of information—understanding and wisdom—to make excellent decisions. But most information management and retrieval systems are not built with this hierarchy in mind. And besides, how would you build a term set to describe tacit knowledge, anyway?

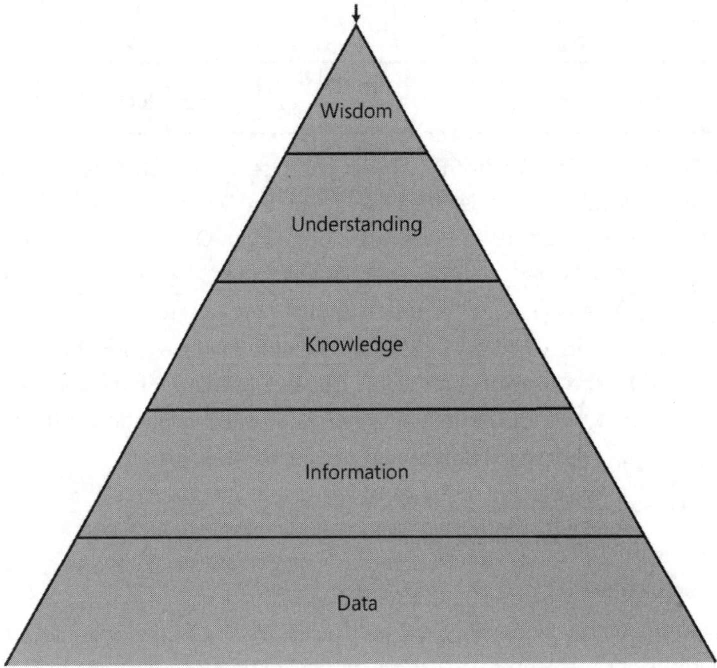

The levels of information can be described as follows:

- **Level 1 – Data** This is just the raw data, such as numbers (1, 2, 3) or symbols (a, b, c, or "this", "car"). I'll create a running example here—we'll use "20" as our data.
- **Level 2 – Information** This is where the Data is given some context. For example, the "20" is useless until it has context, such as "20 dollars", where "20" is data, "20 dollars" is information.
- **Level 3 – Knowledge** This is where information is related to another piece of information—for example, if "20 dollars" is related to the 10 dollar price of

two cappuccinos. At this point, you know you have enough to purchase the two cappuccinos, but perhaps not enough to purchase two concert tickets that might cost 200 dollars.

- **Level 4 – Understanding** This is where Knowledge is put into use or is made actionable. For example, you might decide that asking that special person out for two cappuccinos is a great idea, so you understand that to spend time with that special person, you'll need to spend some of that 20 dollars.
- **Level 5 – Wisdom** This is where Understanding is evaluated and filtered through our intuition, training, and experience. For example, you might decide that it's a wise choice to ask that special person out for two cappuccinos, but after spending time with him or her, you realize that it was not as wise a choice as you initially thought.

Understanding and wisdom come with experience and time. Until you've been there, done that, you don't really *know* what to do in a given situation. But if you've been through similar experiences several times, when the next similar scenario presents itself, you'll have instinctive wisdom about what to do or not do. Combining experience with intuition and relevant data is the essence of wisdom. Not everyone can do this in your organization, but those who can become leaders and decision makers.

> ***MORE INFO*** **SharePoint Online operates in all five levels. It can hold raw data in lists or provide lookups to databases. Information can be related in SharePoint Online, not only by relating lists, but by using the Managed Metadata Service and the User Profile Service. Relating term sets to documents and user profiles to accounts is an excellent example of how SharePoint can enable the relating of data.**
>
> **SharePoint provides knowledge-based environments by supporting document collaboration, document management, and other intelligence-oriented services, such as Power BI, Excel Services, and SQL Reporting Services. SharePoint Online supports Understanding—actionable content—by surfacing the right content to the right people at the time they need it to make decisions. This can be accomplished through a robust Search deployment, complete with accurate content types, result sets, and result templates. Finally, wisdom can be codified through community sites and blogs.**
>
> **SharePoint Online can interact with all five levels of information and become much more than a collaboration tool—it can become an intelligence tool for your organization.**

This is why organizing elements that point to experience and expertise are so important to any organization. For example, if my company is building out the fall marketing campaign, would it not be helpful to me to talk with the leaders of past marketing campaigns so that I can know what *not* to do as well as what to do? If my company employs 10,000 people, finding the right people might be difficult—perhaps they have moved on to different jobs with different titles or perhaps they have left the company altogether.

So organizing people—their experience and expertise—can be a huge benefit to your organization. Consider creating profile fields that allow users to be organized based on the following characteristics:

- Past titles
- Current titles
- Degrees earned
- Industry certificates earned
- Industry licenses and credentials earned
- Awards received
- Projects worked on
- Past reporting relationships
- Hobbies
- Current skills
- Department
- Internal training completed
- Schools attended

The list could go on and on. My point is that you need to find ways to describe what people know and what they can do in a way that helps others who need that knowledge or those skills find them swiftly and easily.

Manage user properties

When you click the Manage User Properties link under the People section, you're taken to the page where you can create, modify, and delete user-profile properties. The default list is pretty extensive, comprising roughly 99 profile fields. Still, you will likely think of more fields to create that will be better descriptors in your environment. To create a new profile field, click the New Property link (not illustrated).

Once the New Property link is selected you'll be presented with a screen to create a new profile property. (See Figure 2-3.)

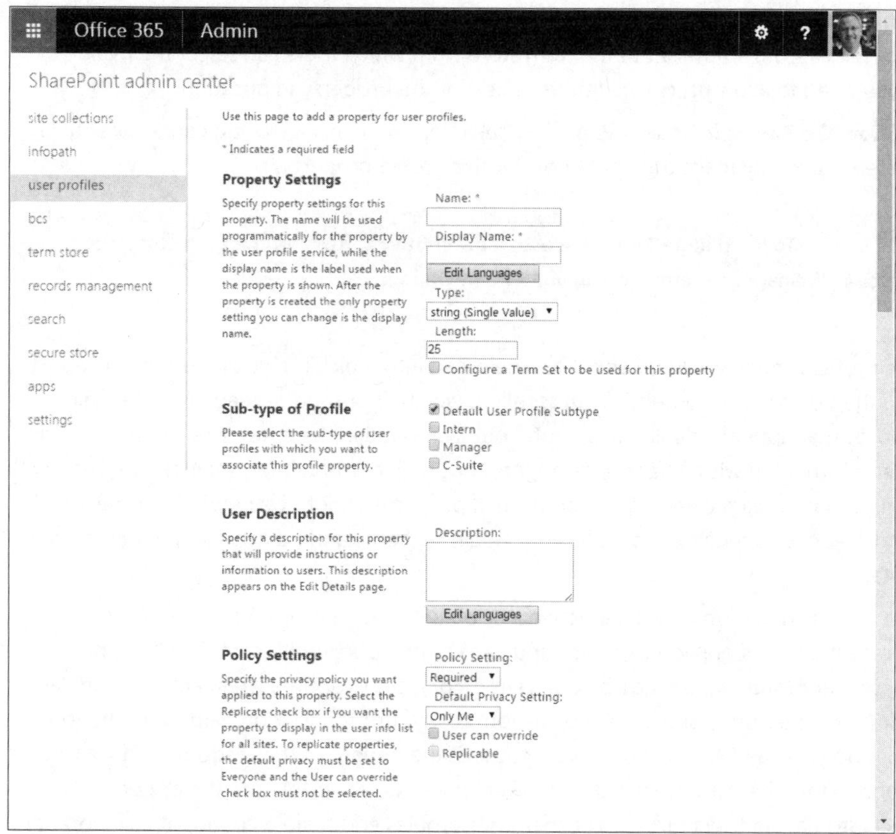

FIGURE 2-3 The new profile creation screen in SharePoint Online

When creating the new profile property, there are several key decision points you should address. If you combine the use of descriptive terms from the term store with the user profiles, you can achieve significant organization and increase the findability of expertise. Use these property definitions to your advantage (I'll discuss the more important configurations here—space limits my ability to go in depth into each configuration option):

- **Configure A Term Set To Be Used For This Property** If the values for this property can be built into a pick-list rather than a free-text value, the list should be built in the term store and consumed by the profile property. Having a standard set of terms from which to pick differentiates *meaning* between each term. Also, it helps ensure everyone uses the same set of terms rather than having each user enter a term that is meaningful to them but lacks meaning to others. For example, in a list of colleges attended, a standard term might be "University of Minnesota," whereas a meaningful term for a person who has attended that school might be simply "Minnesota" or "U of M." Shortcut terms or abbreviations should be avoided in standard term sets so that the terms that appear are both meaningful and clear as to their meaning.

- **Allow Users To Edit The Values For This Property** If you're going to expose a list of values from a term set in the term store from which users can select their values, you need to allow users to edit the values for the property in question.
- **Show On The Edit Details Page** By selecting this check box, you can ensure that users can easily make their selection for this profile property.

MORE INFO **To learn more about the use of descriptive terms and the term store, see Chapter 4, "Managing a term store in SharePoint Online."**

If the profile property values cannot be coalesced into a pick list, you're left with users entering their own values; potentially misspelling words, inputting garbage into the field, or using words that are individually meaningful but lack value in the enterprise. Most users will not enter information with nefarious intentions, but they can unwittingly cause confusion with the terms and phrases they enter. Although such properties might be helpful in some way, I would advise that, as much as possible, you should rely on standard lists for the user-profile metadata.

From a risk and governance perspective, not building out a robust user-profile system can represent a loss of applied expertise and can create opportunity costs in which the same or similar mistakes are made by different employees over time when acting in similar capacities. Acquired understanding and wisdom that your organization paid for in the form of salaries goes unused when people work without the benefit of the wisdom of those who have gone before them. Compliance that lowers the risks represented in the opportunity costs includes having users fully fill out their user profiles and build a culture of collaboration across organizational teams, departments, divisions, and hierarchies. Of course, this assumes that the profile properties can tightly discriminate between users and surface experience and expertise in a way that helps propel your organization forward in fulfilling its strategic objectives.

Manage subtypes

Profile subtypes can be used to create a different set of properties for a different set of users. For example, you can create a subtype that categorizes a user as either an intern or a full-time employee. So, instead of having a one-size-fits-all profile for every user in your organization, each user type (defined by you, the system administrator) can have its own set of profile properties. For example, you might want to create the following sets of profiles: Manager and Intern. Hence, you would draw up something like this:

Profile Property	Manager	Intern
About Me	Yes	No
Department	Yes	Yes
Skills	Yes	Yes

Profile Property	Manager	Intern
Current Job Title	Yes	No
Current School	No	Yes
Degrees Earned	Yes	No
Former Job Titles	Yes	No

While all these properties would be created within the overall user-profile service, the subtypes would allow you to associate each property with one profile type or more and then assign that profile type to the users.

Manage audiences

Creating audiences is a straightforward process. You first create the audience and decide if membership in the audience should satisfy all the rules that will define the audience or any one of the rules that defines the audience. After creating the audience, you need to create the rules that will define membership in the audience.

Membership (shown in Figure 2-4) can be defined in these pragmatic ways:

- Existing membership in an Azure security group, distribution list, or organizational hierarchy
- Existing reporting relationship, such as whether the user reports to another user account
- A particular value assigned to a particular profile property—for example, a user whose Department property in his profile is defined as "Accounting"
- A particular value *not* assigned to a particular profile property—for example, a user whose City in her profile is anything but "Minneapolis"

More than one rule can define membership in an audience, so you can combine multiple rules to create unique audiences. For example, let's say Juan has 120 people who report to him, but they work in three locations: Minneapolis, Indianapolis, and London. You want to build an audience for those who report to Juan but include only those who live in Minneapolis and who are working in the Marketing department. So you create three rules:

- **Rule 1** User reports to ("under" is the word used in the interface) Juan
- **Rule 2** User's Office Location equals "Minneapolis"
- **Rule 3** User's Department equals "Marketing"

The rules are not parsed in any particular order, so they can be taken as a whole. For each distinct aspect of the membership, you should plan to build a rule that defines that aspect and not try to combine two aspects into the same rule.

Audiences are applied at the site and web-part layers. In most web parts, you'll find the ability to assign an audience under the Advanced properties of the web part, which are shown in Figure 2-4.

FIGURE 2-4 Target Audience input box in the Advanced properties section of a web part

Audiences you create in the SharePoint Admin Center will appear as Global Audiences (as shown in Figure 2-5) after you click the Browse button.

Note that audiences don't need to be created only from the Global Audiences. Audiences also can be assigned from distribution groups, security groups, or both from your directory service as well as from SharePoint groups from within your site collection. This gives your site-collection administrators the ability to create audiences without looping through the SharePoint Admin Center.

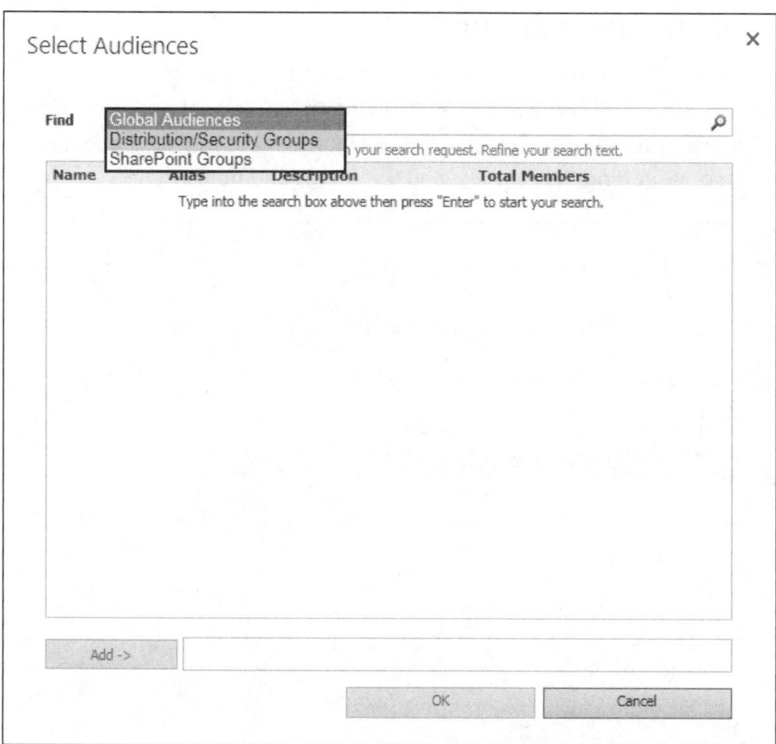

FIGURE 2-5 The Select Audiences screen, where you can create audiences from multiple sources

This is not something that you, the SharePoint system administrator, tries to control. Recall that audiences are not a security feature—they are a view-crafting feature. If it is advantageous to your users within a site collection to create SharePoint groups and then use them as audiences, this should be supported. This is the type of ownership-of-collaboration processes that you'll want to foster in your environment.

From a governance perspective, if end users are selecting groups or distribution lists to build audiences, it would be ideal if they have a way to enumerate the memberships without having to loop through the IT department. Keeping the administration transaction costs low is essential to SharePoint Online being well adopted within your environment. If users don't have a way to do this, they might assign an audience to a resource and either overexpose or underexpose that resource in the interface.

Although this isn't a security issue, it could be an irritant that causes unnecessary support cycles. It is better to anticipate the potential support and process problems in advance and fix them before they cause real problems in your environment and, perhaps, dampen enthusiasm for SharePoint Online adoption.

Manage user profile permissions

When you click the Manage User Permissions link within the People section of the User Profiles page, you'll be presented with a dialog box within which you can set permissions for who can create My Sites (shown as Create Personal Site in Figure 2-6) as well as configure settings for following people, editing their profile, and using tags and notes.

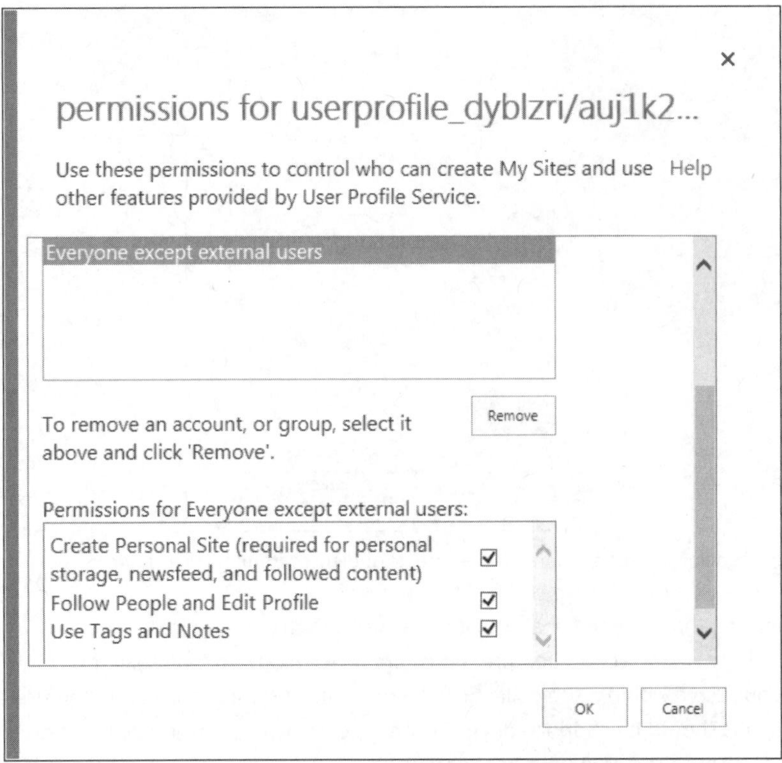

FIGURE 2-6 The dialog box that displays when you click Manage User Permissions

By default, the Everyone Except External Users is applied, which allows every user to perform all these actions, but you can restrict permissions by individual account or by group. The groups can be created within SharePoint Online, Azure Active Directory, or Windows Active Directory (if you're in a hybrid environment) and consumed from a number of sources. These sources appear when you click the Address Book button to select which users and groups you want to manage for this purpose. (See Figure 2-7.) Of course, these sources need to be properly configured and populated before they will be of any value to you. Just because the source appears here—such as Forms Auth—doesn't mean you can click on that source and find groups configured within them.

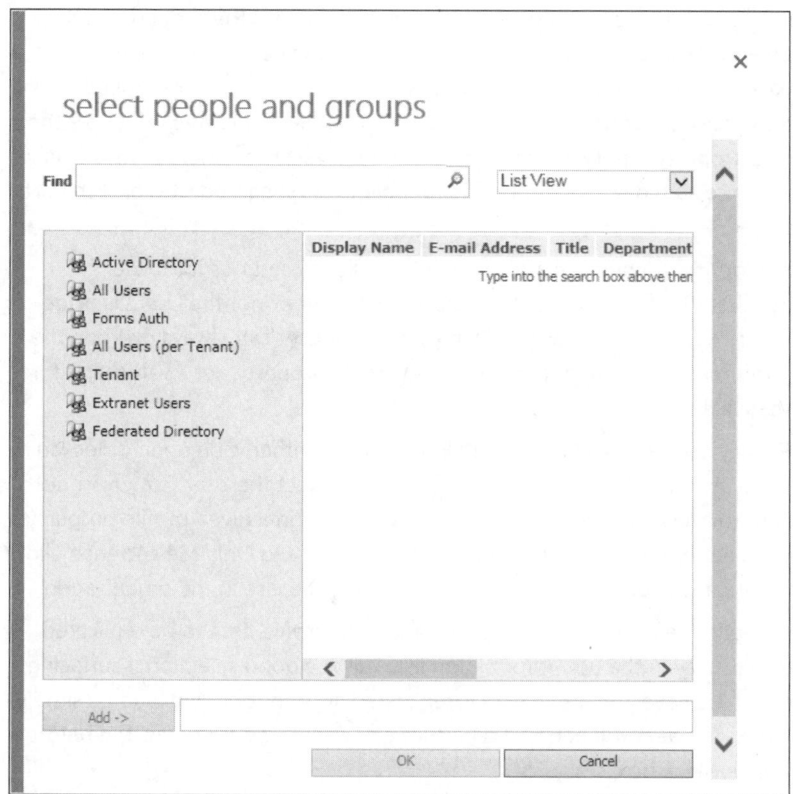

FIGURE 2-7 The Select People And Groups dialog box

Once you select a group, you can assign permissions to it such that membership in that group opens up the features and functionalities stated earlier. A common example of how this is used is for My Site creation and administration. I know of Microsoft customers who created a "Ready For My Site" (or some other name that was meaningful to them) security group in Windows Active Directory and assigned the available permissions to that group (refer back to Figure 2-6). As users attended training specific to My Sites and social technologies in SharePoint Online, their accounts were added into the Ready For My Site security group and thus were given permission to create a new personal site and engage in social activities.

Manage policies

Policies are used to govern the visibility of information in user-profile properties to others in the organization. These policies really represent privacy options that you, as the system administrator, configure on a global basis per profile property. This granularity might require additional administrative effort on your part, but it also enables each profile property to be aligned with your organization's existing privacy and sharing policies.

The policies can be required, optional, or disabled. *Required* means the property must contain information and the information is shared based on default access. *Optional* means the property is created but its values are supplied by each user if they are not supplied automatically. In the case of the former, each user decides whether to provide values for the property or leave the property empty. *Disabled* means the property or feature is visible only to the User Profile Service administrator. It does not appear in personalized sites or web parts, and it cannot be shared.

The User Override option enables users to change the visibility settings for those properties when this check box is selected. Regardless of whether or not the User Override option is selected, when you create a new profile property, the user can always override the setting. Essentially, this means you cannot create a new profile property, set a value, and force users to live with that value.

The two basic Privacy choices are Only Me and Everyone. It's either wide open or locked down to the individual user who the profile is describing. You select the User Can Override check box if you want to allow users to make their own selection on a given profile property. The most common way to use this check box is to set the property to Only Me and then allow users to choose if they want to open up that property to everyone else in the organization.

If you select the Replicable check box, you're allowing user-profile data to be replicated to the various sites to display in the user information list. This is a good selection if surfacing social data is your goal. However, once the data is replicated, it cannot be removed by simply clearing this check box. The data will persist. So be sure you want this data replicated before selecting the Replicable check box.

For confidential or sensitive profile descriptors, it's best to leave it at the setting you select and then clear the User Can Override check box.

NOTE **My Sites are private by default. Make My Sites Public is a privacy setting that an administrator can use to make all users' My Sites public by default. The Make My Sites Public setting is located in the User Profile service application under Setup My Sites. Even if an administrator configures any of these policy settings, these policy settings are overridden if the Make My Sites Public setting is selected.**

Organizations

Similar to how users can have profiles in SharePoint Online, organizations can have profiles too. Where the user fits within the larger organization chart can be exposed using the Org Chart web part that is included in SharePoint Online. It is a web part that must be added to the user's My Site.

The Org Chart web part that was visible under the About Me section of MySites in previous versions of SharePoint is now hidden in SharePoint 2013 by default. But when you view the About Me page of any other employee it is displayed. This behavior is by design, because it leads to better performance.

In previous versions of SharePoint, the profile page always loaded the Org Chart web part. Loading peer, manager, and direct-report data actually requires an extra database lookup, which contributes to a longer page load time. Because most users prefer to have their personal profile page load faster than to see their own position in the organizational hierarchy, the Org Chart web part is hidden when a user views her own profile page.

> ***NOTE*** **You will need Silverlight installed to run the Organization Chart web part.**

Each user will need to add the organization chart to his My Site. A user starts by logging in to his My Site. Because each My Site is a site collection, each user is the Site Collection administrator of his own My Site. Once a user is logged in, he should open Site Settings and select the Quick Launch link under the Look And Feel section. When the user does this, he is presented with the Quick Launch screen (shown in Figure 2-8), in which he can add new headings and navigation links. Have the user click New Heading in the interface.

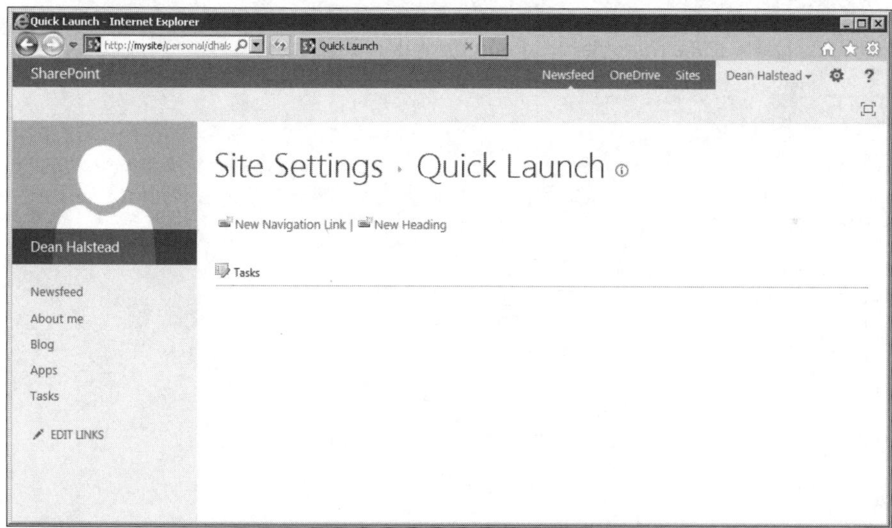

FIGURE 2-8 Quick Launch screen

After selecting New Heading, the user sets the web address to **http://<my site host collection root site URL>/organizationview.aspx** and sets the description to **Organization Chart**.

IMPORTANT **Be sure to have your users enter the exact same description into the Description field so that there is visual consistency across your organization when using this web part.**

You also should prescribe where this entry should appear in the heading hierarchy. By prescribing and enforcing the heading name and location, you'll create a more usable and enjoyable experience for those who use this web part to find experience and expertise within the organization. Because there is no way to *enforce* this prescription within SharePoint Online itself, I think it is best to use spot checks as your enforcement mechanism. So visit the public My Sites for a randomly selected number of users each month and visually check that their organization chart is properly working, titled correctly, and placed in the prescribed sequence within the Quick Launch hierarchy.

After pictures and About Me information is filled in, you'll find the Organization Chart (shown in Figure 2-9) to be rather helpful in traversing your organization chart to find the right individual(s) you need to connect with at any given time.

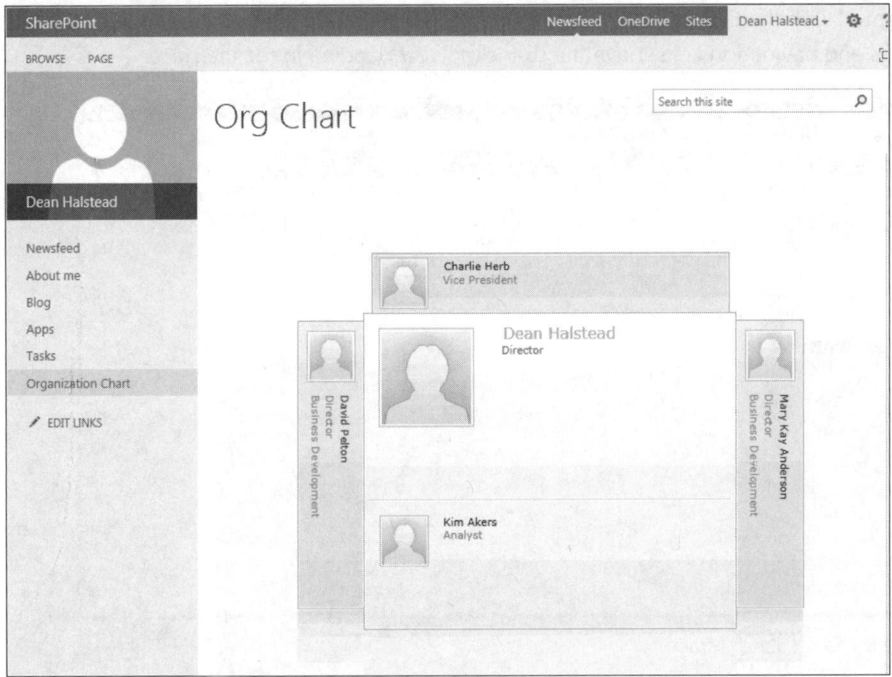

FIGURE 2-9 Organization chart in SharePoint Online

Note that this chart is focused on Harry Truman's place within the organization even though I'm on Millard Fillmore's public My Site. This means the entire chart can be traversed from any user's My Site that has the chart exposed.

Remember, this organization chart is sourced from your directory services. If you haven't filled in the organization information in the directory services, the organization chart can't do its job. In Windows Active Directory, you need to have filled in the Organization tab to achieve a baseline of information with which the Organization Chart web part can work. (See Figure 2-10.) If you're not importing information from Windows Active Directory and you're using only Azure Active Directory, you won't find an Organization page in the user's properties in Azure Active Directory.

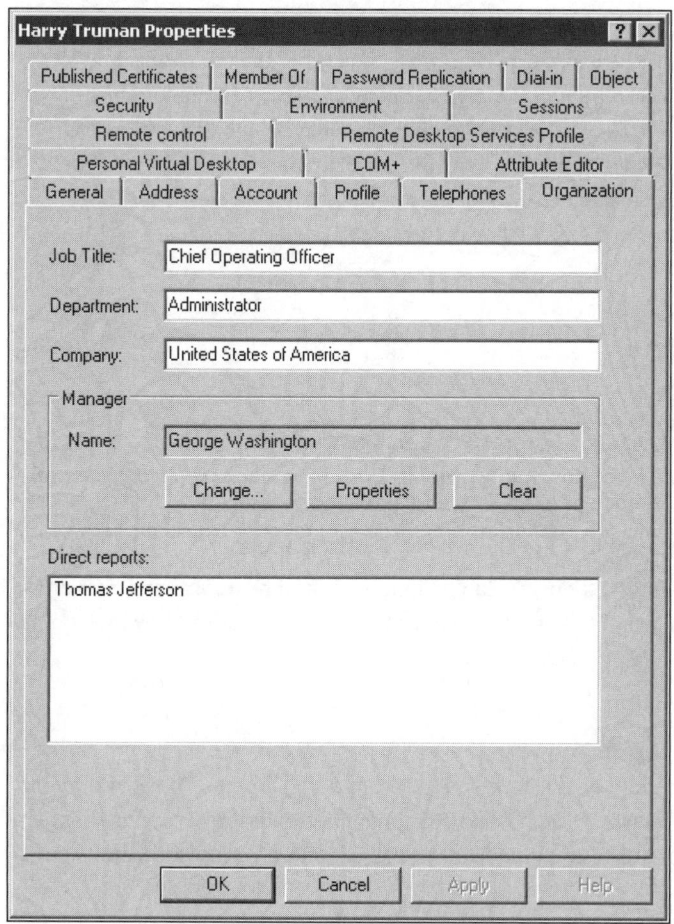

FIGURE 2-10 The Organization tab in the properties of a Windows Active Directory user account

From a governance perspective, you'll want to ensure your employee onboarding processes loop through your Windows Active Directory or Azure Active Directory services teams such that the new employee's organization and other pertinent information is entered into her account as it is initially being created. Although the information can be added later, from a process viewpoint, it is more efficient to add that information to the account as it is being created.

You'll also want the onboarding employee to log in to Office 365 and create her My Site right away, and then add the organization chart to her public-facing My Site.

> ***TIP*** **It is probably a good idea to have developers force this chart onto each user's My Site so that they don't have to add it individually if you plan to have the organization chart exposed on each My Site.**

> ***TIP*** **If you want to expose the organization chart on a page other than the user's My Site, consult with this thread as a starting point:** ***https://social.msdn.microsoft.com/Forums/office/en-US/d31d080f-3f13-4c5b-8ae5-68cb4418d7c0/organization-browser-web-part?forum=sharepointgeneralprevious*****. Note that this thread is discussed from an on-premises viewpoint, not an Office 365 viewpoint, so you'll need to consult with a developer to see if these ideas can be ported to SharePoint Online.**

My Site settings

My Sites are personal portals that allows users to collaborate with others and offer ideas to the enterprise. I've been surprised at how many organizations have demurred from the use of My Sites. I suspect, over time, however, the collaboration and social features will become baked into the core processes such that My Sites will be routinely used.

My Sites must first be set up and then you can configure trusted host locations, manage promoted sites, and publish links to Office client applications. Let's get started by looking at the setup of the My Sites in SharePoint Online.

My Site setup

In SharePoint Online, the setup of My Sites is managed from a single page. The environment is automatically created for you when your Office 365 tenant is created. You cannot change the My Site Host or the Personal Site Location like you can with an on-premises installation.

Preferred Search Center

The setup starts with the option to enter a Preferred Search Center. I find this to be particularly useful if you created an Enterprise Search Center. Having their queries automatically redirected to a global search center is useful if your users want to search for global content from within their My Site. However, if this is not a need, you can leave this input box (shown in Figure 2-11) blank and let users manually traverse to the Enterprise Search Center (assuming you created one) when they want to make global queries.

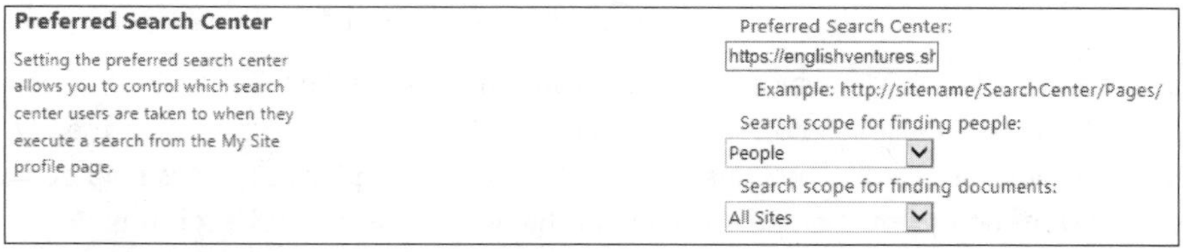

Preferred Search Center

Setting the preferred search center allows you to control which search center users are taken to when they execute a search from the My Site profile page.

Preferred Search Center:

https://englishventures.sh

Example: http://sitename/SearchCenter/Pages/

Search scope for finding people:

People

Search scope for finding documents:

All Sites

FIGURE 2-11 Working with the Preferred Search Center

Note that you can select the default search scopes for finding people and documents. This screen in SharePoint Online is outdated in the sense that it uses SharePoint 2010 terminology (scopes) instead of SharePoint 2013 terminology (result sources). Don't confuse the two. *Result sources* are the updated and more mature version of search scopes and can include real-time queries and filters as well as carving out a portion of the index against which the keyword query is committed.

Read Permission Level

In the Read Permission Level input box (not illustrated), you'll enter the accounts to whom you want to grant the Read permission level for each My Site when it is created. You'll need to ensure that these accounts have the correct Personalization services permission to use personal features and create personal sites. (See the "Manage user profile permissions" section earlier in this chapter.) You'll also need to ensure that the public My Site page in the My Site host site collection has these accounts assigned the Read permission. This configuration is not retroactive. If your users create a number of My Sites and then you change permissions here, those My Sites already created will not inherit the changed permissions from this page.

The default permission group is Everyone Except External Users. By default, all Office 365 users in your tenant automatically have Contribute permissions on all lists and libraries because this group is automatically added to each list and library in each site across your tenant with the permission level Contribute. This means, by default, that all users have Contribute permissions to the document library (named *Documents*) created in each user's My Site.

IMPORTANT **From a risk-management perspective, this is far too generous with regard to default permission assignments. It opens resources to users who might not need to access those resources. Office 365 is built from a departmental, sharing viewpoint. Care must be given to remove this group from the Members group when needed, and site-collection administrators should be trained how to effectively manage permissions within their own site collection. It would be better to leave the default Documents library empty and create new document libraries in which you manually set permissions as needed.**

Newsfeed

You'll have two check boxes with which to concern yourself in this section. The first check box, Enable Activities In My Site Newsfeeds, specifies whether or not to enable activities in the My Sites newsfeeds (not illustrated). If you select this check box, notifications can be generated when certain events occur from people and content the user follows. This check box is selected by default. Unless you have a specific reason to turn this off, leaving it selected is preferred. For example, if John is following Suzie and she follows a site that interests her, that Follow event will appear in John's activity feed.

The second check box, Enable SharePoint 2010 Activity Migrations, enables SharePoint 2010 activity migrations. The word *migrations* is misleading: this selection simply means that if your organization is making use of SharePoint 2010 legacy activities, those can appear in the activity feeds as well. You select this only when you're in a hybrid deployment between your SharePoint 2010 On-Premises farm and your SharePoint Online deployment.

Email notifications

Type the address you want used for sending certain email notifications for newsfeed activities in the String To Be Used As Sender's Email Address input box. This address need not be a monitored mailbox. If you select the Enable Newsfeed Email Notifications check box, you'll allow users to receive email messages for newsfeed activities, such as mentions or replies to conversations they've participated in. You'll need to assess the usefulness of these types of email notifications. If there are too many of them, they just become white noise in the user's inbox and no longer serve their alerting purpose.

My Site cleanup

Fortunately, in SharePoint Online, My Sites are automatically cleaned up after 14 days have passed since a user's profile is deleted. This means that, by default, the user's My Site is deleted and no longer accessible. By default, if the user's manager can be discerned by the system, it will give the user's manager full access rights to the user's My Site. This permission level enables the manager to pull out information needed for the ongoing work of the organization before the My Site is deleted by the system.

However, you can input a secondary name in the Secondary Owner picker box to specify a person who also will have owner access to the My Site after the user's profile has been deleted. I highly recommend you enter an account here to ensure you have a backdoor into each My Site once the profile is deleted.

From a risk and governance perspective, you should have an account designated for this purpose, and the account credentials should be made available to those in a need-to-know situation so that critical information isn't lost. Because the password can be changed by the tenant administrator, each time the account's credentials are passed out, they can be used and then effectively locked thereafter.

Privacy settings

By default, in SharePoint Online, a user's My Site is public, even though the interface says it is private by default. If you leave the Make My Sites Public check box selected, that user's My Sites become public to the other users in the organization. When you deselect this check box, some elements of the user's My Site are no longer shared on an automatic basis, such as the following:

- User's list of followers
- Information about who that user is following
- User's activities

When the check box is selected, user activities automatically become public, such as the following ones:

- New follow notifications
- Tagging of content, rating of content, or both
- Birthdays (if populated)
- Job title changes
- New blog posts

If these activities (and others) are made public, users can still override the default settings as long as they are allowed to manage their own privacy settings within their user profile.

What choices you make here is less a governance question than it is a cultural/collaboration question. The risks posed by opening this up are that users might unwittingly post information or activities in their newsfeed they don't want going public. But the downside of closing this down is that, in a highly collaborative environment, other technologies will supplant SharePoint Online for certain sharing needs. It seems best to transfer to the user the management of which activities appear in the newsfeed instead of using a one-size-fits-all approach—unless that is what your organization wants.

Configure trusted-sites locations

The Trusted My Site Host Locations feature prevents a user from creating more than one My Site in an organization with multiple User Profile service applications. It also is a feature in both on-premises and Office 365 deployments, in which it informs the SharePoint environments where a user's My Site and User Profile is located based on Active Directory groups, and, suboptimally, audiences. To enable Trusted Host Locations, simply enter the URL for Office 365 My Sites for a group of users. You can leverage existing Windows Active Directory security groups for targeting.

The URL entered into a trusted-site location becomes a simple redirect in the client web browser. Therefore, there does not need to be connectivity between the server environment running SharePoint Server on-premises and Office 365 as long as the users themselves can access both locations from their client devices.

Multi-user-profile service environments become more complex. For example, in a server farm deployment that spans geographic regions, you might have separate User Profile service applications for each region or regional server farms in the environment. By default, a user can create a different My Site in each User Profile service application or server farm, which could cause unwanted results from both an administration perspective and a user perspective. Where the potential exists for the user to create multiple My Sites, use of the Trusted Sites Locations is needed to ensure the user can work in different farms but will still have only one My Site.

Many hybrid deployments can place the user's My Site in the SharePoint Online environment while leaving other services and applications running in the on-premises deployment.

Map an account through different membership providers

Federated user identities in Office 365 are prefixed with the membership provider that provides claims-based access. An on-premises user identity of *bill@englishventures.us* might become *i:0#.f|membership|bill@englishventures.us* in Office 365.

The My Site host uses this identity to display the correct My Site or User Profile by including it in the "accountname" querystring on the User Profile URL. An example, a User Profile URL for an on-premises installation might look as follows:

http://my/profile.aspx?accountname=bill@englishventures.us

The formatting differences mean that the two environments will not automatically resolve the requested user identity. So a simple workaround for this formatting is to use an ASP.NET page running on the on-premises farm that can resolve the identities and then redirect the request to the real on-premises or Office 365 location. In the preceding example, some string manipulation would be sufficient to remove the *i:0#.f|membership|* part of the user identity so that it could be resolved on-premises or to add it so that it can be resolved by Office 365.

The script can be placed as inline code in a dummy profile.aspx page in a directory on each SharePoint front-end web. Configure the My Site Trusted Host locations to point to the directory that contains the script, rather than the actual destination, and allow the script to perform the redirect.

Suppose a user browsing the on-premises environment requests a user profile that is stored in SharePoint Online. This is the process that will take place:

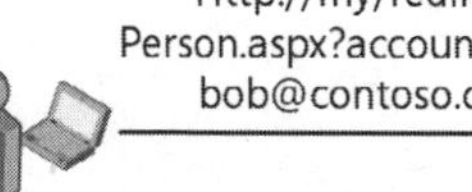

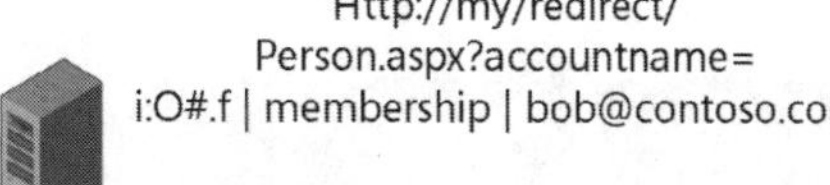

Now, let's suppose a user browsing the SharePoint Online environment requests a user profile that is stored on-premises. This is the process that will take place:

MORE INFORMATION If you're in a hybrid environment and would like to access the redirect code with instructions on how to install and use it, visit Summit 7 System's website at *http://summit7systems.com/code/profile_redirect*. This code is unsupported, but it will get you started in creating the proper redirects for your hybrid environment.

Manage promoted sites

You can promote any URL (not just SharePoint sites) to your user's Sites page so that they see the link when they visit the Sites page. (See Figure 2-12.)

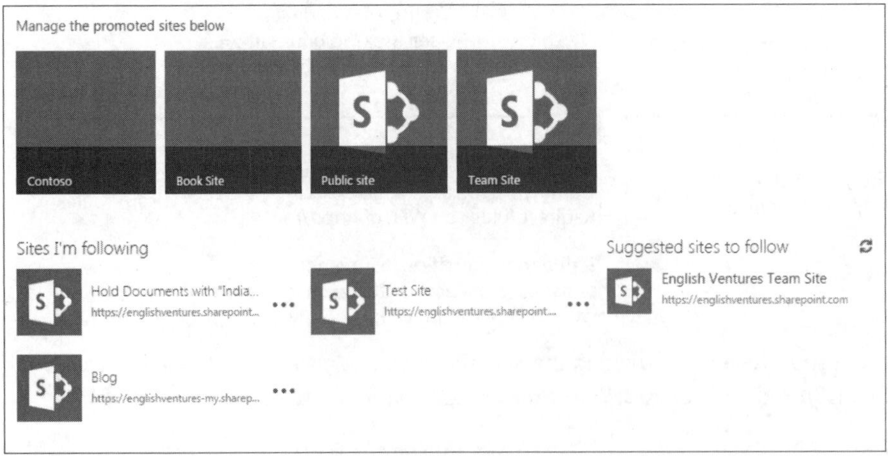

FIGURE 2-12 The Sites page with Contoso as a promoted site

To customize the Sites page, you'll click on the Manage Promoted Sites link under the My Site Settings and then click the New Link link (not illustrated). On the next page (shown in Figure 2-13), you'll fill in the URL, Title, and Owner text boxes and then optionally type a value for the Description box, a URL for the image that will appear with the link on the Sites page, and the target audience (if any). Note that even though the interface does not show it, the owner of the link is a required field, so you'll need to enter an owner for the promoted link to save the entry and promote the link.

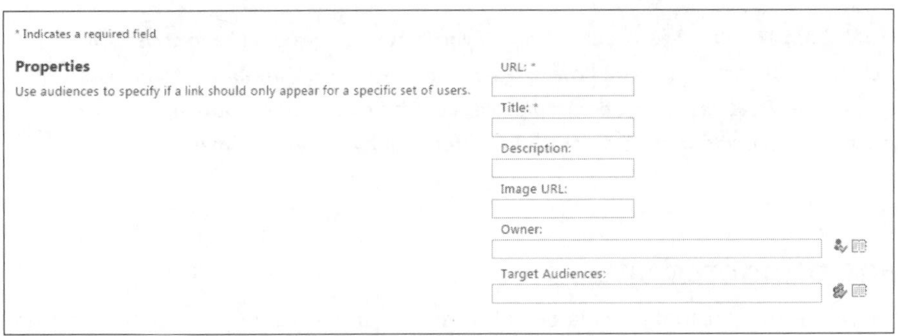

FIGURE 2-13 Managing promoted sites input screen (note the lack of an asterisk next to the Owner selection box even though it is a required field)

> ***NOTE*** **You'll likely need to work with the rendition size of the graphic so that it fits into the square icon area the way you want it to. The default rendition sizes within the Images library do not automatically fit the icon area, so you'll want to work with a third-party graphics program to get the graphic into the size and density you want before uploading it into SharePoint Online.**

From a governance perspective, there isn't much risk here. I would use this feature to promote websites and documents of a global nature to your users. You can think of the Sites page as a type of one-page portal in which you promote certain pages or opportunities. For example, you could promote the summer golf outing or the winter party on the Sites page. You could promote the company-giving campaign to a local charity or community group. Furthermore, you could promote the updating of the human-resources policy manual or a new expense-reimbursement program. This sites page can add real value to your organization. The only real risk is that users might filter out most of the links if they are not of use or interest to them. So, from a governance perspective, I suggest using audiences to refine the interface so that users don't visually filter out unneeded links.

Publish links to Office client applications

When users are opening or saving documents from their Office client applications, you can ensure their most commonly accessed SharePoint Online sites, libraries, and lists appear in the client interface by publishing certain links from this location. Links published here will show up under the My SharePoints tab. The use of audiences for these links is strongly encouraged. Ironically, there is no owner attached to these links, unlike with a promoted-site link. And you can select the type of object to which you're linking using the Type drop-down list (not illustrated).

I suspect your need to create these links will diminish as users implement OneDrive for Business more pervasively. (See my discussion below in the "OneDrive for Business" section.)

OneDrive for Business

OneDrive for Business is an Office 2013 client that replaces the old SharePoint Workspace by giving you the ability to synchronize document libraries and lists from SharePoint Online to your local hard drive. But it also acts as a client you can use to save directly from your local hard drive to a document library or list sitting in the cloud. At its core, however, it is an evolution of the My Site document library. Essentially, OneDrive for Business is a cloud-based, SharePoint-based document library in which individual business customers can save documents that can be consumed by others in the organization.

The OneDrive for Business client installs with the Office 2013 Pro Plus package on your user's workstation or other device. Your users then invoke OneDrive for Business by clicking on the OneDrive For Business link within the Office 365 menu from your Start/Programs/Office 365 menu selections.

When OneDrive for Business installs, it will be automatically added to your user's Favorites in the File Save-As dialog box of the Office client as well as in Windows Explorer. Any interfaces that borrow the File Save-As information will also include the OneDrive for Business information. From a user's perspective, OneDrive for Business will be named using the name of Office 365 tenant. For example, if your tenant was named *something.onmicrosoft.com*, OneDrive for Business will appear in the various interfaces as *OneDrive – Something.*

Once OneDrive for Business is configured, users can use their My Site document library to store documents. And they will have drag-and-drop, cut-and-paste, and other common document-management functionalities between their Windows Explorer and OneDrive for Business when it is opened using Windows Explorer. It will look and feel like another drive in which they can manage their documents.

OneDrive for Business also works with the synchronization capabilities built in to the document libraries and lists within SharePoint Online. Each time a user synchronizes a document library, it is added to the SharePoint folder in the File Save-As interface as well as Windows Explorer. (See Figure 2-14.) The names are long and not configurable. For example, a synchronized document library named Corporate Documents will appear in the interface as *Something Team Site – Corporate Documents* if it is synchronized from a default site collection (where *Something* is a placeholder for the name of your tenant). New site collections will not take on this naming convention, as illustrated in Figure 2-14. Note also that synchronized libraries do not appear with the OneDrive for Business folder in the interface even though they are managed by the OneDrive for Business client.

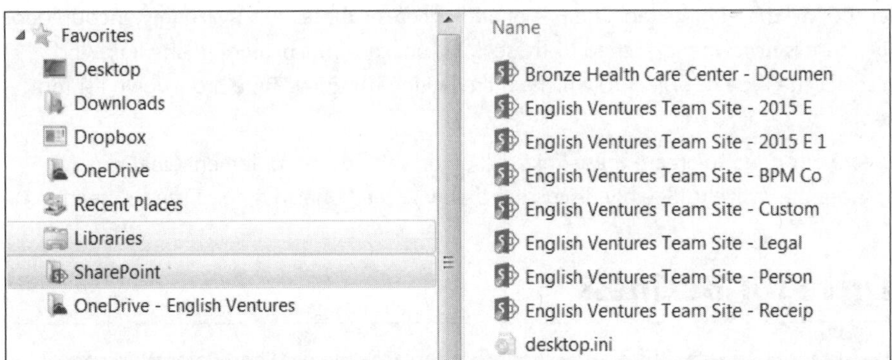

FIGURE 2-14 OneDrive for Business and document libraries interface (illustrating on the right side how some library names are cut off because the combination of the default names)

There are considerable risks with OneDrive for Business. It is nested deeply enough in the more recent Office 365 deployments that it will be difficult to turn off. Hence, it's best to embrace and manage this technology as opposed to attempting to limit it or shut it down, in my opinion. But the risks that I outline here should not be overlooked as you build out your SharePoint Online deployment.

First, by default, the Everyone Group except External Users will have Contribute permissions on each user's OneDrive document library. This is a considerable security risk in that users who don't understand this default setting might copy sensitive information to their OneDrive for Business instance only to find they have widely exposed that information. Training should emphasize the governance rules you set up to mitigate this risk. One governance rule, for example, could be that users are not placed into the group that has My Site capabilities until they have completed both My Site and OneDrive for Business training. (See the section "Manage user profile permissions" earlier in this chapter for more information.)

Second, some users will have the tendency to upload their entire My Documents to OneDrive for Business because of their ability to access their document from multiple clients, such as iPads or Android devices. This can be a real support issue because of the speed at which documents are synchronized. In my own testing, I found that it took *days* to copy nearly 20,000 documents to my OneDrive for Business library. Although faster bandwidth will help, you should not be under any illusions as to how long this will take and the amount of bandwidth that will be consumed. One governance idea to reduce the risk of consuming too much bandwidth is to have people synchronize only a portion of their My Documents in a single administrative activity—say, no more than 1000 or 2000 documents—and to run that process during night or weekend hours, presumably when you have more available bandwidth.

Third, users might want to use document libraries like file servers, because document libraries can be more accessible from the cloud than file servers are from the Internet. The thought will be this: "Since we can synchronize file servers to the cloud, we can make those files more accessible than before." Although that sounds logical, simply grabbing the files on a file server and copying (or synchronizing) them to a document library is not a good idea. Most file servers have old, outdated, and redundant documents. Before your users upload entire sets of documents from a file server, you should require a file server "cleaning out" project to remove old, outdated, and redundant files from the file server. The risk of not reorganizing files on a file server and not scrubbing the system of unneeded files is that whatever misery and loss of efficiencies you're currently experiencing with your file servers will be transferred to your Office 365 tenant. This transfer of problems will artificially increase your tenant costs and do nothing to introduce efficiencies into your work processes.

Fourth, at the time of this writing, Office 365 does not have endpoint security solutions or any type of a compliance center. While it is possible today for users to download and take sensitive, company information to their local, personal devices, OneDrive for Business makes it even easier to do this. Once files are copied from the network, they are out of your control, for all practical purposes. One idea on governing the downloading of company documents onto personal devices is to require personal devices be set up to work with your company's rights-management solution. So at least there would be some enforced privacy on certain documents even when they are copied off network to a personal device. This isn't a solution that will always work, but it is one idea to work with. Another governance idea is to purchase third-party software that inputs a watermark onto downloaded documents that contains security warnings and other needed information.

Last, the introduction of OneDrive for Business is likely to contribute to confusion at the desktop as users wonder where they should be storing which files. The solution to this problem depends on your Enterprise Content Management (ECM) architecture—understand what your major "buckets" of information are, which platforms are used to host and manage those buckets, and how your processes use information for both inputs and outputs. As Office 365 is rolled out, it's best to take the time to define when users should use file servers, document libraries, OneDrive for Business, My Documents, and so forth and to define, at least in broad terms, what documents should be hosted within which technology. Lower overhead costs come from the standardization of processes, not their randomization. OneDrive for Business and Office 365 might introduce ECM randomization if it is not properly managed, and that will drive up overhead costs.

Summary

In this chapter, I introduced the management of user profiles and discussed the usefulness of these profiles for finding experience and expertise within your organization. We looked at how to create new user profiles and why you might want to create user subtypes to make unique profiles or different profile types in your environment. We discussed organization profiles and how to set up My Sites.

I have not delved into the client side of My Sites; instead, I have focused on the server administration aspects of getting My Sites going in your deployment.

In the next chapter, we'll consider Business Connectivity Services and how they can help your Office 365 deployment aggregate data to increase collaboration and productivity.

CHAPTER 3

Working with Business Connectivity Services

Business Connectivity Services (BCS) provides a way to consume information that is hosted in other repositories in Microsoft SharePoint Online. When you use BCS, SharePoint Online becomes a client to the data that doesn't live in SharePoint Online. For example, this external data might be in a database and accessed by using an out-of-the-box BCS connector.

BCS also can connect to data that is available through a web service, data that is published as an OData source, or many other types of external data. Connectivity is achieved by using the connectors that install with BCS and SharePoint Online or by creating your own custom connector. A *connector* is merely the communication bridge between SharePoint Online and the external system that hosts the data.

Data can be presented in a number of ways in SharePoint Online. Because nearly everything in SharePoint Online is a list (at least architecturally speaking), a common way to present external data is to use an external list. External lists look and feel like regular SharePoint lists and also can write back to external data sources. But you're not limited to the list level. If you want to integrate data from an external source into a list hosting internal data, all you need to do is use an external data column and import data from an external source into a list that is hosting local content.

When the external data is available in the SharePoint Online interface, you'll be able to perform common operations on that data, which are represented by the acronym CRUDQ (Create, Read, Update, Delete, and Query). Synchronization of the changes you make to external data within the SharePoint Online interface sometimes can be written back to the external source.

The possibilities that BCS opens to your organization are immense. It's not uncommon for critical data to reside in multiple disparate systems across multiple locations. Much of this data doesn't reside in SharePoint Online or even in an On-Premises deployment of SharePoint 2013. Associating the right data at the right time within core processes of an organization is more art than science, especially when the company doesn't control the production or hosting of the data. For processes to be lean, they must be supplied with the right data and data that is accurate, accessible, useful, usable, valuable, desirable, findable, and credible. And this data must represent the right inputs needed by the process if the process is going to output a transformed version of the input data. It all has to work together. In most organizations, there is no one person in charge of any given process (no matter how critical that process is), so data integration into the process (if the process is even defined) becomes a constant source of irritation, work slowdowns, and sometimes work stoppages.

A common workaround to this cultural and procedural problem is to have the developers create custom applications that take data from disparate sources and expose that data to their users. Processes are sometimes adjusted to how the data is surfaced, usually making the process more "fat" (or inefficient, as compared to more "lean," or efficient). BCS can be used to further technology-centric management of information and processes, or it can be used to support process-centric consumption of information.

BCS has a traditional server/client architecture. However, you are not bound to a strict server/client architecture when building your BCS solution. This means that your BCS solutions can contain only server-side components, only client-side components, or both. If you build a server-side solution, that information will be stored in an External Content Type (ECT). If you build a client-side solution, that information will be stored in a Business Data Connectivity (BDC) model on the client in the BDC client cache. If you build a solution that involves both server and client components, the information is stored as two separate entities, using both an ECT model and a BDC model.

The benefits of using Business Connectivity Services

Business Connectivity Services (BCS) has been available ever since Microsoft SharePoint Office Server 2007 Enterprise under the name of the *Business Data Catalog*. BCS evolved through Microsoft SharePoint 2010 and Microsoft SharePoint 2013, and it has been available not only to Enterprise licenses but also to SharePoint Foundations, albeit with fewer features. Today, BCS provides a stable suite of services your organization can use to benefit from having external data available to search, view, and use within SharePoint On-Premises as well as SharePoint Online.

Every organization has selected business applications for their processes, such as Microsoft Dynamics CRM or Salesforce.com for their sales department. Each department, or business unit, might be using entirely different systems with their own data repositories. The fact that this data is stored on separate machines that could both be on-premises or in the cloud presents an issue when your users need to gather business data.

Using Business Connectivity Services, that data can be searched along with all SharePoint content, looked up via an external data column, and stored as metadata against SharePoint lists, items, and documents. It also can be displayed on SharePoint pages to provide insight to the external data via Business Data web parts, and it can provide an interface for updating the data via external lists.

Microsoft Office client applications also provide Business Connectivity Services integration. Microsoft Outlook can display contacts, tasks, and calendar events from external data sources. Microsoft Excel can be used to display lists of data for further data analysis via BCS, and Microsoft Word can integrate with BCS via Quick Parts, allowing external data to be looked up from external data sources from within the Word document itself.

This functionality makes it possible to use SharePoint Online as a central hub for all business information, which can be accessed securely.

External lists

External lists show external content to users through a familiar interface. Because users of SharePoint Online should already be familiar with regular SharePoint lists such as tasks and announcements, working with external data in SharePoint should be intuitive. Users with sufficient permissions will be able to create views, apply filters, and sort.

> ***MORE INFO*** **Some functionality you are accustomed to is not available, such as data-sheet views, item-level permissions, RSS views, and workflows. The following article displays all the differences between a regular SharePoint list and an external list:** ***https://support.office.com/en-gb/article/Differences-between-native-and-external-lists-6601eda9-b722-4bf8-a2bf-ce25cf3d2fd0?CorrelationId=b5265806-cefd-4404-941a-b307b5097b78&ui=en-US&rs=en-GB&ad=GB.***

These capabilities are lacking because the data is linked to, and not imported into, the list itself. Linking to the data is a major benefit, though, because importing external data into SharePoint lists causes record-synchronization issues and unnecessary duplication and overinflation of SharePoint content.

Much of the functionality within a SharePoint external list is available only as the result of planning and building the External Content Type (ECT). For instance, the Edit Item option is available only if you build an Updater method within your ECT. The Delete Item option is available only if you provided a Deleter method within your ECT, a Create Item method is available only if you built a Creater method, and so forth.

You must build two required methods for an external list to work: the Finder and Specific Finder methods. The Finder method returns all the rows of data from the data source, and the Specific Finder method displays a single item. The Finder method is called for the main view within an external list, and the Specific Finder method is called when you choose the View Item menu option.

You should build filters into your Finder methods. You can create different types of filter operations, such as Limit, Wildcard, and Comparison. As an administrator, when you import a BDC model into SharePoint, you will be presented with a warning if your Finder method does not contain a limit filter. The model will work, but this warning informs you that you might suffer performance issues within the external list without a limit filter.

> **MORE INFO** Some limits for external lists within SharePoint will depend on the data source you are connecting to. The following article explains these limitations and the errors you might come across: *http://lightningtools.com/bcs/business-connectivity-services-end-user-implications-part-one-threshold-limit-errors/.*
>
> External system throttling also can be modified using Microsoft Windows PowerShell. Information on how to do so can be found here: *http://lightningtools.com/bcs/business-connectivity-services-end-user-implications-part-two-changing-external-system-throttling/.*

When you are creating the External Content Type, you can build more than one Finder method. Each Finder method will be presented as a separate view within an external list. For instance, you can display a list of your customers from a Customer Relationship Management system regionally using different views of the Customers table. Each Finder method will need to have a default filter—for instance, *Country = United States*. This also can overcome the external-list limitations, because you can design your Finder method filters to always return fewer than 2000 rows. Figure 3-1 shows how these operations can be available in the same interface.

ProductID	ProductName	SupplierID	CategoryID	QuantityPerUnit	UnitPrice	UnitsInStock	UnitsOnOrder	ReorderLevel	Discontinued
1	Chai	1	1	10 boxes x 20 bags	18.0000	39	0	10	No
2	Chang	1	1	24 - 12 oz bottles	19.0000	17	40	25	No
3	Aniseed Syrup	1	2	12 - 550 ml bottles	10.0000	13	70	25	No
4		2	2	48 - 6 oz jars	22.0000	53	0	0	No
5	Chef Anton's Gumbo Mix	2	2	36 boxes	21.3500	0	0	0	Yes
6	Grandma's Boysenberry Spread	3	2	12 - 8 oz jars	25.0000	120	0	25	No
7	Uncle Bob's Organic Dried Pears	3	7	12 - 1 lb pkgs.	30.0000	15	0	10	No
8	Northwoods Cranberry Sauce	3	2	12 - 12 oz jars	40.0000	6	0	0	No
9	Mishi Kobe Niku	4	6	18 - 500 g pkgs.	97.0000	29	0	0	Yes
10	Ikura	4	8	12 - 200 ml jars	31.0000	31	0	0	No

FIGURE 3-1 A BCS external list providing the View Profile and View item operations

External Data column

The External Data column provides a lookup to the external data from a SharePoint list or library similar to that of managed metadata and looking up terms from a term store. The advantage to looking information up from your external data is that your users might be associating documents or list items with data that already resides within external data sources. An example is associating a customer proposal with the customer record within Microsoft Dynamics CRM. When you search for that customer within SharePoint, you will receive consistent search results, including documents for that customer. If you use a Single Line Of Text column, your users might input data inconsistently, resulting in poor filters and search results.

A consideration for your planning of the External Content Type is the Item Picker. The Item Picker is a dialog box accessed from both the browser and from within Microsoft Office applications when selecting the data. Each column you want to include in the Item Picker should have the property *ShowinPicker* set to *True*. Additionally, the Item Picker can display only 200 rows of data. You can use a wildcard filter to enter the first few characters of a company name or other column value and return the rows under the 200-item limit.

Figure 3-2 displays a document library containing documents with metadata set from the external data source. This is a document library with multiple External Data columns, which allows users to select their own matrix of customers and products from the external data source.

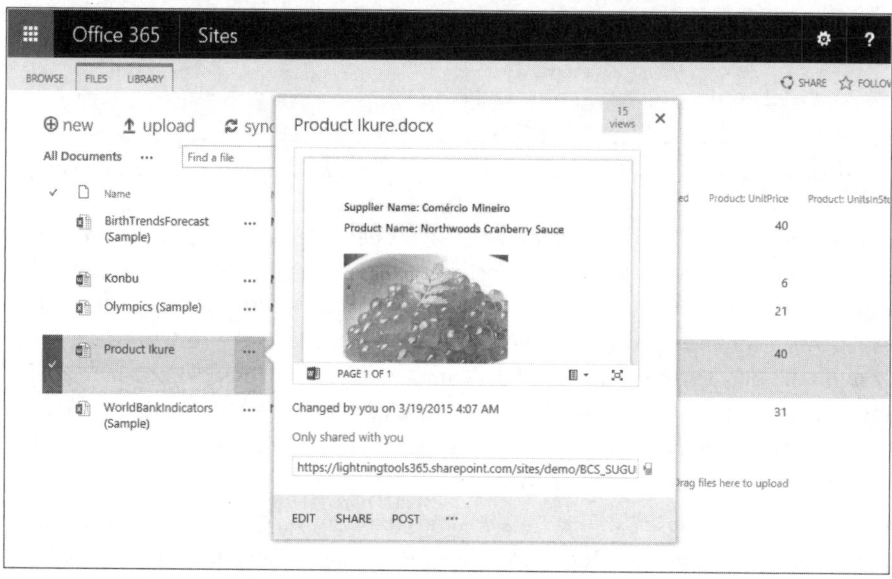

FIGURE 3-2 A document library with multiple External Data columns allowing for customers and products to be selected from the external data source

When you edit the properties of the document or list item, an icon is displayed next to each External Data column, which the user can click to display the picker, as shown in Figure 3-3. If you know the identifier for the row of data, such as the customer ID, enter it and then click the Check If External Item Exists icon.

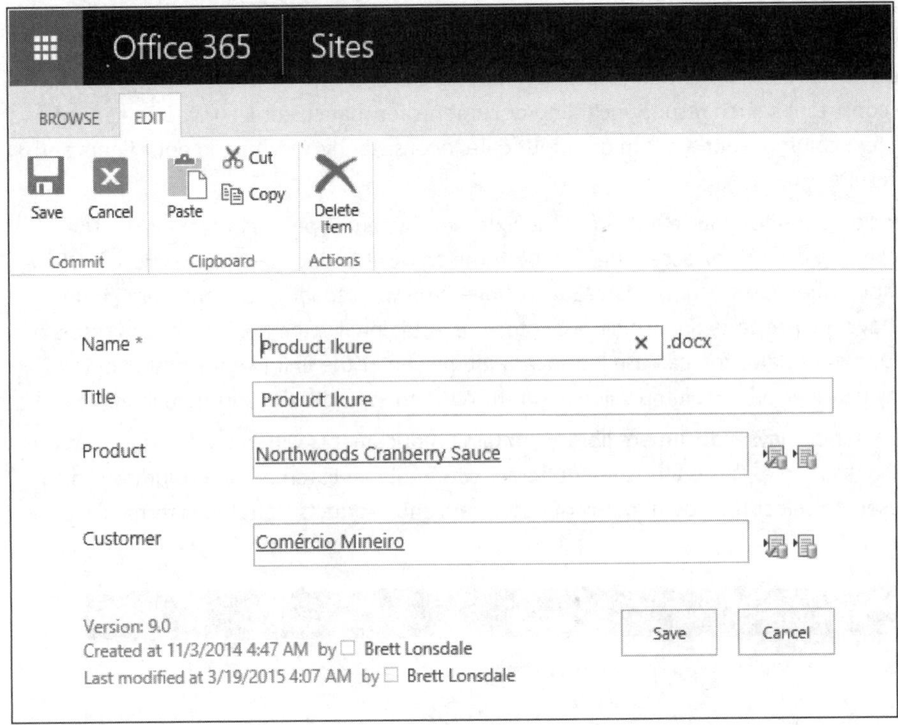

FIGURE 3-3 Looking up external data from two external data sources within a document's properties

Unlike the SharePoint external list, after the data has been selected using the Item Picker, the values are stored against the list item or document as metadata. They will not reflect any changes made to the external data. Therefore, if you change a customer name, the old customer name will continue to display against the document. You can refresh the data, but you can do this only for the entire set of data. If your document libraries contain tens of thousands of documents within a view or folder, they will all be processed together, which could result in a long operation. The refresh icon is shown on the column header (referring back to Figure 3-2) next to the Customer column.

Microsoft Word allows these External Data columns to be set via Quick Parts that can be inserted into a Word Document or Document Library template, as illustrated in Figure 3-4. The Quick Parts can then be used to set the column values by performing a lookup directly from Microsoft Word. The Document Information Panel also will display any External Data columns as read only.

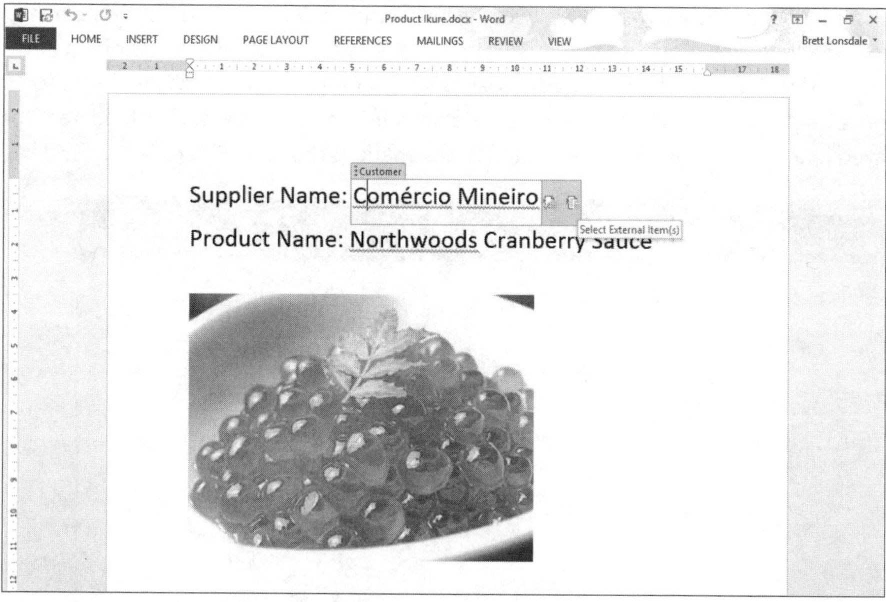

FIGURE 3-4 Microsoft Word Quick Parts that allow external data to be looked up and set from the external data source

Business Data web parts

Several BCS web parts can be added to a SharePoint page to display a read-only view of the external data. The web parts include the following:

- Business Data List
- Business Data Related List
- Business Data Item
- Business Data
- Business Data Item Builder
- Business Data Actions
- Business Data Connectivity Filter

Each web part displays in the Business Data category and can be inserted into any SharePoint page. The Business Data List web part displays the results of a Finder method. Users will be able to set the filters for that Finder method if they were created via a toolbar. The toolbar is not available if a Filter method has not been created. If you created an association between two entities, such as Customers and Orders, you will be able to use the Business Data Related List web part. The Business Data Related List web part will display the many sides of any association. The web parts are connected using web part connections, which allows Customer data to be selected from a Business Data List web part and the associated Orders data displayed in the Business Data Related List web part.

You also can join the Business Data List web part or Business Data Related List web part to a Business Data Item web part. The Business Data Item web part will display a row of data in a columnar format. This is powerful because it allows for summary columns to be displayed in the Business Data List web part, and then more detailed information about a selected item to be displayed in a Business Data Item web part. This scenario is shown in Figure 3-5.

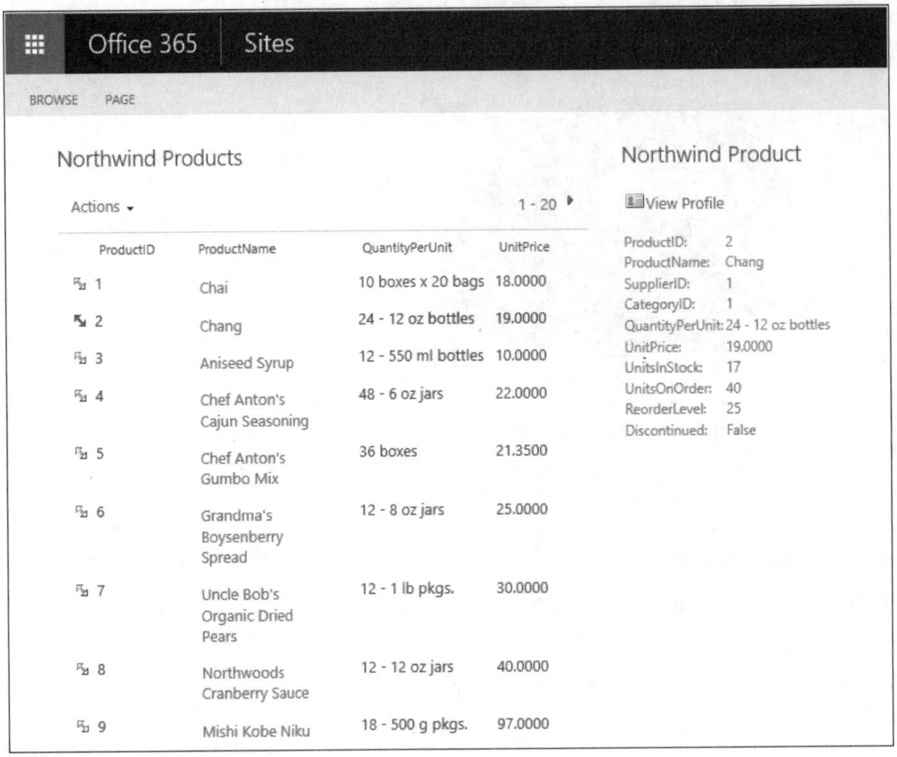

FIGURE 3-5 The Business Data List web part joined to the Business Data Item web part

If you select Edit Web Part from the Business Data List web part to display the tool pane, you will notice an Edit View link appears within the web part itself. Within the Edit View properties, you will be able to set the filter options for the web part. Notice that in the Items To Retrieve and Item Limit sections, the option buttons are unavailable (grayed out) in Figure 3-6. These option buttons are available only if you properly planned and created your filters on the Finder methods within the External Content Type.

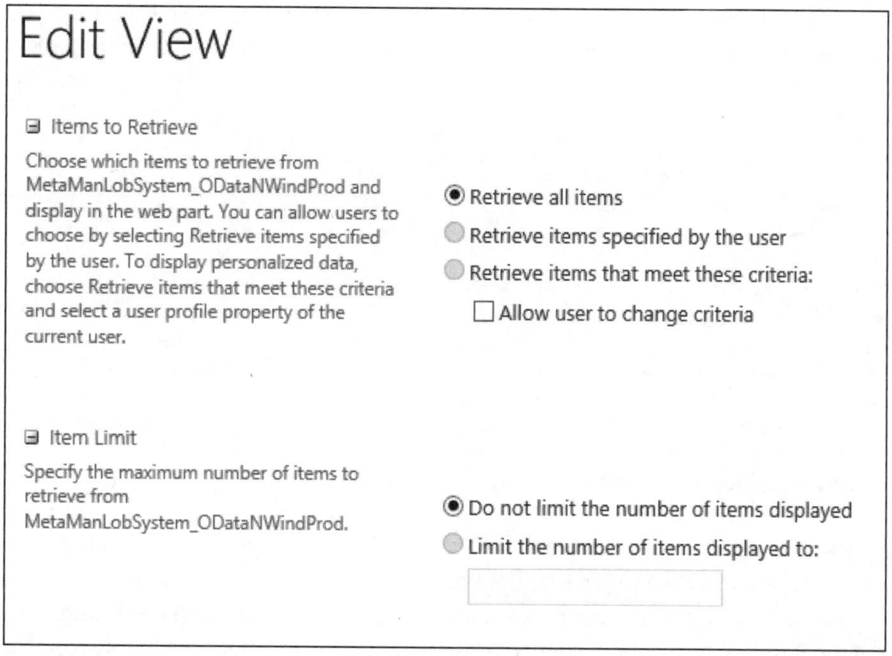

Edit View

Items to Retrieve

Choose which items to retrieve from MetaManLobSystem_ODataNWindProd and display in the web part. You can allow users to choose by selecting Retrieve items specified by the user. To display personalized data, choose Retrieve items that meet these criteria and select a user profile property of the current user.

- (●) Retrieve all items
- ( ) Retrieve items specified by the user
- ( ) Retrieve items that meet these criteria:
  - [ ] Allow user to change criteria

Item Limit

Specify the maximum number of items to retrieve from MetaManLobSystem_ODataNWindProd.

- (●) Do not limit the number of items displayed
- ( ) Limit the number of items displayed to:

FIGURE 3-6 The Edit View option of the Business Data List web part

If you create a Wildcard or Comparison filter on the Finder method, you can set the Items To Retrieve properties. You then can allow the user to set the value to be filtered by using the web parts toolbar, or you can set the filter value within the web parts view itself and, optionally, allow the user to override the default filter value. The Item Limit option is grayed out if you have not created a Limit filter on the Finder method. If you have created one, you can set the limit for the number of items to be displayed.

Custom actions and view profile

Each of the Business Data web parts, as well as the external list, can show custom actions. A *custom action* is a hyperlink made up of a URL and a value from a selected record. For example, consider a list of customers displayed within a Business Data List web part. A user might need to look up a particular customer on the Linked In website or search for the customer using Bing. If this is a common requirement among users of your system, you can create a Search Customer custom action users can use to search for the customer in Bing by clicking a Custom Action button. If you create the custom action in the External Content Type, it will display automatically within the Business Data web parts.

You also can create a Profile page for each External Content Type. The Profile page can be created from within the SharePoint administration page. The View Profile custom action also is displayed automatically in the Business Data web parts and allows users to show a columnar view of the row of data they selected. Within a SharePoint On-Premises installation, when a user searches for external data, the search result will link to the Profile page. In Figure 3-7, you will see the Create/Upgrade option in the Profile Pages area for each External Content Type.

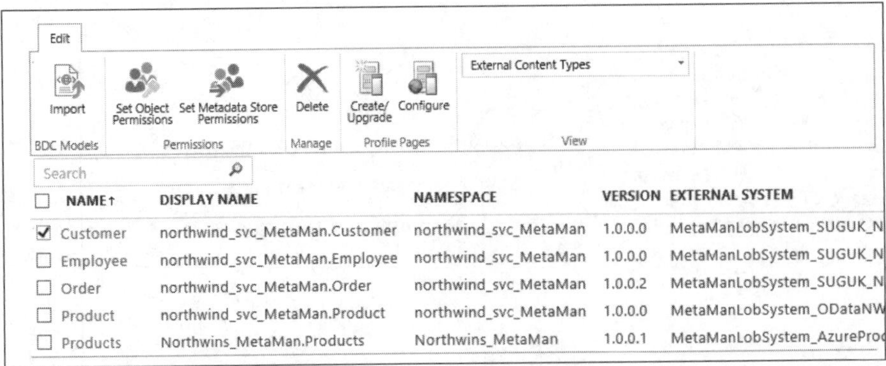

FIGURE 3-7 Create/Upgrade the Profile page for each external content type

Once the Profile page has been created, it will display as a custom action by default on any newly added Business Data web parts. The Profile page comprises two Business Data web parts: the Business Data Item web part and the Business Data Item Builder web part. The purpose of the Business Data Item Builder web part is to retrieve the identifier for the row (such as a customer ID) from the URL and pass it to the Business Data Item web part via a web part connection. The Profile pages look bland by default, but they can be branded and customized using XSLT. In Figure 3-8, you can see the View Profile custom action within the Business Data Item web part.

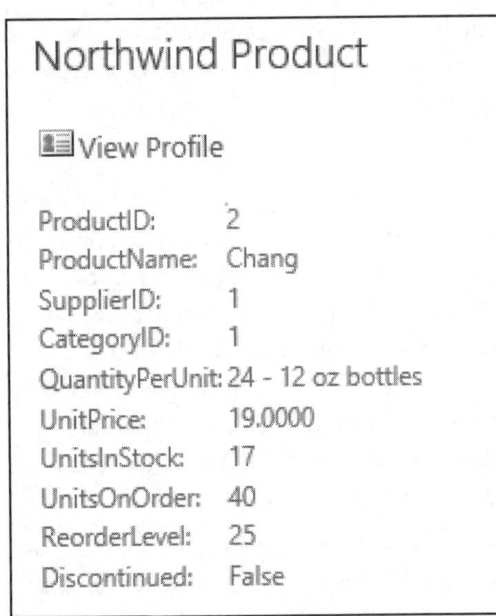

FIGURE 3-8 View Profile custom action within a Business Data Item web part

Searching external data in SharePoint Online

At the time of this writing, you cannot search external data using SharePoint Online as you can with SharePoint On-Premises. It is not possible to configure the SharePoint Online Search function to index an external data source. However, if you use a hybrid SharePoint environment, your SharePoint On-Premises Search functionality can search both SharePoint Online content as well as external data sources.

What is an administrator's role with Business Connectivity Services?

Now that I have established what Business Connectivity Services provides, I'll discuss how Business Connectivity Services is configured. However, a lot of the configuration is not just part of an administrator's role. The configuration of the end-user elements—such as the external lists, Business Data web parts, and External Data columns—are performed by the Information Worker role. However, certain settings must be correct within the External Content Type and within the SharePoint Admin Center because they directly affect how well the end-user elements perform.

The roles involved within Business Connectivity Services include the following:

- Database Administrator
- SharePoint Administrator
- SharePoint Developer
- Information Worker

Before you can consider even building the External Content Type, you must establish a connection string to the data source and an account with the relevant privileges to the database you are connecting to. You also should consider building new database views or stored procedures to maximize performance rather than connecting directly to tables, which are likely to grow.

The Database Administrator must create an account with at least Read permissions, which you will use to connect to the database. If you are considering using Windows authentication, several accounts will likely require permissions to the database. The method to do this, of course, will differ depending on the data source. You might well be connecting to Microsoft SQL Azure, OData, or a Windows Communication Foundation (WCF) Service.

You likely will need to use the Secure Store Service for authentication. In such a case, this also must be created by the SharePoint Administrator prior to the External Content Type being created.

After you establish how you will connect to the data source and you have an account that will authenticate and authorize you to access the database, you will be able to create the External Content Type. The ECT is typically created by a SharePoint Developer. However,

Microsoft Visual Studio, SharePoint Designer, and third-party Business Data Connectivity products have become less dependent on developers skills. Quite often, External Content Types can be created by a person with little or no programming knowledge.

What is required by the developer of the External Content Type is an understanding of the database schema so that the correct tables, views, and stored procedures can be used.

Once the External Content Type is created, the SharePoint Online Administrator will import the BDC Model file into SharePoint Online and set the relevant permissions to each External Content Type. Nobody will be able to use the data in any way until permissions have been granted to SharePoint users.

Profile pages also will be created via the SharePoint Admin Center after the BDC Model file is imported and privileges have been set.

Finally, Information Workers can begin to create the end-user elements such as the external lists and External Data column.

Data aggregation in SharePoint Online

You have a number of ways to aggregate data in SharePoint Online. The data aggregated by these technologies can be entirely inside or outside your SharePoint Online environment, depending on the individual technology involved. Consider the following aggregation technologies that you can use without developing any custom code:

- BCS
- Power BI
- Search
- Performance Point Services
- Content Query web part
- Image Viewer web part
- Apps that aggregate data

As you can see, BCS is only one way to aggregate data in SharePoint Online. But the core advantage to using BCS as opposed to other aggregation technologies is the External Content Type (ECT) and what it represents from a management perspective. External Content Types persist housekeeping data about the external data source, such as where the data is, how you will connect to it (including the authentication protocol and the credentials used to log in to the external data source), and what you can do to manage the information. Similar to SharePoint content types, ECTs can be stored and managed in a central location, secured, and reused across your SharePoint Online deployment. And the data that is exposed via BCS can be indexed by SharePoint Online. Managing a single container (ECT) that includes the details to work with external content is much easier than managing all those details separately.

Connecting to external data sources

Using SharePoint 2013, you can connect to almost any external data source using Business Connectivity Services. However, with business slowly moving to the cloud, data often is stored on the premises, but SharePoint Online is in the cloud. This presents a challenge when attempting to connect to the databases on the premises.

If your database is stored in SQL Azure, you'll find that it is simple to connect to and generate an External Content Type. You have a choice of tools such as Microsoft SharePoint Designer 2013, Visual Studio 2012 or newer, and various third-party tools.

If the data is stored on the premises, you might need to expose the data via OData or a WCF Service. Both of these options are likely to require some development work to make the data available. Alternatively, you could replicate the data into a SQL Azure database using a service bus.

MORE INFO **Visit this link to learn more about the Azure service bus:** ***http://azure.microsoft.com/en-gb/services/service-bus/.***

Connecting to OData

OData is an open protocol you can use to create and consume queryable RESTful APIs in a simple way. Using Visual Studio, you can create an ADO.NET Entity Data Model, which exposes on-premises data as an OData service. Then using Visual Studio or a third-party app like *BCS Meta Man,* you can create an External Content Type based on your OData service. Unfortunately, Microsoft SharePoint Designer 2013 cannot create an External Content Type based on OData.

TIP **For the purpose of this chapter, we will use a Northwind database that is already exposed as OData via OData.org. OData.org is publicly available, and you can make use of the site in your own testing using the sample data. If you want to use this database as a test while you follow along in this section, you are welcome to do so.**

SharePoint Online provides two methods to work with OData. One method is to import a BDC Model File that has been created manually using Visual Studio or a third-party tool. This will allow all the features of Business Connectivity Services to be available for the OData source. The other method is to build a SharePoint App External Content Type using Visual Studio. This approach involves building and deploying an external list as an app. However, it will be available only within the site you deploy the app to, and it won't be available as an External Data Column lookup or be available to the Business Data web parts.

SAMPLE BCS MODEL FILE Within the resources of this book is a BDC Model file that is already configured to work with Northwind via OData.org. called *ODataNWind.BDMC*. However, if you would like to build your own model, you can use the ODataV2 services with BCS, which is available using the following link: *http://www.odata.org/odata-services/*.

Importing an OData BDCM file

Your Business Data Connectivity Model (BDCM) file is an XML file made up of the following information:

- LOBSystem Type set to ODATA
- ODataServiceMetaDataURL (Url of the OData Service)
- ODataServicesVersion
- LOBSystemInstance Name
- ODataServiceURL
- WCFAuthenticationMode
- ODataFormat
- Entity Description
- Finder, Specific Finder Methods

To import the BDCM file, navigate to the SharePoint Admin Center within your SharePoint Online environment and follow these steps:

1. Select BCS from the Quick Launch pane on the left side of the screen.
2. Click the Manage BDC Models And External Content Types link.
3. Click the Import icon in the BDC Models Group on the Edit ribbon, as shown in Figure 3-9.
4. Under BDC Model, click the Browse button to browse to the BDCM file.
5. Leave Model selected as the default File Type.
6. Leave Localized Names And Properties selected under Advanced Settings.
7. Click Import.

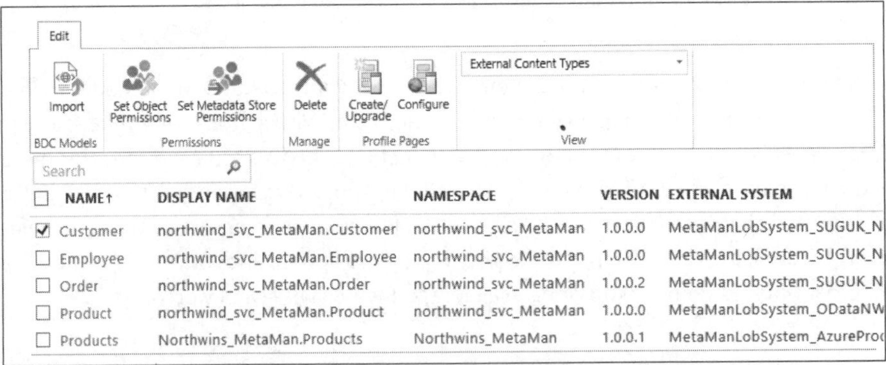

FIGURE 3-9 The Import icon appears in the BDC Models group of the ribbon

Building an External Content Type using Visual Studio

To build an External Content Type for OData using Visual Studio, you need to create a SharePoint Hosted App. Note that the app will provide only a site-scoped external list and the other features described, such as Business Data web parts and an External Data column. Follow these steps to create a SharePoint Hosted App:

1. Create a new Visual Studio 2012 Project.
2. Select App For SharePoint 2013, as shown in Figure 3-10.
3. Provide a name and solution name for your SharePoint app and then click OK.

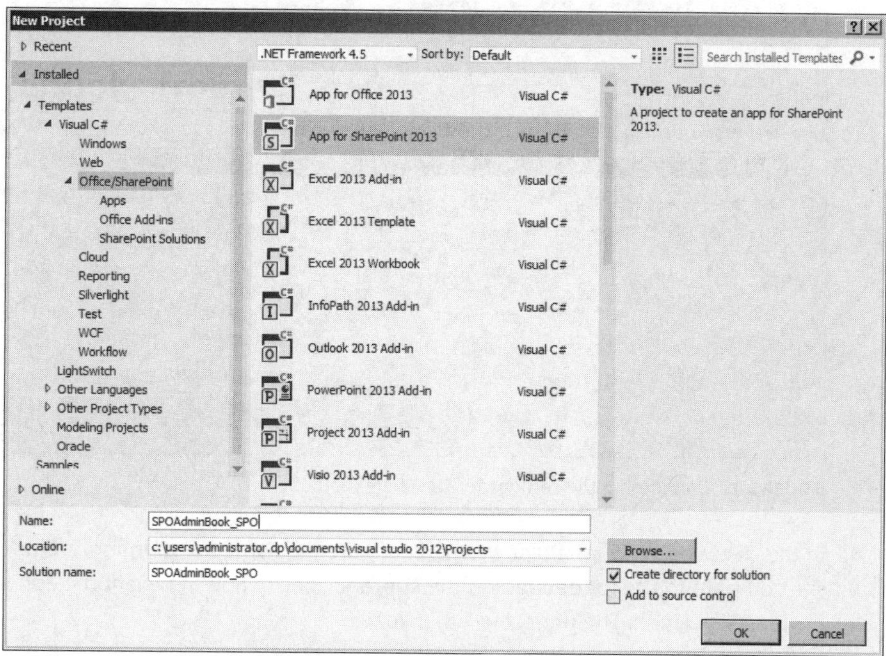

FIGURE 3-10 Selecting App For SharePoint 2013 in Visual Studio to build a new project

4. The new project screen will allow you to select App For SharePoint 2013 to start a new project in Visual Studio 2012. Set the URL for your SharePoint Site that will be used to test the app.

5. Select SharePoint-Hosted as the type of app, as shown in Figure 3-11.

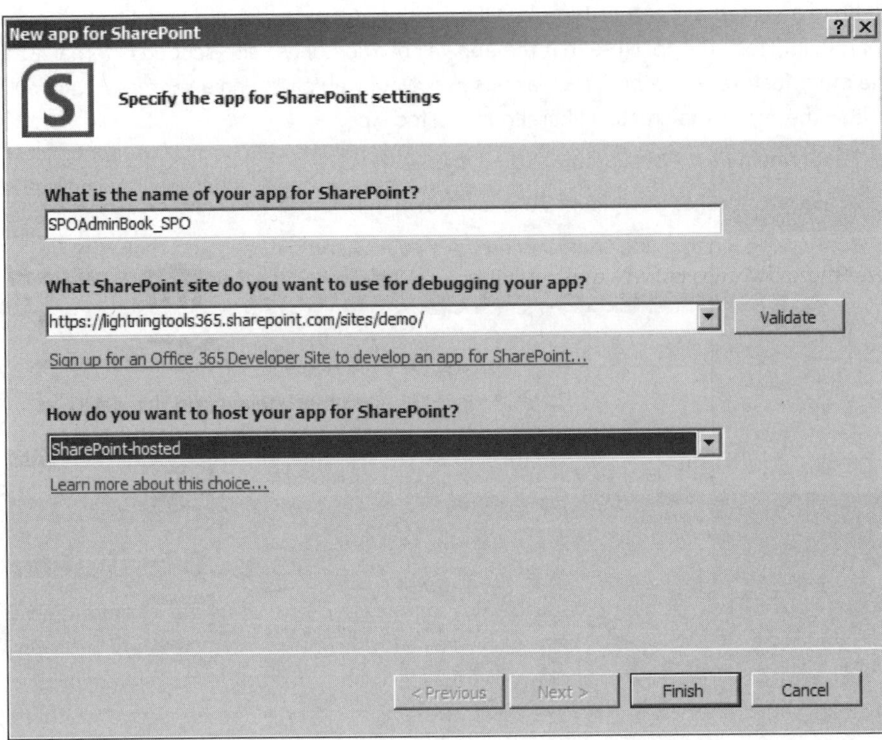

FIGURE 3-11 Configuring the settings for the SharePoint app

6. In the New App For SharePoint wizard, configure the name for your app, identify the site you want to use for debugging the app, and specify how you want the app to be hosted. Click Finish. The project will then load.

7. Right-click your project in Solution Explorer, and choose Add, Content Types For An External Data Source as shown in Figure 3-12.

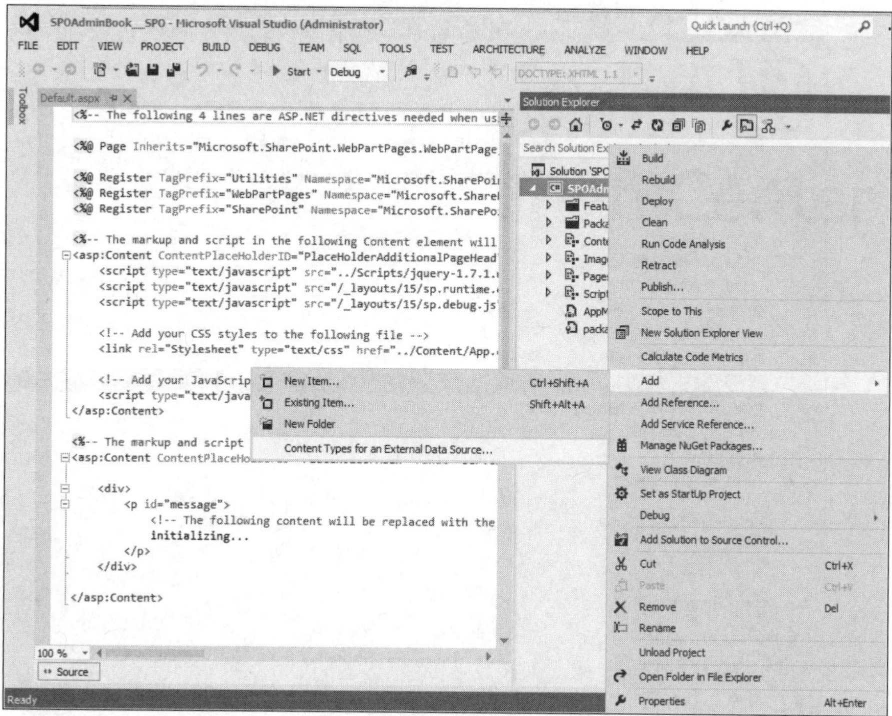

FIGURE 3-12 Adding a new content type for an external data source

8. Provide the URL for your OData source. For the purpose of this exercise, use the following: *http://services.odata.org/V2/Northwind/Northwind.svc/*.

9. Set the name of your Data Source Name—for example, **SharePoint OnlineAdmin_NWind**.

10. After clicking Next, Select the data entity that you would like to display, as shown in Figure 3-13.

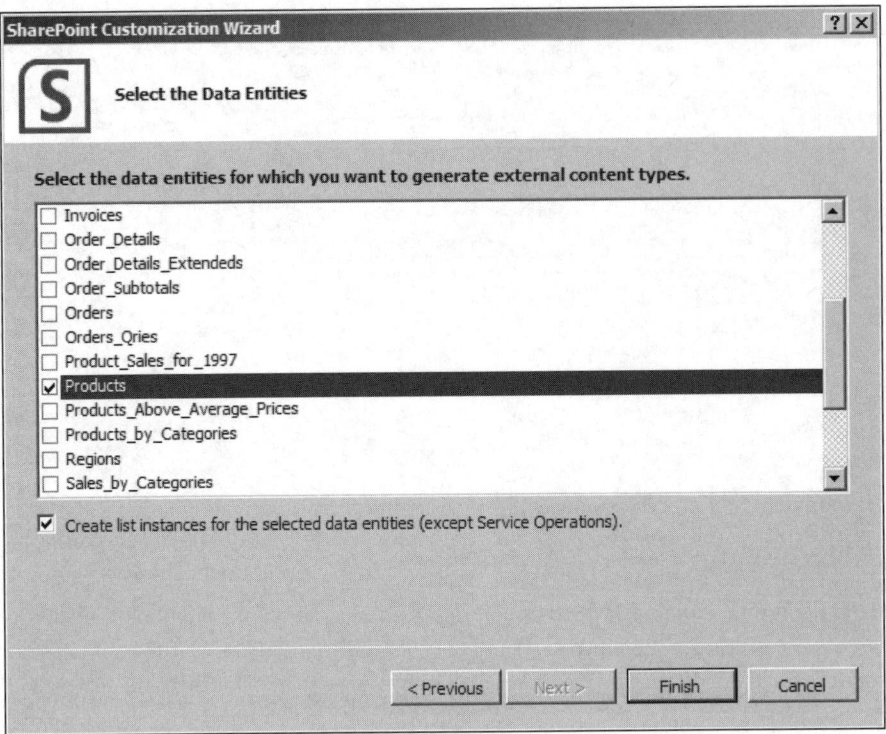

FIGURE 3-13 Selecting the Products data entity to display

11. Click Finish.
12. Open the APPManifest.xml file in Visual Studio, and set the start page to SharePoint OnlineAdminBook_NWind/lists/products instead of the default SharePoint OnlineAdminBook_NWind/Pages/Default.aspx.

    Making this change will ensure that the external list of data is displayed as soon as the app is opened.
13. Build your app by clicking Start on the toolbar. The app will deploy to your site. Alternatively, you can upload the app package to your Organizations App Store within SharePoint Online.

MORE INFO **For more detailed steps, please go to *https://msdn.microsoft.com/en-us/library/office/jj163967.aspx.***

Build an External Content Type using SharePoint Designer 2013

Using SharePoint Designer 2013, you can create an External Content Type that consumes a WCF service or connects to a SQL Azure database. Open SharePoint Designer 2013, and open any site within your SharePoint Online site collection. You must also have the URL for the SQL Azure database and the credentials to connect to it available. Using SharePoint Designer 2013, follow these steps:

1. Click External Content Types from the Navigation pane.
2. Click New External Content Type from the New group on the ribbon. (See Figure 3-14.)
3. Set a name, display name, and namespace for your External Content Type.

> ***TIP*** **Keep the display name and namespace very user friendly because these will display to users who are configuring the user elements of Business Connectivity Services.**

4. Click the Click Here To Discover External Data Sources And Define Operations link.
5. Click Add Connection.
6. Choose SQL Server.
7. Enter the name of your database server—for example, **zjrjowkxq9.database .windows.net**.
8. Select Connect With Impersonated Windows Identity.

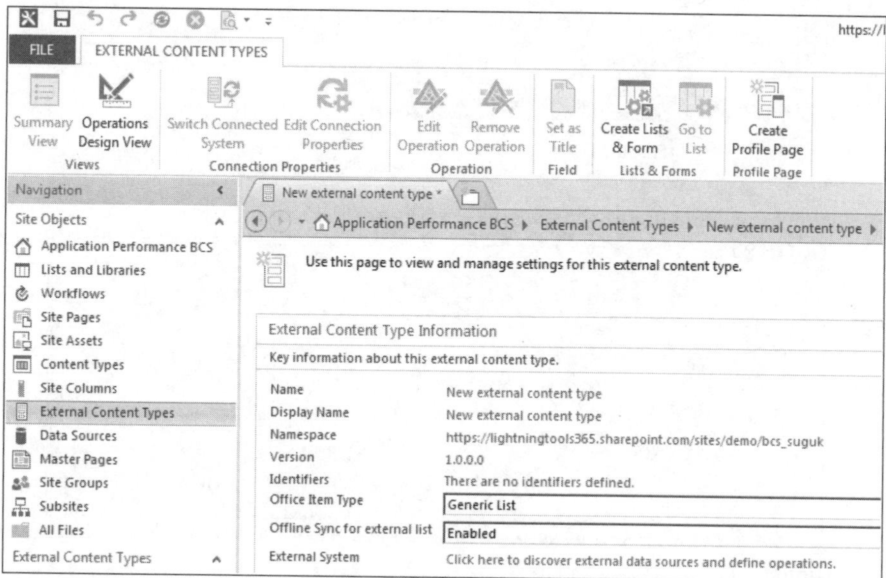

FIGURE 3-14 Creating an External Content Type with SharePoint Designer 2013

9. Set the Secure Store Application ID. (We will explore creating Secure Store configurations in the next section.)
10. Expand Tables, and then right-click the Products table and choose Create All Operations.

> ***TIP*** **If you are unsure of the server name, database name, or credentials, you can navigate to the SQL Azure database in your Azure portal and choose Connection Strings from the links on the right. Connection Strings for ADO.NET, JDBC, ODBC, and others will be displayed. You can gather all the required information from the connection string.**

11. Click Next to create all operations, such as Read List, Read Item, Create, Update, and Delete.
12. Accept the defaults on the Parameters Configuration page. All columns will be selected.
13. Click Next.
14. Click the Add Filter Parameter button.
15. Name the filter, and choose Limit as the type. (See Figure 3-15.)
16. Choose ProductID in the Filter Field drop-down list.

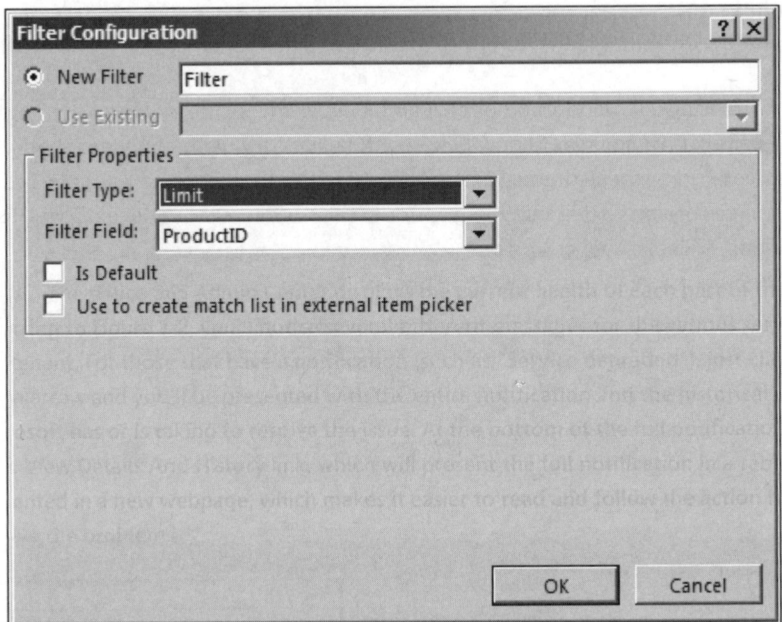

FIGURE 3-15 Creating a limit filter

17. Optionally, create Wildcard filters for reasons explained at the start of this chapter.

18. Click Finish.
19. Click the Save icon within SharePoint Designer 2013 to save the External Content Type.
20. You might need to set permissions on the External Content Type to allow users to access the data.

Authentication

Authentication within Business Connectivity Services is quite complex. Within a SharePoint On-Premises environment, many administrators struggle with authentication issues because of double-hop issues or poorly configured Kerberos environments. Within SharePoint Online, the issues are typically not present because users are authenticated against a SQL Azure instance or an OData source.

It is recommended that you use Secure Store to authenticate users against SQL Azure because SQL Azure will not support mixed modes from SharePoint Designer 2013. Using the Secure Store, create a target application that consists of users who can be authenticated using the target application and the credentials used to access the data store. When you are configuring the target application, you can create fields that are required to pass information to the data store. For example, in addition to using Username and Password fields, you might also require additional fields of information such as Consumer Key and Consumer Secret when connecting to sources such as Salesforce.com.

Secure Store works by mapping groups of SharePoint users to a single set of credentials. This approach allows, for example, all salespeople in a sales group to access a database such as Dynamics CRM using a Sales account. Other groups of users in SharePoint might be mapped to another account providing different permissions to other non-sales-related tables.

Configuring Secure Store

To create a Secure Store target application, select Secure Store from the SharePoint Admin Center:

1. Click New from the ribbon to create a new target application.
2. In the Target Application ID text box (shown in Figure 3-16), enter a name for the target application, which will be used within the BCS connection.
3. Enter a name for the target application in the Display Name field.
4. Enter an email address in the Contact Email text box.
5. Optionally, add additional fields if you need to. For SQL Azure, you will not need additional fields.
6. In the Target Application Adminstrators area, enter the name of the administrator of the target application.
7. Specify the groups or individual user accounts that will be authenticated using this target application.

8. Click OK.

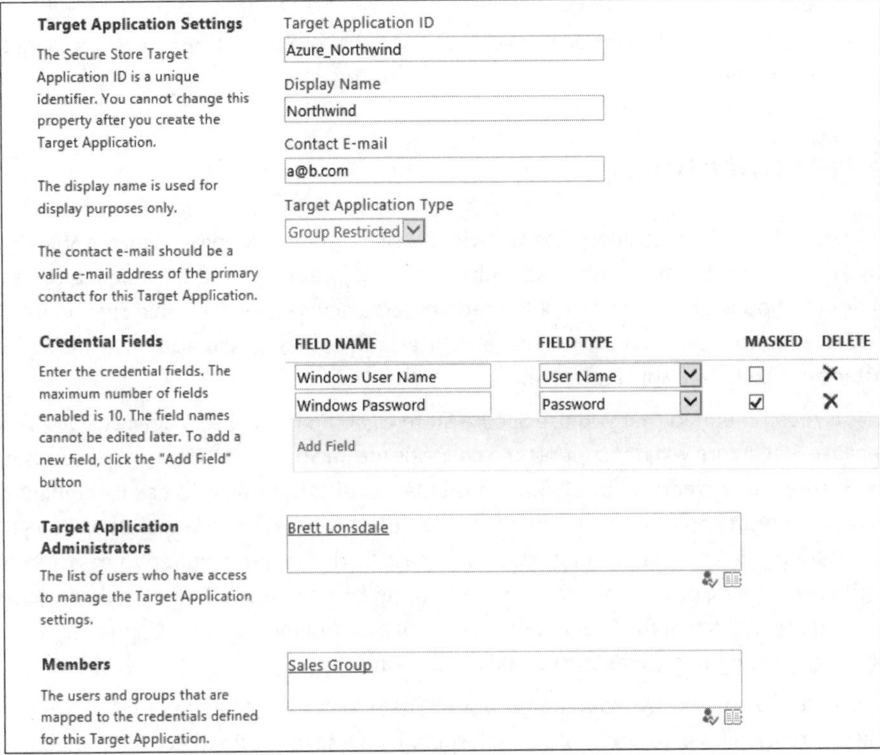

Target Application Settings
The Secure Store Target Application ID is a unique identifier. You cannot change this property after you create the Target Application.
The display name is used for display purposes only.
The contact e-mail should be a valid e-mail address of the primary contact for this Target Application.
Target Application ID
Azure_Northwind
Display Name
Northwind
Contact E-mail
a@b.com
Target Application Type
Group Restricted
Credential Fields
Enter the credential fields. The maximum number of fields enabled is 10. The field names cannot be edited later. To add a new field, click the "Add Field" button
FIELD NAME
FIELD TYPE
MASKED
DELETE
Windows User Name
User Name
Windows Password
Password
Add Field
Target Application Administrators
The list of users who have access to manage the Target Application settings.
Brett Lonsdale
Members
The users and groups that are mapped to the credentials defined for this Target Application.
Sales Group

FIGURE 3-16 Creating the Secure Store target application

9. Select the check box for your target application, and choose Set Credentials.
10. Enter values in the Username and Password text boxes to access your SQL Azure database.
11. Click OK.
12. When you configure a BCS connection, the target application ID will be the value which you use when configuring the External Content Types using Microsoft SharePoint Designer 2013, or also some third-party tools.

Authorization

As well as being authorized at the database level, users of SharePoint Online also need to be authorized against the External Content Type itself. By default, even the Tennant Administrator role will not have permissions to execute a BCS External Content Type, even though the person in that role can administrate the External Content Types. Four permissions can be assigned to users for each External Content Type:

- Execute
- Edit
- Selectable In Clients
- Set Permissions

The permissions have a different meaning in the context of the metadata store, each model, the External Content Type, and method. Table 3-1 describes each permission on each object.

TABLE 3-1 SharePoint External Content Type Permissions

Object	Definition	Edit permissions	Execute permissions	Selectable In Clients permission	Set permissions
Metadata store	The collection of XML files, stored in the Business Data Connectivity service, that each contain definitions of models, External Content Types, and external systems.	The user can create new external systems.	Although there is no Execute permission on the metadata store itself, this setting can be used to propagate Execute permissions to child objects in the metadata store.	Although there is no Selectable In Clients permission on the metadata store itself. This setting can be used to propagate these permissions to child objects in the metadata store.	The user can set permissions on any object in the metadata store by propagating them from the metadata store.
Model	An XML file that contains sets of descriptions of one or more external content types, their related external systems, and information that is specific to the environment, such as authentication properties.	The user can edit the model file.	The Execute permission is not applicable to models.	The Selectable In Clients permission is not applicable to models.	The user can set permissions on the model.
External system	The metadata definition of a supported source of data that can be modeled, such as a database, web service, or .NET connectivity assembly.	The user can edit the external system. Setting this permission also makes the external system and any external system instances that it contains visible in SharePoint Designer.	Although there is no Execute permission on an external system itself, this setting can be used to propagate Execute permissions to child objects in the metadata store.	Although there is no Selectable In Clients permission on an external system itself, this setting can be used to propagate these permissions to child objects in the metadata store.	The user can set permissions on the external system.

Object	Definition	Edit permissions	Execute permissions	Selectable In Clients permission	Set permissions
External content type	A reusable collection of metadata that defines a set of data from one or more external systems, the operations available on that data, and connectivity information related to that data.	Although there is no Edit permission on an external content type itself, this setting can be used to propagate these permissions to child objects in the metadata store.	The user can execute operations on the external content type.	The user can create external lists of the External Content Type.	The user can set permissions on the External Content Type.
Method	An operation related to an External Content Type.	The user can edit the method.	Although there is no Execute permission on a method itself, this setting can be used to propagate Execute permissions to child objects in the metadata store.	There is no Selectable In Clients permission on a method.	The user can set permissions on the method.
Method instance	For a particular method, describes how to use a method by using a specific set of default values.	The user can edit the method instance.	The user can execute the method instance.	There is no Selectable In Clients permission on a method instance.	The user can set permissions on the method instance.

Figure 3-17 shows how to set permissions for each user. Note that the permissions can be propagated down to sublevels.

Creating a BCS solution in a hybrid environment

When you build a BCS solution in a hybrid environment, you'll create either a one-way inbound or a two-way SharePoint hybrid configuration. The desired result is to make on-premises data available in SharePoint Online, and also to allow content from SharePoint Online to be searched along with external data in SharePoint 2013 On-Premises.

All users that will require access to the BCS data will need to be available within a Federated Azure Active Directory. A Secure Store Target Application will be configured to authenticate users. An ODataEndPoint will be created, allowing the data to be made available to SharePoint Online.

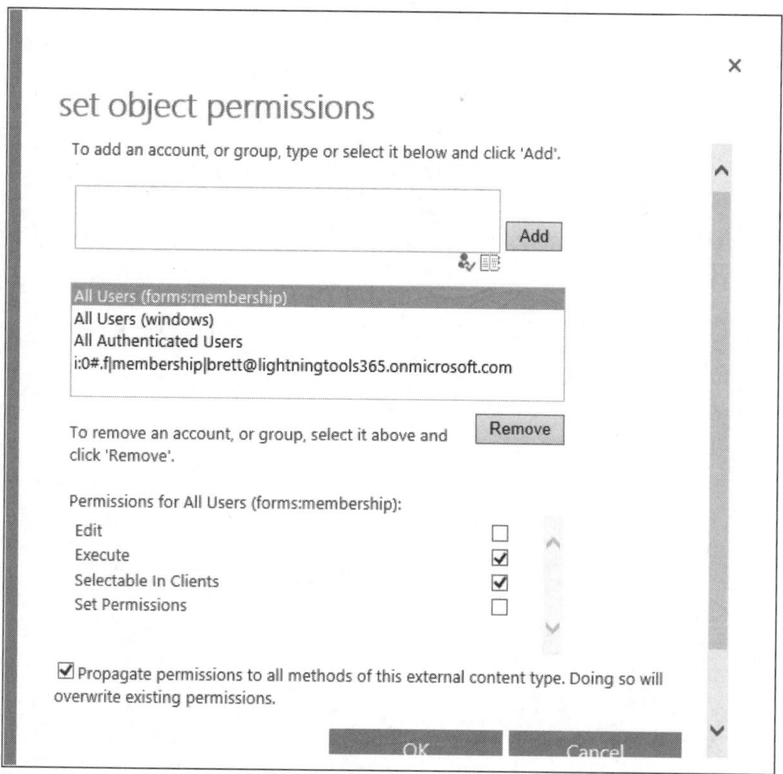

FIGURE 3-17 Permissions configuration screen

> ***MORE INFO*** If you would like to follow the exact steps for setting up a BCS solution in a hybrid environment, the following article describes the full steps: *https://technet.microsoft.com/en-us/library/dn197236.aspx.*

Summary

Within this chapter, we explored the different methods that are available to aggregate data within Microsoft SharePoint. We then explored the benefits of using Business Connectivity Services and described each service within the BCS suite of services. There are several methods to create External Content Types. We explored using Visual Studio and SharePoint Designer to connect to SQL Azure and OData. Finally, we explored Authorization and Authentication options, such as Secure Store and permissions.

CHAPTER 4

Managing a term store

What is known as the *managed metadata service* in Microsoft SharePoint 2013 is called the *term store* in SharePoint Online. From a macro viewpoint, the core SharePoint services involved that support a full information-management solution include the search and indexing service application, records management, document management, and the managed metadata service. This chapter is focused just on the term store, so at times you'll find that I don't dive into next-step topics that would naturally follow if the focus of this chapter was broadened.

To achieve a full information-management solution, organizations need to be engaged in the following:

- Developing content that is placed into collaboration sites
- Assigning metadata to that content through the term store
- Indexing the content
- Finding the content through search results and various web parts
- Securing content
- Connecting content to value-creating processes
- Life-cycling content so that it remains *lean* and usable and doesn't slow down existing processes

When combined, the search and the term-store technologies provide velocity to information flow in a SharePoint system. If you combine records management, document management, collaboration, and social technologies, you'll find SharePoint Online to be a core platform your users will need to use in the core processes that form their daily job duties.

Being able to find information is a core element if a business is going to implement its strategies and achieve its goals. Every core process, strategy, or goal in a business depends on obtaining the right information at the right time in a secure fashion. But a robust solution that provides excellent *findability* is highly dependent on a robust *putability* solution.

Putability

Putability is the industry word for describing how information goes into an information-hosting system, such as SharePoint Online. Putability is the front end to findability, which is concerned with how information is retrieved from the system. Putability encompasses all that goes into the input of information into an information system, including tagging, input tools, and user training. The more important it is to find a document or a content item, the more important it will be to focus on how that information goes into SharePoint Online. The more effort you put into obtaining quality metadata assignments, good location selection, and good navigation on the content item *at the point of capture when it is being placed into SharePoint Online*, the better your findability solution will be. In fact, it is not an exaggeration to say that if you can't find information, it's because you have not put enough time, effort, processes, and people around the putability solution in your organization—not because the search functionality isn't working.

Rather than simply allowing users to upload documents into any document library with little or no metadata, or letting them put documents wherever they please without regard to how people might navigate to find those document items, a strong putability solution will first design the information-management system and then train users on how to manage their information within that system. It is important to ensure that when documents are stored in SharePoint, users do the following:

- Store documents in an appropriate location.
- Use the appropriate document template where required.
- Provide sufficient metadata to help other users find the document.
- Provide appropriate and consistent metadata to help other users locate the document.
- Avoid having too much metadata, so that users are able to find relevant documents using search.

As I discuss at the beginning of Chapter 6, the same word can have vastly different and disparate meanings in different contexts. As the number of documents in your index increases, the more difficult it is to return a relevant result set using the keyword by itself because it is more likely that the same word is used in different contexts with different meanings. Hence, the same word is used across disparate documents in disparate content domains to refer to different concepts, objects, or elements. This is why meaning is often expressed in phrases, idioms, and the unique use of words. For example, "good grief" can be an expression of several emotions. "Give it a go" is often an expression of hope and optimism in trying out something new. Finding the right data at the right time is essential to good decision-making in any organization and to running your processes in a lean, cost-effective way.

The proper and consistent use of metadata is essential to overcoming this problem. But metadata will only be effective when the metadata has been created, the documents have been correctly tagged, users know what the metadata terms mean, users know how to use the metadata, and users have a realistic expectation that the query will result in a relevant result set.

SIPOC is highly dependent on good information

Many readers of this book will be familiar with the SIPOC (Suppliers, Inputs, Process, Outputs and Customers) and DMAIC (Define, Measure, Analyze, Improve and Control) models in Six Sigma and project management. (See Figure 4-1.) SIPOC is one way to visualize a process map or a project scope. The idea of process flowcharting goes back to as early as 1921 and has advanced ever since. SIPOC helps you understand the starting and endpoints, and it helps ensure that what you do between them transforms the inputs into the outputs in a way that is cost-effective and one that customers are willing to pay for.

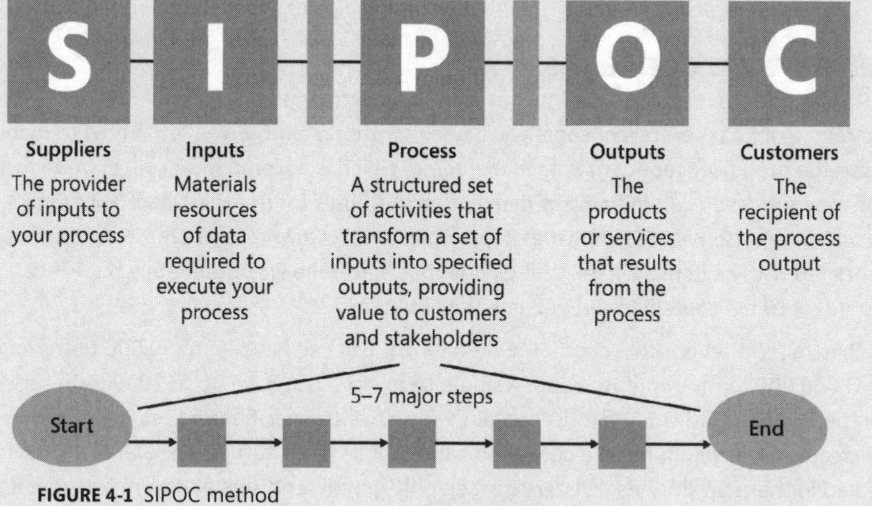

FIGURE 4-1 SIPOC method

So why bring this up in a SharePoint Online book? Because you can't divorce process and business issues from technology issues. If you, as the system administrator, don't understand or appreciate how your business processes consume, transform, and output information, you'll be forever missing the mark on managing platforms like SharePoint, because they become the provider of data

into your processes. Often, the outputs of those processes involves writing the transformed data back into SharePoint. Depending on the type of data involved, *customers* can be internal personnel or actual customers who are purchasing goods and services through an e-commerce solution. Regardless, always keep in mind that your customers *experience a process* even though they *purchase a good or service.*

Software platforms, like SharePoint Online, are written to support mission-critical processes in your organization and, as such, are necessary to the success of those processes. But SharePoint should never take a front seat to the needs of the business to create value for your customers. Bad information management can make lean processes slow and frustrating. Decision-makers at all levels in the organization need the best information possible as they make decisions. Because many decisions occur within processes that are supplied by information, it stands to reason that if the information inputs into the process are using outdated or wrongly tagged information, the quality of the decisions made will be lowered, and this results in the organization incurring a soft, or *opportunity*, cost. Hence, our discussion on putability. You cannot go wrong focusing a major portion of your information-management effort on putability.

Term-store concepts

The term store has several concepts you'll need to understand as you learn how to manage it. First is the broad concept of *managed metadata,* which is a hierarchical collection of centrally managed terms you can define and then use as attributes for items in SharePoint Online. Second, a *term* (sometimes known as a *managed term*) is a word or a phrase that can be associated with an item in SharePoint Online that is in some way descriptive but is not always redundant to the content in the document or list item.

Third, a *term* set is a collection of related terms. You can have up to 30,000 terms in a term set (1,000,000 terms per term store). A single term store can have up to 1000 term sets. You will specify that a site column must contain a term from a specific term set. *Local term sets* are created from within the site collection when publishing is turned on. *Global term sets* are created in the term store itself. Users can see only global term sets and term sets that are local to the user's site collection.

A *term group* is a group you create that contains one or more term sets. It is also the security and management boundary within the term store. *Enterprise keywords* are words or phrases added to SharePoint items via social technologies, such as tagging and notes. All enterprise keywords are part of a single, nonhierarchical term set that is named the *keyword set* and appears under the System folder in the term store.

You can nest terms inside of terms up to 14 layers deep. Also, note that term sets and terms are not securable items, nor are they indexed. Only when terms are used in the field are the terms indexed. Metadata is never securable apart from the content element it describes, so everyone has read-only governance on the term store.

From a governance perspective, the store-wide, read-only aspect can be a serious risk to confidentiality if the terms are, in and of themselves, confidential in nature. With an on-premises deployment of SharePoint 2013, if you need to secure metadata because the terms are confidential, you can always create a new term store (a second managed metadata service), quarantine the confidential content in its own web application, and then associate that web application with the second managed metadata service. Although there were drawbacks to this architecture, it was an excellent solution to ensuring confidential terms remained confidential and available to only those with appropriate permissions. But with SharePoint Online, you don't have the option to create a second web application and metadata services. It seems to me that the only other solution is to use a local term set created from within a site collection. Then ensure permissions are applied correctly to the content that is being described by those confidential terms.

In my estimation, this second solution is not as secure as the first one because of the increased opportunity to unwittingly apply the wrong permissions. But in SharePoint Online, this is really your only option.

Term-store administration

You will use the term-store manager to create and manage term sets and terms. Specifically, you can

- Create or delete a term set
- Add, change, or delete terms
- Arrange managed terms in a term set into a hierarchy
- Define synonyms
- Import terms
- Move enterprise keywords into managed terms by moving them into a term set

MORE INFO When the publishing feature is activated at both the site-collection layer and site layer, you will be able to create one or more local term sets that are managed by the Site Administrator Term Store Manager. They will not be visible to you, the system administrator, when you view the term store through the administration interface. Term-store managers can build multiple terms sets and terms within their local term store and pin terms from global term sets into their local term sets. This effectively creates a federated metadata solution in which global terms can be managed through the term store and local terms can be managed directly by the content owners in their local term sets.

If you're familiar with working in the on-premises version of the Managed Metadata Service, the interface will be familiar to you. In Figure 4-2, notice the name of the store is system generated with "Taxonomy_<GIUD>" as the name. This is not configurable. Notice also that the default search dictionaries are created for you, as are the three common system term sets. There are configuration options on the term store itself that you need to consider. Figure 4-2 illustrates the options I'll discuss next.

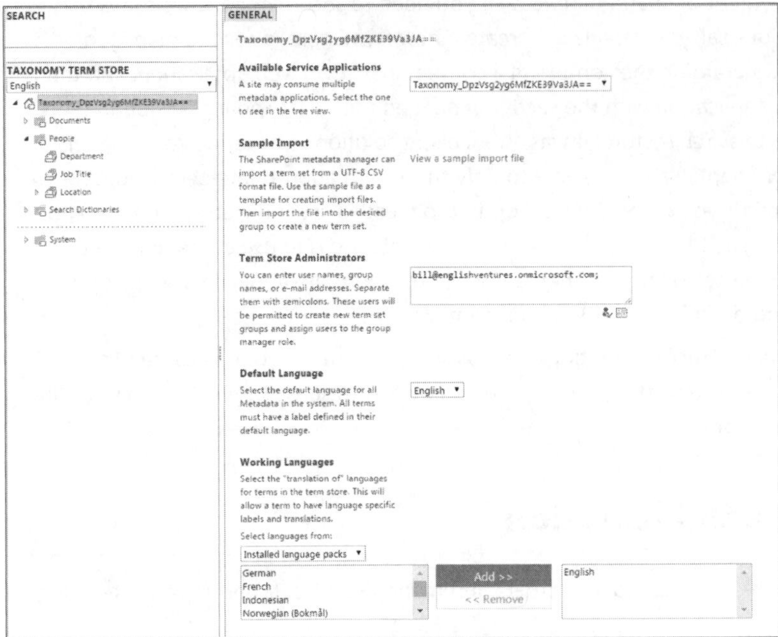

FIGURE 4-2 Term-store configuration options

First, although you can't change the name of the service application, you can download and populate an import file you can use to import and enter the term set into the term store. To download the file, just click the View Sample Import File link and SharePoint will send you a CSV file already laid out the way it needs to be in order to populate the content and then upload it.

> ***TIP*** **You will download the sample CSV file from the Store level, but import it at the Term Group level. You'll need a separate Microsoft Office Excel file for each term set you import. If you try to import multiple term sets from the same spreadsheet, the import process will hang and no error message will be given to you.**

Second, you should input the names, group names, or email addresses of those whom you want to serve in the role of Term Store Administrator. This role has full permissions to create, delete, and modify term groups, term sets, and terms plus all of their configuration settings.

Third, select the default language of your tenant, understanding that a plethora of language packs are installed with most Office 365 tenants. If you need the term store to host terms in more than one language, simply select the language in the left box under the Working Languages section and click the Add button to move it into the box on the right. The languages listed in the box on the right are those your information can be hosted in and your sites can be presented in.

> ***TIP*** **If you don't see the language you need for use in the term store, click the down arrow next to the Installed Language Packs and select Other locales. Then scroll to find the language you need, click it, and select Add. When you select a second language and save your selection, the interface will change a bit. First, a system-generated prefix will be added to all the accounts listed in the Term Store Administrator's account-picker box. It will appear as *i:0#.f|membership|<account_name>*. Second, the name of your store will change to "Managed Metadata" even though the Service application will continue to be named "Taxonomy_<GUID==". You will also see a language picker for the entire term store just above the term-store name so that different administrators can view the entire store in their native tongue.**

Managing term groups

To create a new term group, click the down arrow that will appear when you hover your mouse over the name of the term store and click the down arrow that will appear. You'll see a Create Group link, which you can click (not illustrated). A new folder will appear beneath the System folder. Type in the desired name to the right of the folder and then click outside the input area and the new folder will appear.

> ***TIP*** **If you are the tenant administrator but still don't see the drop-down arrow to create a new term group, be sure to add yourself as a Term Store Administrator.**

Deleting a folder is just as easy. Simply hover your mouse cursor over the folder, click the down arrow that appears while you're hovering the cursor over it, and then select the Delete Group option. Objects inside the group will be deleted as well and cannot be recovered, so remember this is a one-time, one-way action that has no rollback option.

The management options on a term group are related to permissions that specify who can commit which actions on the term sets and terms hosted within the term group. As you can see in Figure 4-3, the configuration options allow you to do the following:

- Set the group name.
- Type descriptive text about the group to help users better organize and use term sets in the group.

- Assign group managers who will have Contributor permissions and be allowed to add other users into the Contributor role for the term group.
- Assign contributors who will have full permissions to create, modify, or delete term sets and terms within the term group.

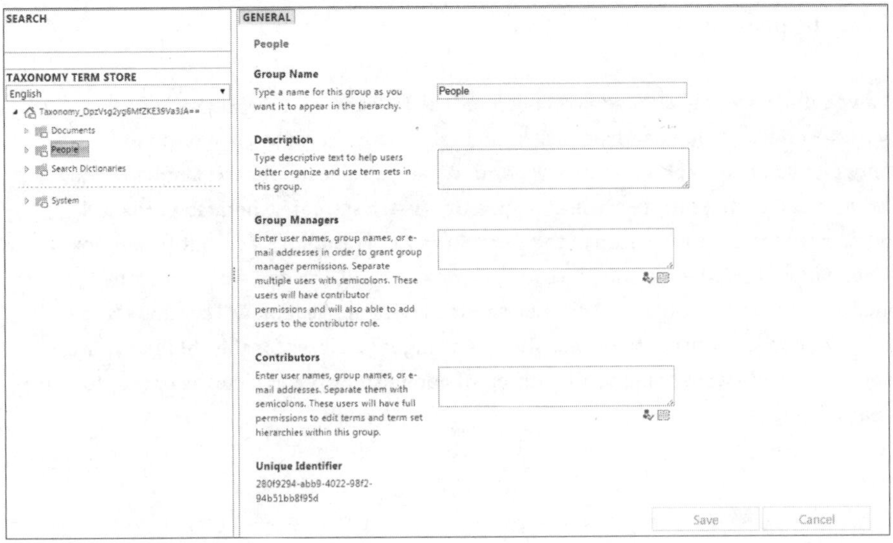

FIGURE 4-3 Management options for a term group in the term store

Managing term sets

Term sets are created inside term groups. Recall that you can create a term set simply by importing the information for the term set from an Excel spreadsheet. But you also can create new term sets by clicking the down arrow of the term group in which you want to create the set and clicking New Term Set. Name it as you wish, and press the Enter key. The term set will be created.

Term sets have a number of configuration options in the right pane that will appear when you set focus on the term set in the left pane. There are a number of configurations you'll want to consider as you build your term sets. First, you can set the term set name and enter a description of the terms that will be hosted by this term set. Second, you can set who the owner is for the term set. From a business standpoint, you'll want to input the account that will have responsibility for keeping the terms updated. Third, you should probably type an email address in the Contact text box so that suggestions for improvement on the terms in the set can be submitted. If this is a local term set, type the name of the Term Store Manager for the site collection. (The Term Store Manager is not a security role, but a given set of responsibilities to manage the term store—either at the global level or the site collection level.) If this Contact box is left empty, the suggestion feature will be disabled. Fourth, enter the names of the users and groups who should be notified before major changes are made to the terms into the Stakeholders text box.

Finally (as shown in Figure 4-4), you'll need to choose either the Open or Closed option and configure the term set accordingly. Open sets are those that accept term submissions from users as they are working with the set in the field. Closed sets are more traditional in that they do not allow users to enter terms directly into the term set; hence, they are a top-down, "one-size-fits-all" term set.

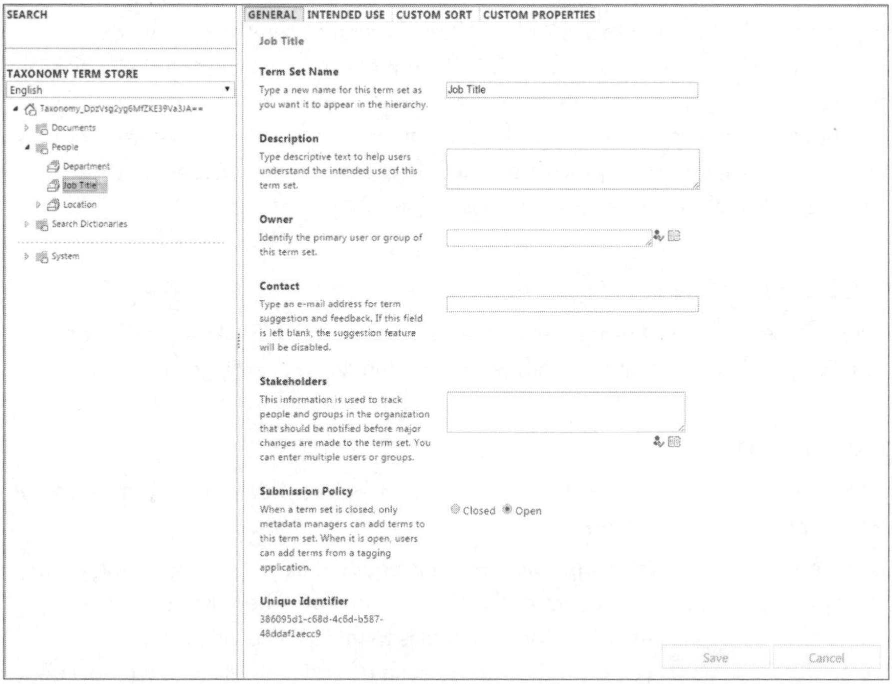

FIGURE 4-4 Term set properties

The advantage of having an open term set is that users can enter terms directly into the term set from the client interfaces. Wherever they can select a term from the term set, they will have the ability to enter their own terms and have those uploaded directly into the term set. This enables an iterative collaboration effort on the development of the term sets. The downside is that people sometimes use abbreviations and acronyms and misspell words—all leading to the need for a Term Set Manager to review and, if necessary, modify, merge, deprecate, delete, or create new terms that the larger writing and consuming teams can work with.

Having said this, many system administrators like closed term sets precisely because they are not modifiable by the end users. They don't like new terms being added and potentially misspelled. They don't like the extra effort required to find out what an abbreviation or acronym means and then going in and updating the term. They don't like this busy work.

Yet one of the main downfalls of closed term sets is the result of what George Zipf called the *Principle of Least Effort*. This principle postulates that people will naturally choose the path of least resistance or effort. As a linguist, Zipf theorized that the distribution of word use was the result of the tendency to communicate efficiently with the least effort, and this tendency accounts for why 50 percent of the words we use come from a list of 50 words. So in a closed term set, people will sometimes select terms from the list that approximate the description they would naturally choose. But if they perceive that effort to be too difficult, they might very well just choose *any* term from the list so that they can move on with their day.

Presenting a standard set of terms in a metadata field for a discreet set of data doesn't necessarily mean that content creators will select the right term or even care about which term they select. However, if an open term set is available to them, they are more likely to either care about the terms presented to them or input one of their own. Generally speaking, when users have some input into a process or when users feel a personal connection to a process, they tend to make positive contributions within that process.

Term set properties

There are three additional tabs of properties for the term sets. They are displayed on the Intended Use, Custom Sort, and Custom Properties tabs (which you can see back in Figure 4-4).

Intended Use tab

This tab (not illustrated) has three check boxes you use to indicate how you want the term set to be used. Your choices are as follows:

- **Use The Term Set For Tagging Content** This option makes the terms in the term set available as metadata on content items and documents when site columns are connected to the term set. What's helpful here is to understand that even when you get a new content type from the hub, you can extend it locally with your own metadata and, hence, use the metadata entered in the localized term sets with your extended content type.
- **Use The Term Set For Site Navigation** This option allows the values in the term set to be used for managed navigation in a publishing site. Note that this set must also have been added to the list of publishing pages as metadata in order for this feature to work. When you select this option, the Navigation and Term-Driven Pages tabs appear in the properties of individual terms, and the Term-Driven Pages tab appears in the properties of the term set.
- **Use This Term Set For Faceted Navigation** You can configure the term set to be used for faceted navigation, which means that when content items appear in the result set whose metadata is, at least in part, derived from this term set, terms within the set will appear down the left side of the page. When this option is selected, it will filter the results for those content items that only have the selected term assigned to them.

Custom Sort tab

You can use the default alphabetical language sorting of child terms, or you can set up a custom sort order to ensure the terms appear in a consistent, customized way that you, the system administrator, decides is best for your users. You should consult with your users before doing this, because introducing a customized sort order of terms without end-user consultation might slow down their work and cause unneeded frustration for everyone involved.

You will be given a pick list and can order the terms manually using the numeric drop-down menus for each term in the term set, as illustrated in Figure 4-5.

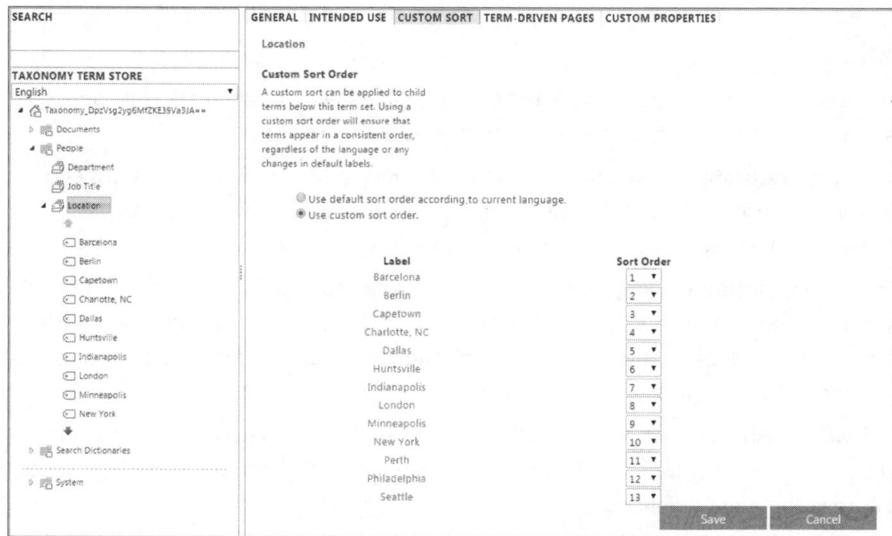

FIGURE 4-5 Custom Sort tab in the properties of a terms set, which shows how the default list is automatically sorted alphabetically and how you can manually change the sort order to suit your needs

Term-Driven Pages tab

When a term is selected within a managed navigation hierarchy, you can specify which publishing pages to load for that term. You use the Term-Driven Pages tab (not illustrated) at the term-set level to specify a single publishing page that is the default for all the terms in the term set.

The second configuration option on this page is the Catalog Item Page Settings. You use these settings to specify the publishing page that loads when terms from a term set that are used as metadata on catalog items are clicked in the managed navigation interface.

For both selections, the Browse button will surface only the local libraries in the tenant administration site and you won't be able to input an absolute URL to point to an individual page in a different site collection within the tenant. This is why using local term sets is the way to go when working with managed navigation. Cross-site publishing is where managed navigation really shines, but that topic is outside the scope of this book.

MORE INFO Individual terms can override these settings you configure for the term set.

Custom Properties tab

The Custom Properties tab (not illustrated) allows you to enter new metadata fields and their custom properties to help describe the term set. These metadata assignments are also shared across all terms in the term set. This way, you can store any metadata with each of the terms, which can then be used at runtime to drive additional logic.

Translation

If you have more than one language selected for your tenant, a Translation tab will appear (not illustrated). You can select to have words translated using one of three options:

- **Machine Translate** This option sends the contents to Microsoft's online translation service to translate content into different languages. The content will then be sent back to your site and appear in the configured location.
- **Create Translation Package** You can create a *translation package* for content that is exported to an XLIFF (.XLF) file. (*XLIFF* stands for XML Localization Interchange File Format.) This is a format that translation software can read. The software translates the content and saves it to the XLIFF file.
- **Upload Translation** Once the translation software has translated the content and saved it back to the XLIFF format, you can upload the XLIFF file and the content will be placed in the right Variations feature.

MORE INFO To learn more about how translation services works for SharePoint online, reference this online Office support article on SharePoint variations: ***https://support.office.com/en-us/article/Create-a-multi-language-website-da0b5614-8cf5-4905-a44c-90c2b3f8fbb6.***

Managing terms and term properties

Terms are created inside term sets and can have nesting up to 14 layers deep. *Terms* are the words that will be made available for metadata on content items and documents. You can perform the following actions (as shown in Figure 4-6) on terms:

- **Copy** A copy of the term will be created within the same term set. The new term will be named using the following format: Copy of <*original term name*>. No child terms for the source term will be copied.
- **Reuse** This option adds the reused term beneath the selected term in the tree view pane. You must have Contributor rights for the group for any term you want to reuse.

- **Pin** Similar to reusing a term, pinning a term allows the term to appear in other term sets with the following differences: the destination pinned term will be read-only, and child terms of the pinned term will be synchronized back to the source term.
- **Deprecate** This action makes this term no longer available for tagging. Child terms are not deprecated. To make the term available again for tagging, select Enable Term from the drop-down menu that appears when you click the down arrow next to the term itself.
- **Merge** The selected term—along with its synonyms and translations—will be merged into the selected target term. The original IDs of each term are preserved so that tags that used the old term IDs still work for search, but the old IDs will not be available for new tagging. Content tagged with the merged term will not be updated, but it will be returned in searches for the term that is the merge target. You can merge only siblings in the term set.
- **Move** This moves the selected term and any child terms to the target location, even if it is another term set.
- **Delete** This action deletes the term and any child terms below it. If this term is a source term for terms that are reused in other locations, it will be placed in the Orphaned Terms term set in the System group. If the term is not reused elsewhere, it is completely deleted. If this is a reused term, this action removes the term from the current term set.

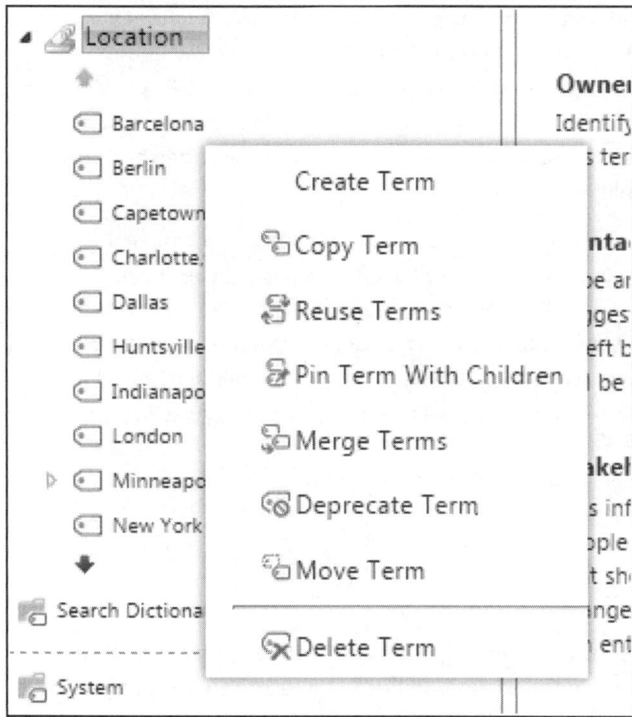

FIGURE 4-6 The context menu that appears when you click the drop-down arrow for a term in the term store

Pinning vs. reusing terms

If you want a particular term to exist in multiple term sets or at multiple levels within your term store, you'll want to *reuse* the term. (This action applies to all child terms of the term too, effectively reusing all the child terms as well.) This action is more than simply making a copy of a term and its child terms. If you make a change to the properties, modify aliases, or add aliases to the term, either in the source term or the reused term, it synchronizes with the other location or locations where it is used. This linkage holds true across however many instances or locations you reuse the same term.

> ***NOTE*** If you want to reuse a term without this action applying to the child terms, you'll need to use Microsoft Windows PowerShell or perform this action programmatically through the relevant APIs. Note also that new children added to the source term or the reused term are not automatically added to the linkage that was set up when the source term was initially reused.

Pinning a term is essentially the same as reusing a term. When you select to pin a term, the term, along with its child terms, will be copied to the target location. However, the link between a pinned term and source term is not as complete as the link for a reused term. For example, the only thing that can be altered at the destination term is whether or not it is available for tagging, and optionally you can choose the Custom Sort Order option for the child terms. Similar to the reused terms, those two properties can be changed, but they are not synchronized between the source and destination pinned terms.

One quirk is that new child terms created at the source are copied to the pinned term as child terms, unlike reused terms. From a governance perspective, if you need changes in the child terms to be consistently replicated between the source and destinations, use pinned terms. But if property changes are more important to be synchronized, reused terms seems to be the better option. In addition, pinned terms are commonly used to create custom navigation hierarchies by selecting terms from multiple term sets.

Term properties

Similar to the properties I discussed with the term groups and term sets, there are properties that can be configured on the terms. In this section, I'll briefly discuss these properties. The configurations you set on an individual term will override any conflicting configurations at the term-set level, term-group level, or both.

General properties

When you set focus on a term in the term store, you'll be presented with several tabs in the right pane. The first tab is the General tab (shown in Figure 4-7). On this tab, you can configure a number of basic properties for the term.

First, you'll see a check box that specifies the term is to be made available for tagging. By default, this check box is selected, which means the term is available for tagging in the client interface. To remove this term from serving in a tagging role, clear the check box.

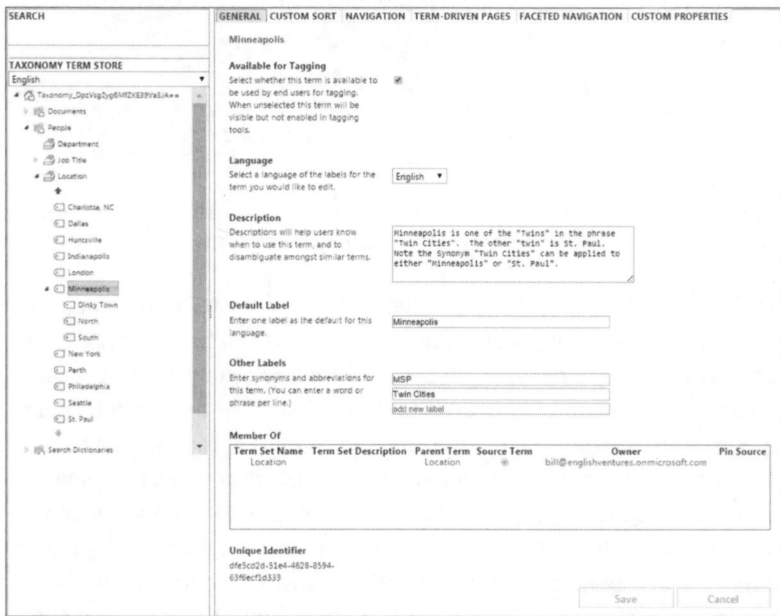

FIGURE 4-7 General properties tab for a term in the Term Store

Second, as you can see in Figure 4-7, you can select the default language in which you want the term to appear. Use the drop-down pick list to select the default language for this term. Note that only the languages you have enabled at the term-store layer (which is discussed in the section "Term-store administration") will appear in this drop-down list.

Third, you can write up a description of the term to help define what the term means and how it is to be used in your larger tagging architecture. The description will appear for your users when they hover their cursor over the term in the Select Term dialog box, as illustrated in Figure 4-8. This dialog box was produced by editing the properties of a document in a team site, where one of the properties is a site column that is connected to the Locations term set in the term store. When the user browses for a value, the terms produced are coming from the term set. Adding a description helps the user understand how to use the term appropriately.

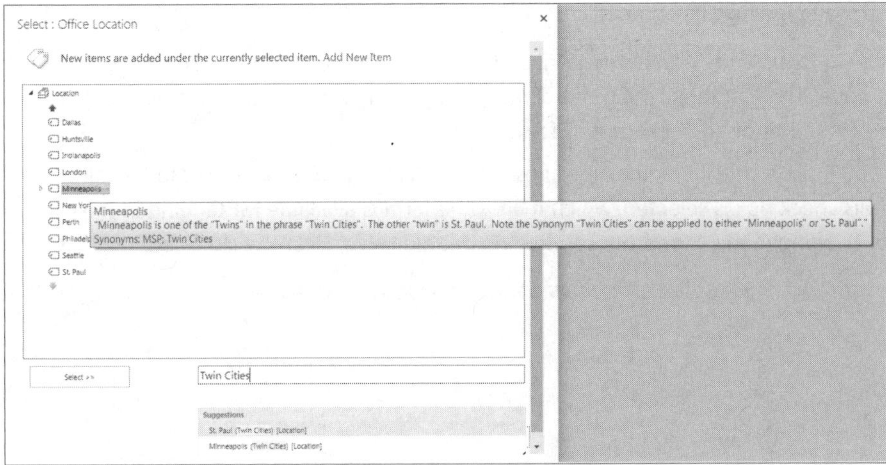

FIGURE 4-8 Text displayed in a box when the cursor hovers over an option, which differs from Figure 4-7 in which the description and synonyms are input on the General tab for the term's properties

Next (as shown in Figure 4-7), you can change the default label of the term by typing in a different label for the term in the Default Labels input box and input one or more synonyms, including abbreviations and acronyms, by typing in one or more labels in the Other Labels input box. If you worked with SharePoint Server 2007 and earlier, you can think of this Other Labels section as replacing the Expansion Sets in the Thesaurus XML files that we had to manage manually. (It's not a one-to-one equivalent, but in concept, it's roughly the same.) To this end, if the term is "Minneapolis," you can enter a synonym as "MSP" and a search on "MSP" should produce documents that contain "Minneapolis," even if the document is only tagged with "Minneapolis" and doesn't actually contain the synonym in its content. In a sense, this allows your term-store administrators to group common terms under a single term and also provide more refined meaning around a term set.

The difference between using a synonym (for example, "Minneapolis" or "MSP") and a nested term (for example, "Minneapolis:MSP") is that a nested term is its own term and is generally thought to be a clear defining extension of the parent term. It's a matter of hierarchical logic vs. lateral similarities. For example, although you can use the airport code "MSP" as a synonym for "Minneapolis," "MSP" is not a subset of "Minneapolis." However, the names of various areas of the city of Minneapolis could be considered a subset of the parent term "Minneapolis," such as "North Minneapolis" or "South Minneapolis." In the term set, it will appear as illustrated in Figure 4-9. However, in the term-selection box, the nesting would appear as "North [Location:Minneapolis]," where "Minneapolis" is the parent to the term "North" in the Suggestions area of the Select dialog box and other interfaces where a term can be manually entered into a metadata field that is connected to a term set.

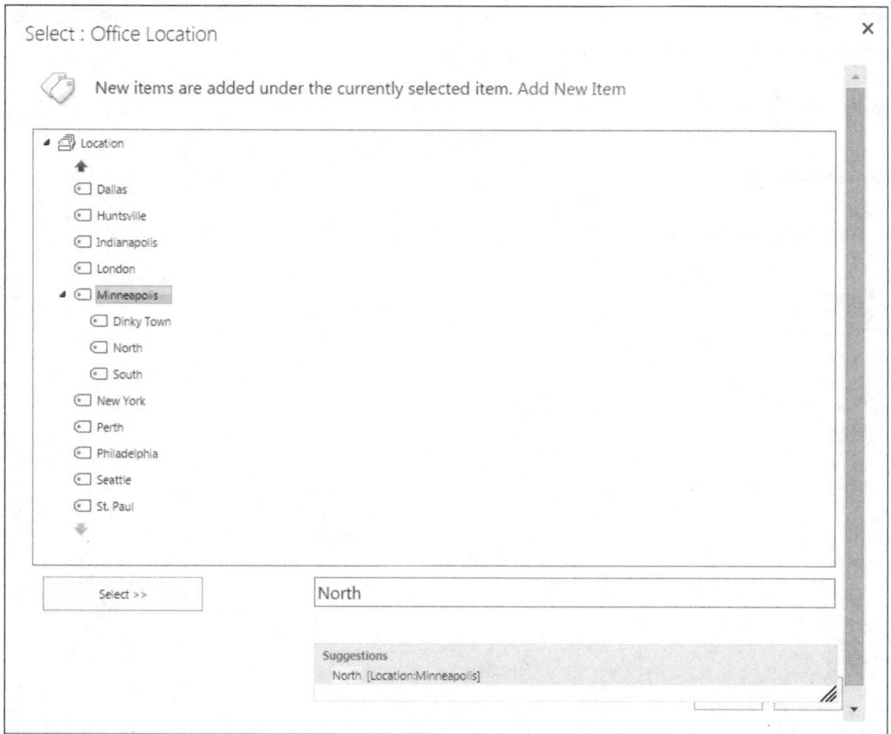

FIGURE 4-9 Illustration of a nested term in the Location term set

Finally, in the Member Of information box (shown earlier in Figure 4-7), SharePoint will present you with certain vitals concerning the term in focus. It will report the name of the term set that the term is a member of, the term set's description, the parent term (the term set name will be the parent term for first-level terms within a given term set), whether it is a source term, who the owner of the term set is and, if the term is pinned, the source of the pinning. In this area, you can see that the term "North" has the parent term of "Minneapolis" and is created in the "Location" term set.

Navigation

On the Navigation tab, there are several configurations for individual terms. (See Figure 4-10.) First, the Navigation Node Appearance area is where you set a title for the term. This allows a different label to be used in managed navigation menus. The default title is the term itself, but you can change it so that a different word or string of characters appears in the navigation menu while keeping the root term the same. You can think of the Navigation Node Appears setting as an alias that can be entered that represents the original term. Note that the Managed Navigation feature uses only this property or the default label of the language matching that which the web was originally provisioned in. Different labels for different languages will not be used based on the locale of the site, nor based on a browser locale detected in combination with alternative supported languages. For this reason, there is not a Navigation Node Title option for each language.

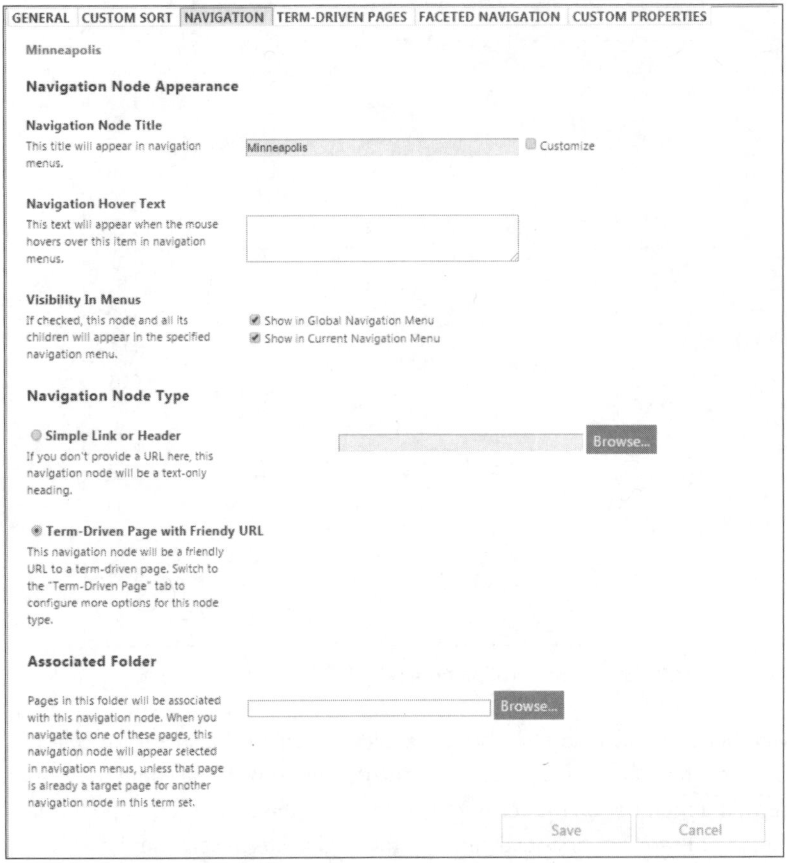

GENERAL | CUSTOM SORT | NAVIGATION | TERM-DRIVEN PAGES | FACETED NAVIGATION | CUSTOM PROPERTIES

Minneapolis

Navigation Node Appearance

Navigation Node Title
This title will appear in navigation menus.
Minneapolis
Customize

Navigation Hover Text
This text will appear when the mouse hovers over this item in navigation menus.

Visibility In Menus
If checked, this node and all its children will appear in the specified navigation menu.
Show in Global Navigation Menu
Show in Current Navigation Menu

Navigation Node Type

Simple Link or Header
If you don't provide a URL here, this navigation node will be a text-only heading.
Browse...

Term-Driven Page with Friendly URL
This navigation node will be a friendly URL to a term-driven page. Switch to the "Term-Driven Page" tab to configure more options for this node type.

Associated Folder
Pages in this folder will be associated with this navigation node. When you navigate to one of these pages, this navigation node will appear selected in navigation menus, unless that page is already a target page for another navigation node in this term set.
Browse...

Save | Cancel

FIGURE 4-10 Navigation property configurations for a single term in the term store

Because managed navigation menus can be configured for either the Global navigation menu (links across the top of the page) or Current navigation menu (links down the left side of the page), you can choose to set this term (and its child terms) to be available in either the Global or Current navigation menu or both. The default is both. Clear the check boxes you want to remove from using this term and its child terms in the managed navigation menus.

In the Navigation Node Type area, you can transform the term into a link by selecting the Simple Link Or Header option and then specifying a URL that the term will link to. The URL need not be internal to your tenant. So you could build a term set with terms that are links to external resources often accessed by your tenant users. For example, if you're working in a parts-distribution company with 500,000 parts from 40 different vendors, you could create a term set with those vendor names and then set a link for each vendor name. Then the list can be exposed in the sites as a managed navigation item such that users simply click the term and they are taken to the vendor's website.

If you leave the default Term-Driven Page With Friendly URL option selected, the term will not point to any default page and you'll need to use the Term-Driven Page tab to specify the publishing page to which you want the term to link.

If your site already has webpages organized into folders, you can associate each folder that contains pages with a term in the navigation term set. When a user views one of the pages, the term's node in the navigation hierarchy will appear as if it had been selected. Use the Associated Folder field on the Navigation tab in the Term Store Management tool to associate a folder on the site with a navigation term.

Term-driven pages

Similar to the Term-Driven Pages configuration for term sets, this page gives you the ability to set several configurations for the terms that flow through to the functionality of the site. The term's term set is selected for managed navigation. Each term in a navigation term set has a friendly URL that loads a physical page in the context of that term. Terms in the navigation term set can be configured to do one of the following:

- Point to the same page as other terms
- Point to a unique page for each term
- Point to a URL or appear only as text

On this page, you can select your target-page settings. The first setting specifies an individual page that loads when this term is selected in the managed navigation hierarchy. Second, you can select a different page that loads for child terms of this term.

If this term is used as a category for a catalog list, you can specify the target catalog item page you want to appear for this term and, if needed, a different catalog item page for child terms of this term.

Faceted navigation

The Faceted Navigation tab (not illustrated) will appear only when you select the Use This Term Set For Faceted Navigation check box on the Intended Use tab in the Term Set properties. You'll do this when your users need to refine search results whose content items are described, in part, with the term set in which the term resides. Refining gives users the ability to narrow down the result set, making it easier to find what they are looking for. *Faceted navigation* is the ability to define different refiners for different terms.

By customizing the refiners that are associated with a term, when a content item that is described with this term appears in a result set, the other refiners will appear as well to help users refine their result set more thoroughly. By default, all child terms will inherit what is set on the term in focus.

> ***MORE INFO*** To learn more about how to configure Faceted Navigation, refer to this MSDN blog post: *http://blogs.msdn.com/b/faceted_navigation_in_sharepoint_2013/archive/2012/11/23/10371130.aspx.*

Custom Properties tab

On the Custom Properties tab (not illustrated), you can configure customized shared and local properties for a term. Shared properties are those that are available on all reused or pinned instances of the term, regardless of where those instances reside within the term store. The local properties are those that are available only on this instance of the term and are not shared with reused or pinned instances of it. In either case, just enter the property name and value and it will be saved. The Name text box cannot contain any of the following characters: " ; < > | and Tab. However, the Value text box does not have any character restrictions.

Content types and the Content Type Publishing Hub

Traditionally, content types are created in the content type gallery of a site collection. With the advent of the Managed Metadata Service in SharePoint 2010, we were able to create content types in the *hub* and then have them syndicated to all of the content type galleries in each site collection around our farm. The hub was little more than a specified site collection somewhere in your farm that was designated as the "hub." Once designated as the hub, that site collection was given additional functionality recognized by the other site collections in the farm. The obvious advantage to creating content types in the content type hub is that you create the types once and reuse them many times.

Content types are the backbone of the publishing model and provide the underlying plumbing for data movement within the farm. Getting this part right is vital to delivering a quality publishing solution for your organization.

In SharePoint Online, you need to understand that the content type hub has been set up automatically for you. You just have to know where to find it. You can't get to it from Tenant Administration like you might expect. Instead, you can find the location by going to the Site Settings page of any site collection and then clicking the Content Type Publishing link. Once you do this, you're presented with the Content Type Publishing Hubs page in the local site collection. (See Figure 4-11.) By default, SharePoint Online creates the hub in the /sites/contentTypeHub site collection when the online platform is initially provisioned. This URL is hidden from the Site Collections interface and the Sites page.

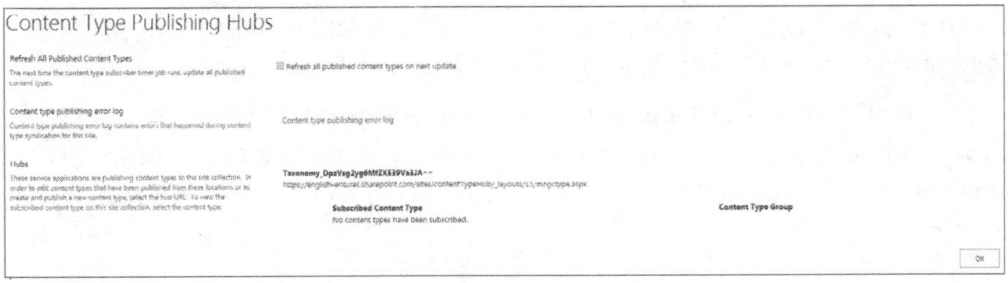

FIGURE 4-11 The Content Type Publishing Hubs page

MORE INFO Only the original Office 365 account creator has access to the Content Type Publishing Hub site collection. Accessing it with another user will get you an "access denied" error message even if you are a global administrator. A workaround for this is to use the following URL to access the site. Just replace "tenantname" with your Office 365 tenant name. Once you are in, you should be able to assign yourself as a site collection administrator to the Content Type Hub.

```
https://tenantname-admin.sharepoint.com/_layouts/15/online/
TA_SiteCollectionOwnersdialog.aspx?site=https://tenantname.sharepoint.com/
sites/contentTypeHub
```

For more information, you can reference the following blog posts:

```
http://www.jasperoosterveld.com/2014/06/sharepoint-online-cant-access-the-
content-type-hub/
```

```
http://dotnetmafia.sys-con.com/node/2172946/mobile
```

A *content type* is nothing more than a data element with metadata fields wrapped up into a template that is used, in turn, to create a content item. Content types have an inheritance model, so lower-layer content types can inherit the settings from upper-layer content types. Lower-layer content types can be extended to include metadata not found in the upper-layer content types, and all content types can be used to create or derive new content types within a given content type gallery.

For example, the default Document content type inherits from the Item content type, which inherits from the System content type, which is not accessible or configurable. You can't get to the root content type—it is not exposed.

WARNING Do not modify the default content types because they might be overridden with an update from Microsoft. Best practice is to create a new content type if you need to customize a content type.

When you create a new content type, you'll need to specify a name for the content type and select the parent content type via the two drop-down lists in the interface. You'll also need to decide which group within the content type gallery you're going to place it in. If you're creating many content types, you'll need to think through your naming conventions as well as your groupings.

From a risk and governance perspective, content types can swiftly become confusing if you don't have a good process-based strategy for creating and maintaining content types, and for defining their purpose, use, and metadata assignments. Ironically, I have found that those who implement robust content type deployments usually keep track of the details outside of SharePoint or they write custom code to surface the information they need to manage the content type topology effectively. It's not enough to simply know the content is created in the gallery. What's needed is to understand its settings and ensure that wherever the content type is used, those settings are consistent with the processes being used within the site collection. From a management viewpoint, you'll want to document the following:

- Content type name
- Purpose
- Metadata fields (site columns)
- Term set usage
- Inheritance information
- Responsible party (who asked for it to be created?)
- Document template information
- Document information panel
- Workflow associations
- Information security policy settings

Content type settings

A content type has several settings that will require your attention. Let's consider each one individually.

Name, description, and group

This page is identical to the page you used to create the content type. However, it's nice to know you can come back and change the name, description, and grouping of the content type after it has been created.

Advanced Settings page

This is a core page (which is shown in Figure 4-12) for managing content types, and it is the only page exposed to a consumer of a published content type. On this page, you can set a document template for the content type, choose whether or not the content type is modifiable, and decide if changes to this content type will be pushed down to child content types. Note that, in effect, the Update Sites And Lists option allows you to break inheritance from the *parent, not the child.* Although seemingly elementary, these settings are important to understand.

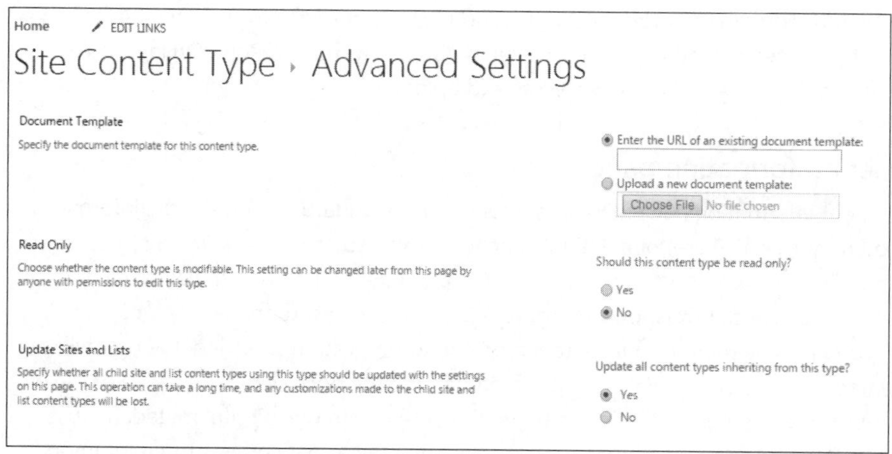

FIGURE 4-12 Content type advanced settings

Publishing a template with a content type

In many scenarios, you'll want to include a template with your content type. You can upload the template directly to the content, or you can reference a URL location from which the content type template can be downloaded and used to create the content item. Ideally, you'll want this capability to be applicable across site collections, so uploading a template to the content type will ensure the template is available when the content type is used to create a new content item.

Even though the interface doesn't tell you this, you can't put a document in a library, point the URL of the content type to the library document, and then expect to use it across site collections. It just doesn't work like it appears that it should work in the interface. If you want to enter the URL directly of a document template, you'll need to engage a developer, who will need to write a solution that is deployed around your farm. Because most organizations aren't going to do this, I suggest that this is not the way to manage document templates for content types. Instead, it's easiest to upload the template directly to the content type. After you have done this, it will be assigned directly to the content type and the template will be syndicated out to all the site collections with the content type. Part of your tracking and management process for this part of content types will be to keep a copy of the template you uploaded to the content type in a source location and ensure you have a process in place for updating the content type's document template when the template itself is updated.

Workflow settings

On the workflow settings page (not illustrated), you can associate one or more workflows with a content type and, assuming your workflows will exist in the consuming site, every time a content item is created using the content type, the workflows will be available for use with the content type. The workflows will need to be propagated separately around your farm. Content-type syndication does not syndicate the workflows themselves.

You can add more than one workflow by using the web interface to build the basic workflow. If you need something more than what appears with SharePoint Online, you'll need to have a developer write the workflow and upload it into your tenant.

Document information panel

The document information panel (DIP) is one of the more underused tools in the information-management quiver of SharePoint. I highly encourage you to use this feature. By selecting the Always Show Document Information Panel On Document Open And Initial Save For This Content Type check box (shown in Figure 4-13), you can ensure that every time an Office document is opened from a content type configured with this setting, the user will be presented with the opportunity to input metadata on the document. This is one of the easiest ways there is to ensure that users tag their content with meaningful metadata. Just by giving users an interface in which they can select metadata that comes from a common location, over time, they will be more apt to adopt the process of tagging their content with meaningful metadata.

You can use the default DIP, or you can use a customized interface. The customized interface can be placed at a specified location, or you can upload an existing InfoPath form that will attach itself to the content type. The good part with using an InfoPath form is that the input boxes in an InfoPath form can have code behind them so that, depending on the values entered, certain code either fires or doesn't fire. You'll have three options for setting a document information panel. This setting must be made first on the content type before it appears in the client interface.

> ***MORE INFO*** **If you want to learn more about the differences between URLs, UNC, and URNs, reference this RFC:** ***http://tools.ietf.org/html/rfc2396.***

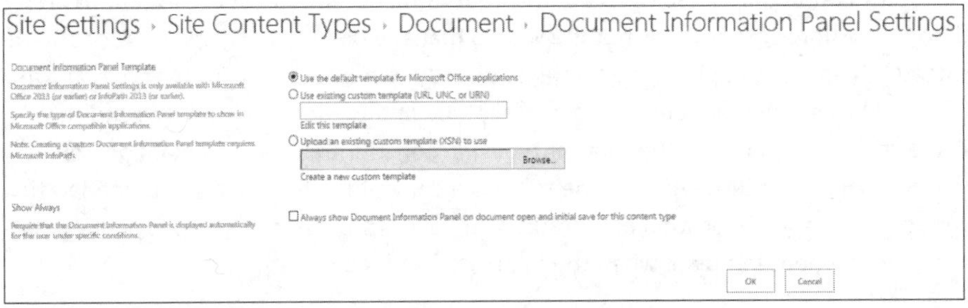

Site Settings › Site Content Types › Document › Document Information Panel Settings

Document Information Panel Template

Document Information Panel Settings is only available with Microsoft Office 2013 (or earlier) or InfoPath 2013 (or earlier).

Specify the type of Document Information Panel template to show in Microsoft Office compatible applications.

Note: Creating a custom Document Information Panel template requires Microsoft InfoPath.

- Use the default template for Microsoft Office applications
- Use existing custom template (URL, UNC, or URN)
  Edit this template
- Upload an existing custom template (XSN) to use
  Browse...
  Create a new custom template

Show Always

Require that the Document Information Panel is displayed automatically for the user under specific conditions.

- Always show Document Information Panel on document open and initial save for this content type

OK Cancel

FIGURE 4-13 Document Information Panel settings with three different options for configuring the panel

Figure 4-13 shows a document information panel in an Excel spreadsheet. In Figure 4-14, the content type that was used to create this spreadsheet has an additional site column titled "Year" and, because the DIP was selected in the content type, it appears in the DIP between the ribbon and spreadsheet.

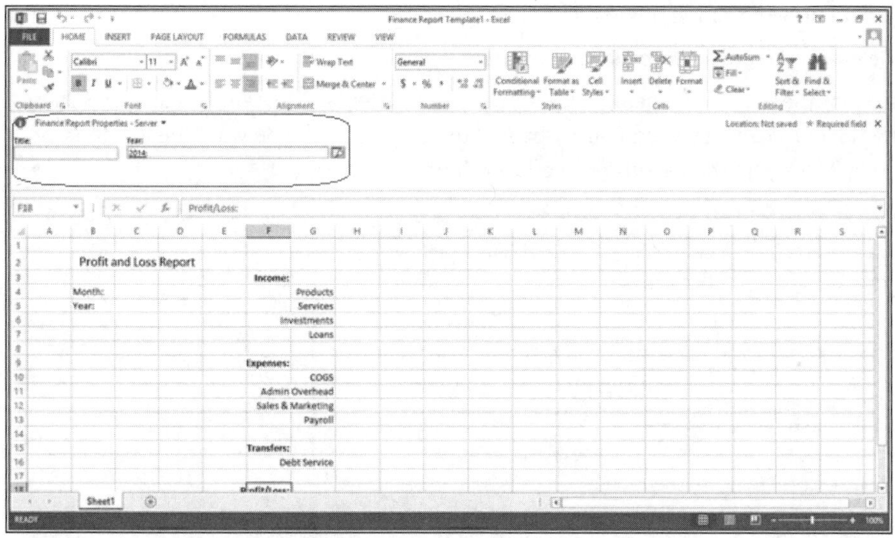

FIGURE 4-14 The document information panel in an Excel 2013 spreadsheet

Information-management policy settings

The information-management policy settings allow you, the administrator, to implement life-cycle management for every content item that is created using the content type. Because these content types can be syndicated around your tenant, you can enforce the item's through these information policy settings. In addition to setting life-cycle management policies, you also can set policies concerning auditing, barcoding, and labeling. If you do enough work up front, you can nearly eliminate old and outdated documents and content items in your SharePoint tenant.

RETENTION SETTINGS

Retention settings (shown in Figure 4-15) are built from a combination of events, actions, and recurrences. You can specify the stage to be based on the time the content item was created, modified, or declared a record. The amount of time after which that event has occurred can be specified in terms of years, months, or days. The actions that can be taken include the following:

- Move the item to the Recycle Bin.
- Permanently delete the item.
- Transfer the item to another location.
- Start a workflow.
- Skip to the next stage.
- Declare the item a record.

- Delete previous drafts of the item.
- Delete all the previous versions of the item.

If you want the action to repeat, you simply need to select the Repeat This Stage's Action Until The Next Stage Is Activated check box and then select when you want the action to be repeated by specifying the Recurrence Period setting.

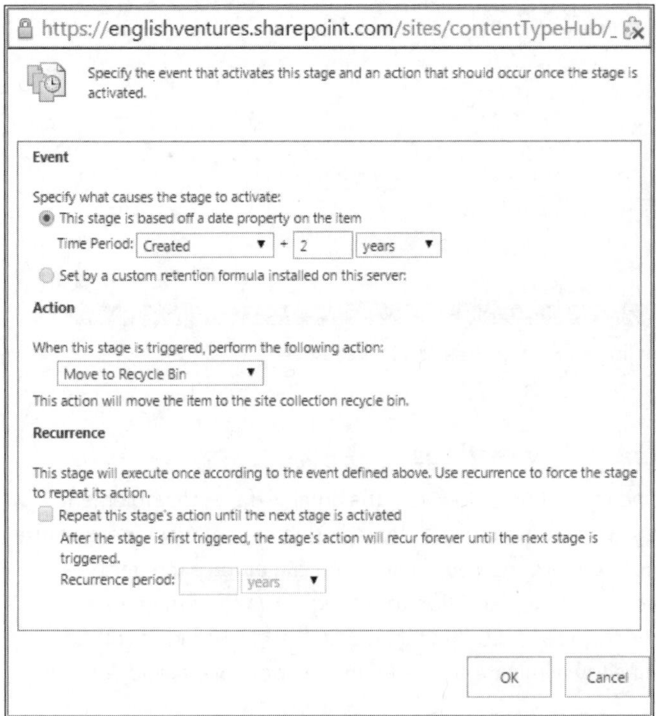

FIGURE 4-15 Configuring a retention stage in the information-management properties of a content type

From a governance perspective, by setting up a simple process visualization that will allow you to understand the life cycle of particular types of content items, you can forecast what will need to happen with the content item as it moves through its life cycle and processes.

Moreover, you'll want to build workflows that will ensure that when the document is moved from one life-cycle stage to the next that it is moved through an approval process where the decisions are tracked within the SharePoint system. For core, mission-critical documents that are most likely to be subjected to an eDiscovery process, it is best to use workflows instead of manual intervention to move the document from one stage to the next. (eDiscovery is part of a legal process where opposing counsel is given permission to find, or discover, information from their opponent that will help them make their arguments in court.) The task lists behind the workflows will give you a decision (in most cases, an approval) history of what has taken place as a document or content item is moved through its life cycle and processes. This will also give you an opportunity to show, in case of an eDiscovery event, that proper processes were followed as the document was created, how it was hosted, how it was published and consumed, and how it was archived.

Governance is less about enforcement of rules and more about risk mitigation. Having the system track what has happened can be a deterrent to users interacting with the system in an unauthorized way.

AUDITING

Auditing can be set at the content-type layer, where the auditing settings are enforced regardless of where the content item is created. These settings will override any site-collection auditing settings because they are applied at the content-type layer. Through the auditing features in SharePoint Online, you can track virtually every click in SharePoint if you really want to. You can track the following actions:

- Opening or downloading
- Editing
- Checking out
- Checking in
- Moving or copying
- Deleting or restoring items

This means that if you need to know what has happened with a particular content item, you should set up the auditing at the content-type layer, and even if auditing is configured differently at the site collection layer, the auditing set on the content type will be enforced.

Managing publishing

If you're working with the Content Type Publishing Hub , the Manage Publishing For This Content Type setting will be the area you use to publish a particular content type from the hub. Bear in mind that the SharePoint Online version of the Managed Metadata Service (MMS) is fundamentally different than SharePoint 2013 On-Premises.

In SharePoint 2013 On-Premises, just because a content type is published from the MMS does not mean that the content type is automatically published to all the other site collections within the farm if the web application is associated with the MMS service application. In SharePoint Online, each site collection's content-type gallery is exposed for direct administration. So, if you want to create new content types or extend existing ones in a given site collection within your tenant, you can do so within the site collection itself. If you want to create a content type that is syndicated to all the site collections, you'll need to work within the content type publishing hub. Just enter the URL for the gallery manually, which is *<site_URL>*/_layouts/15/mngctype.aspx.

When it comes to working with content types in the Content Type Publishing Hub, understand that what you do at the hub will need to be manually published to the other site collections in the tenant. When you publish from the hub, notice that your three choices are to publish, unpublish, or republish. (See the following list for more information.) When you initially get this screen for the first time for any given content type, the publishing button will be selected automatically. The way that you will know that the content type has not been published is that there will be no date or time after the last successful published date-notification area of the screen. If you simply click OK at this point, the date and the time will automatically appear and you will know that the content type has been published. The elements of an enterprise content type that get published include the following:

- Content type with all the corresponding columns
- Document template (for document content types)
- Document set content type
- Information-management policies
- Workflow associations, but not the workflows themselves

If your enterprise content type defines workflows, you will need to ensure the workflows are available in the site collections, where the content types are going to be syndicated. Once those content types land in the destination gallery, they will be re-associated with the workflow(s). If the workflow doesn't exist in the destination site, no assignment is made and the content type will function to the extent it can without the workflow.

For the content types that are on the hub site collection, you can perform the following actions:

- **Publish** This is the action used when the content type is being syndicated for the first time.
- **Unpublish** This means that the content type should no longer be in syndication. The effect of an unpublish action is that the content type is made read/write at the local level and is still available for use at the local level, but it is no longer available in a read-only version from the hub.
- **Republish** This action is used when changes to the content type have been made and you want to push those changes out to the consuming audience.
- **Roll-Up Errors From Consuming Site Collections** It is possible, in a scenario where there are thousands of content types being published from a single hub, that some content types will contain errors. In those instances, all of the consuming sites will report their errors back to the hub so that the content types can be fixed and republished.

Consuming a content type

From the consuming side of the content type publishing, you can perform these actions either within the content type gallery or from the Content Type Publishing Hub administration page:

- **Extend a published content type** Consuming sites can add more columns to the content type in order to give that content type more specificity in the local environment.

- **Derive from a published content type** This means you can use a published content type as one from which to inherit in order to create new, local content types.
- **View import errors** This will allow the consuming site to view the errors that it is reporting back to the hub.
- **Refresh all content types from the hub** This action allows the consuming site to erase all the syndicated content types and perform a new, full download of the existing published content types from the hub. This can be especially helpful when the hub has been down, the consuming site has been down, or connectivity has been lost and there is a need to capture all the new, updated changes from the hub.

You click the Content Type Publishing link in the Site Collection Administration menu to find the last two options (which are shown in Figure 4-16). The dialog box shows you where your hub is in your tenant. The site collection that hosts the hub is hidden by default, but it is accessible from this page.

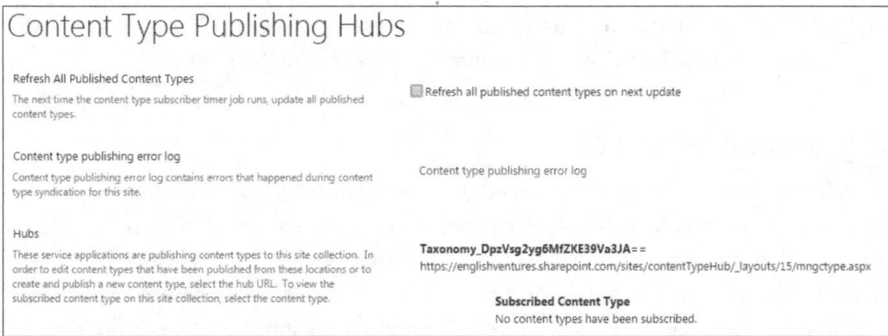

FIGURE 4-16 Content-type publishing hub information at the site-collection level

Managing navigation and local term sets

In SharePoint 2013, Microsoft abstracted the navigation of a site from the site's page and site-collection structure. This abstraction persists in SharePoint Online. Managed navigation is available only when the publishing features are activated at the site collection and site layers. You'll use managed navigation in any site in which you want the structure of the site navigation to be separate from the structure of the site's pages and its content. The navigation elements are consumed from a term set in the term store. If the term sets you need for managed navigation are not available to you from the global term sets in the term store, you can create your own term sets that are local to your site collection.

Normally, when a new publishing page is created and then published, the URL name of the page is inserted into the navigation of the site if the site-collection administrator has chosen to show pages in either the Global or Current navigation (or both). The create and publishing action of the page also creates new terms in the navigation with a one-to-one relationship between the page that is created and the navigation term. This technology's pedigree traces back to the old Microsoft Content Management Server platforms and, essentially, has persisted through today.

The downside of this architecture is that those who create the pages must pay attention to the names they give to the them. By using managed navigation, you can get away from the one-to-one relationship of a single term to a single page, change the navigation term set, and have those changes appear on your site without having to add new pages or change the physical structure of the site and its content.

Note that in SharePoint Online, when a new page is created from the Gear/Create Page menu option, a new term is not created in the managed navigation because this action does not create a new publishing page. Instead, it creates a new wiki page. When publishing is activated within a site collection, one of the results of that activation is a new Pages library, which is substantively different than the Site Pages library. The Site Pages library will hold the nonpublishing, wiki pages. Do not confuse the two. The Pages library hosts the publishing pages that can be included in the managed navigation hierarchy. The Site Pages library hosts the wiki pages, which cannot participate in the managed navigation hierarchy.

Creating a local term set

Local term sets are created by site-collection administrators directly from within the Site Settings interface. Local term sets look, feel, behave, and are administered the same as global term sets. They are created in the term store but are reserved for, or local to, the site collection from which they were created. At the Site Administration layer, there is a link—*Term Store Management*—that allows a site user with sufficient permissions to administrate the term sets and terms that are hosted in the local term store.

To create a local term set, click the Navigation link in the Look And Feel section of Site Settings. The Navigation Settings page will appear. In Figure 4-17, I selected the Managed Navigation: The Navigation Items Will Be Represented Using A Managed Metadata Term Set option button for the Current Navigation. Once I do this, the screen refreshes and a Managed Navigation: Term Set element is added to the *areanavigationsettings.aspx* page (which is shown in Figure 4-17). The navigation screen displays the graphical interface to browse the term store and select the term set you want to have appear as the managed navigation hierarchy. It will also give you the ability to create a new, local term set.

So, to create a new local, term set, just click the Create Term Set button. Within the interface, one new term group and two new term sets are automatically created for you. The term group is named Site Collection - *<Root tenant URL>*, and the two term sets created are *<Tenant Name>* Team Site Navigation and Wiki Categories. To manage these elements, click the Term Store Management link.

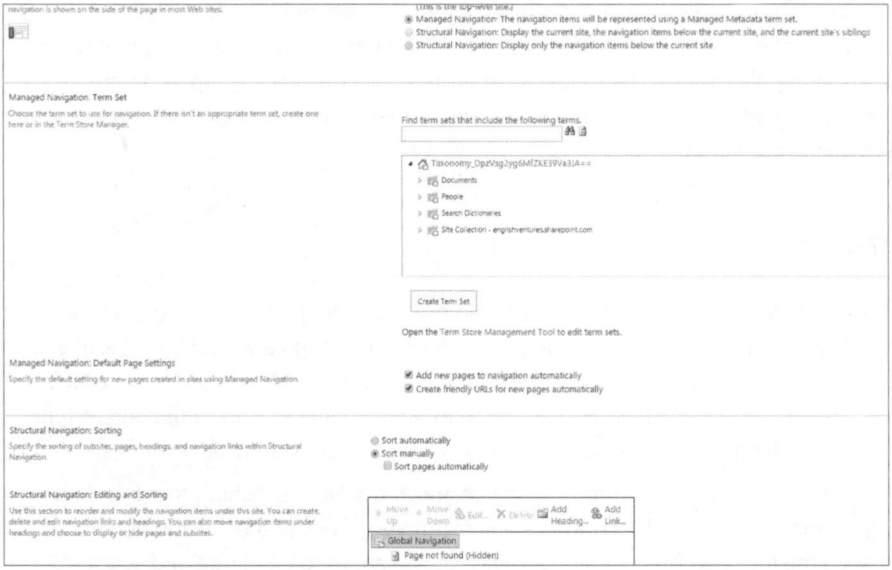

FIGURE 4-17 Managed Navigation: Term Set element that appears when the Managed Navigation option button is selected

When you do this, you're taken back to the term store, but now with a new twist: your local term group appears beneath the System folder. If you expand it, you'll see the newly created term sets in which you can create new terms. You also can create more term sets if you'd like and then go about the business of copying, reusing, pinning, or creating new terms between the global terms sets and your local term sets. Note that you cannot copy an entire global term set directly to your local term group, so if you need those terms in your Local Term Group, a nice workaround is to perform this three-step process:

1. Copy the global term set. Click the down arrow for the global term set you want to copy, and select Copy Term Set. This will create another global term set that is a full copy of the original term set. It will have the name "Copy of *<Term Set Name>*."
2. Then click the down arrow for the copied term set, and select Move Term Set. Select your local site collection term group into which the copied term set should be moved. Click OK.
3. After you move the term set, rename it as needed. It's now available for use as a local term set. Note that all the terms in the term set will be reused from the original term set.

Once you have the term sets created the way you want them, you can configure the Term-Driven Page settings to point to your Home page (or any other page, whether it's a site page or a publishing page) as a global default and then configure individual terms to point to specific pages.

If you have a library or list with a metadata column that was pointing to a global term set, you can reconfigure the column to point to the local term set without losing metadata assignments by simply copying the global term set to your local term group as described earlier. Once you have made it a local term set, you're then free to configure the properties as needed to meet your needs.

Summary

The term store is more detailed and involved than most people think. It is designed this way so that it can help you better manage your information design and architecture. In this chapter, I briefly discussed term-store concepts and the administration of the store itself. I also took some time to look at how to manage term sets and terms, work with content types within the hub of the metadata service, and explain how to work with local term sets.

The term store is so deeply nested with Search and Cross-Site Publishing that it is difficult to know (at some connection points) where one technology ends and the other begins. So I tried to keep the focus on what system administrators can do to configure and support the term store from the Administration area of Office 365. This meant not covering obvious next-step topics, at least in most cases. One of the next-step technologies that I can discuss in conjunction with the term store is the Search Service, which I do in chapter 6. First, let's delve into records management, which is the topic of the next chapter, including how to syndicate content types and create routing rules based on the properties of the content type.

CHAPTER 5

Records management

More and more, we're seeing the management of digital artifacts become a normal part of business. It is expected and assumed by both business and government agencies alike that nearly any communication or decision could become a point of inquiry or litigation. Definitions of what constitutes a record abound, but there seems to be two consistent characteristics in the definitions I reviewed prior to writing this chapter:

- A record is an artifact—whether tangible or digital—that represents proof of existence of something and that can be used to re-create or prove the state of existence or an action taken (or not taken).
- A record is often created in response to legal obligations or regulatory compliance.

Both characteristics, it seems to me, are evidentiary in nature: a record provides truthful, reliable evidence of a state of existence, of actions taken or not taken, or of adherence to (or diversion from) an established process. Note that the format and media type of records is generally irrelevant for the purposes of records management. Records must be managed, regardless of their form.

Records must be uniquely identified and distinguished from non-record artifacts. How and when artifacts become records and how records are managed throughout their life cycle are the main concerns of a Records Information Management (RIM) program. Just as a Center of Process Excellence can host various established processes and thereby define the core capabilities of an organization, similarly one or more *record centers* can host and surface truthful, reliable evidence of past communications and actions of an organization, thereby truthfully informing interested parties as to past words and actions.

Microsoft SharePoint Online has a records center solution. The solution is easy to set up and use. What will be difficult about using this solution is that you'll need tight processes around records management in your organization. SharePoint cannot resolve conflicts related to business processes, but it will likely surface those conflicts as users with different process agendas use SharePoint Online.

In-Place Records Management

The SharePoint Online In-Place Records Management feature allows users to create records from existing artifacts without having to move those artifacts to the records center. So it makes some sense to enable site-collection administrators to activate the In-Place Records Management feature to allow artifacts to be declared as records.

From a process perspective, it would be nearly impossible for organizations to move all potentially related documents and artifacts to a records center once a retention population is defined by legal counsel. In most litigation efforts, the artifacts become a matter of record well after their creation. Because it's impossible to know in advance what type of litigation might materialize for a given organization, it's impossible to predict what documents, email messages, and other content items should be preserved "just in case." So instead of creating processes to move a population set of content items into a records center that was not reasonably anticipated, it's easier to simply declare those items as records where they reside and then mine the SharePoint databases for those items.

Enabling users to declare records in their current location, without having to copy or move them to an official records center, allows for a more granular approach to managing records. However, this means that records and non-records will exist in the same location. For files to be declared as records where they exist, the In-Place Records Management feature first must be activated at the site-collection level.

Record declaration settings

When the In-Place Records Management feature is activated in the site collection features, you will have a Record Declaration Settings area (shown in Figure 5-1) under the Site Collection Administration section in Site Settings to manage how records are declared. This is a site collection–by–site collection setting and is a site-collection administration page, so what you set here applies to all lists and libraries in the site collection. There are no global tenant settings for how records are declared in SharePoint Online. The settings include the following:

- **Record Restrictions** In this section, you define how restricted normal document-management actions are on artifacts declared as records. The options include No Additional Restrictions, Block Delete, and Block Edit And Delete (which is the default setting).
- **Record Declaration Availability** Here you choose whether lists and libraries inherit settings from the site collection (Available In All Locations By Default) or define their own settings (Not Available In All Locations By Default).
- **Declaration Roles** In this section, you define who can declare and undeclare records.

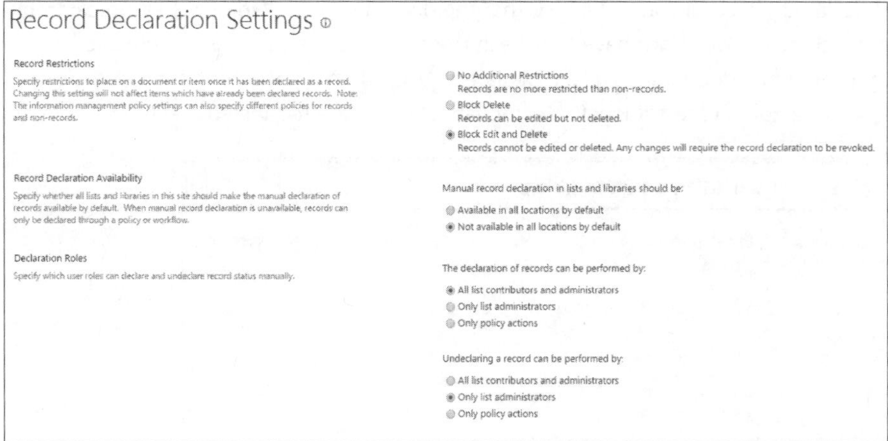

FIGURE 5-1 Record Declaration Settings page

Record restrictions

The first set of configuration options deals with the restrictions on what you can do with the artifacts *after* they have been declared a record. The default option is Block Edit And Delete, but you can back this down to Block Delete only or have no additional restrictions.

From a governance perspective, there is little reason to allow users to declare something as a record and then allow that record to be modified. If a modification is needed, a new record should be created. It is an anathema to records managers hither and yon to allow a record to be modified. It simply goes against best practices for records management. Although the software will allow you to do this, I highly recommend that you first check with your legal team to see what setting they want to have enforced here.

Another governance issue is that there is no method to know what has been set in each site collection without manually checking each site collection. If you have only 10 or 15 site collections and want to do spot checks on them, manually checking site collections is probably an acceptable way to manage this. But if you have hundreds of site collections in your tenant, you'll need to either use PowerShell or write some type of custom code to find out what the setting is or purchase third-party software that can report and possibly fix any wrongly configured record restrictions.

Record declaration availability

By default, SharePoint Online does not make available the manual declaration of records in all lists and libraries. If you want to change this, select the Available In All Locations By Default option. This will allow the manual declaration of records on individual documents or list items. After doing this, if you click into a document's properties, you will notice a new link named Compliance Details. Clicking that link will allow you to declare the document or content item a record (as shown in Figure 5-2) by clicking the Declare As A Record link. Once the document has been declared a record, you will notice that the document is locked, which is indicated by a small padlock icon. (You might have to refresh the screen to see this.) By default, a locked document cannot be edited unless it is undeclared. Also, when a document is a record, it can become part of a hold process if legal or compliancy details are requested.

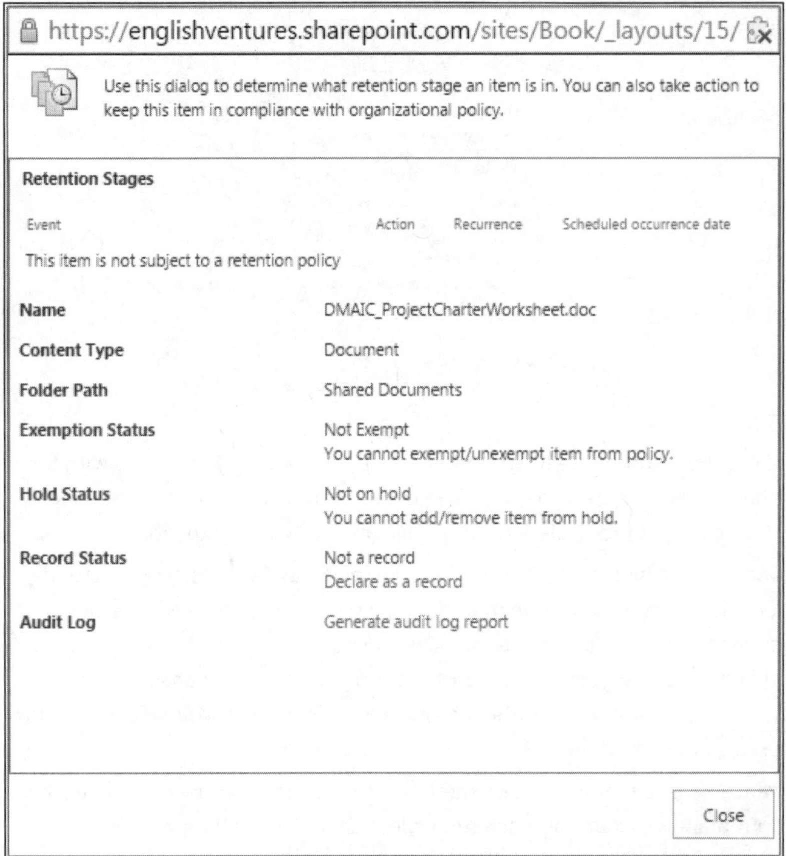

FIGURE 5-2 Dialog box in which you can manually declare a content item as a record

You also have the ability to undeclare the record if the document no longer needs to be treated as an official record. Simply go back into the item's compliance details and select the Undeclared Record link, and the record status on the document will be removed.

Once a document or content item has been declared a record—even if it is undeclared at some point—the ability to delete the list or library will be removed from the settings area of the list or library. This is removed because you don't want to delete entire lists with documents or content items that have records declared in them. And the ability to delete a list or library that once held a record would damage the chain of custody of that record. So be aware of this limitation.

Declaration roles

Referring back to Figure 5-1, you'll see that you can specify which user roles can declare and undeclare records manually. Your choices are as follows:

- All List Contributors And Administrators
- Only List Administrators
- Only Policy Actions

The policy action applies to custom code running as the System Account. But it also applies to information-management policies that are configured to declare an item a record as part of a retention stage or the moving of a document or content items from one stage to the next.

Automatic declaration

For some lists or libraries, you will want to make different configuration choices than what has been set at the site-collection level. This need is most common when you want documents or content items to be declared a record as soon as they are created within or moved into the list or library. To do this, you'll need to navigate to the library or list settings and click the Record Declaration Settings link. Doing that will bring up a page similar to Figure 5-3. Note that the default for the manual declaration of records will be to use the site-collection's default settings. But you can select two other choices:

- Always Allow The Manual Declaration Of Records
- Never Allow The Manual Declaration Of Records

In addition, you can select the Automatically Declare Items As Records When They Are Added To This List check box. If you select this check box, a notification screen will be displayed informing you that a check-in is required in order to change the document to a declared record and checkout is required before you can edit the document. Note also, as illustrated, that the Never Allow The Manual Declaration Of Records option is automatically selected when you click the check box because the system will be declaring new items as records. This takes away your ability to manually declare records.

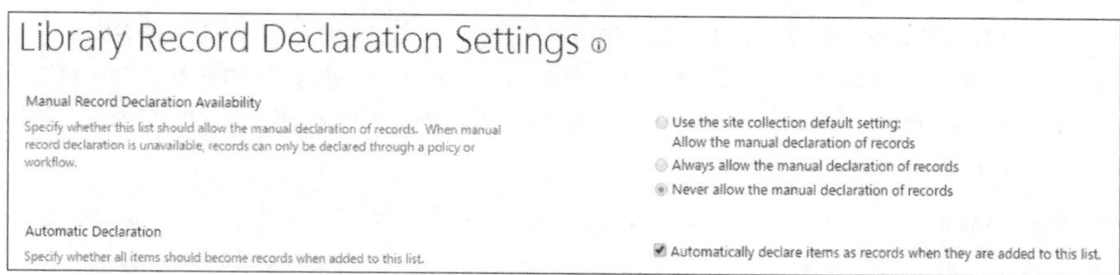

FIGURE 5-3 Library Record Declaration Settings page

> ***MORE INFO*** **After you set up automatic record declaration in a list or library, any existing items will need to checked out and then checked back in to apply the lock. For all new items, the process is automatic as you check in the document.**

Creating and managing records in the records center

A records center can meet your needs for longer-term record storage and compliance. It can act as the central repository for your organization's records. It takes forethought and planning to set up well. To that end, I highly recommend that you have your organization's legal counsel establish the retention policies related to the types of content in your organization. Then you can fully implement those policies. Some of those policies will need to be reflected in a *file plan*, which is a matrix that lists the document's life-cycle stages and the various metadata to be filled in or followed by the document at each life-cycle stage. A file plan is little more than a table written in Microsoft Word or Excel. An example of this file can be found on the books' companion webpage at *http://aka.ms/SPO/files*.

This table is given to stir your thinking. You can use it as-is or modify it as needed. The point is that creating file plans for each of your mission-critical document types and then applying the plan within your processes when the document is created will help your organization improve its information management and give you a more successful records-management implementation in SharePoint Online.

In the following pages, I'll illustrate how to set up a common process your organization might want to use to declare records. If this doesn't exactly fit your organization, I supplied the Raw Visio 2013 documents for download, which you can use to modify the processes to meet your needs.

The first process illustrated (shown in Figure 5-4) is for setting up records submission. I could have presented it as a checklist, but I thought some readers of this book might need to have it outlined in a process format so that the organizations they work for can change, update, or use the steps to add to their process repositories. The second process defines how users will send documents to the records center and have them declared as records automatically. If completed correctly, the second process should be very simple and rather transparent to the end user. The configuration process is the part that will involve some detailed work on your part.

Bear in mind that in the first process, you do *not* need to follow these steps in this precise order. But I give you this process so that you have a repeatable roadmap to follow if you need it.

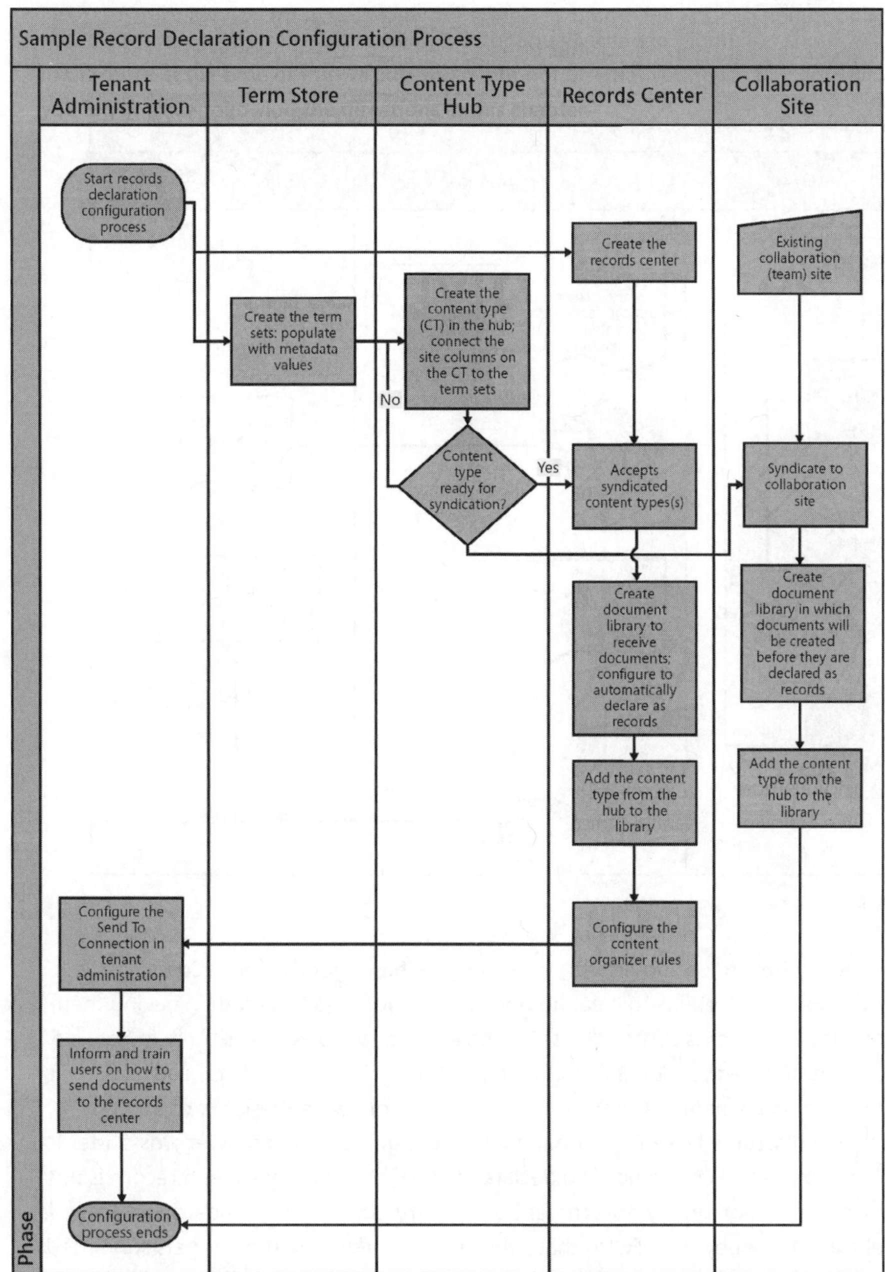

FIGURE 5-4 Basic configuration process to allow users to send documents to a records center and have the documents automatically declared records

The configuration process illustrated in Figure 5-4 will result in the following records-submission process in which your users can engage. (See Figure 5-5.)

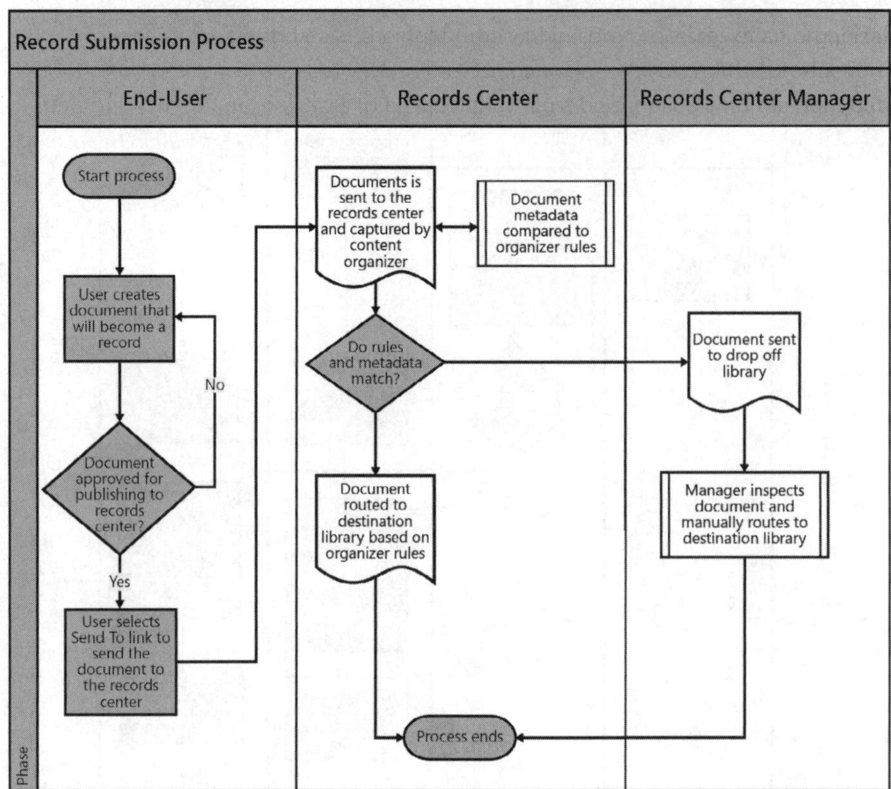

FIGURE 5-5 Records-submission process

I'll now discuss how to use these two processes to achieve good information velocity in your organization as it pertains to creating documents and artifacts and then having them become records in a records center. I'll use a simple scenario—one that is likely to be used in many organizations—the submission of an annual budget request. I'll use a spreadsheet for a fictitious company named Contoso. I'll play the role of a Vice President of Business Development and assume I need to submit my final budget to an internal records center for review by the Contoso CFO. The need to declare my final budget request as a record is not dictated by a legal action or any government or industry-compliance standard. Instead, it is an internal standard set by the CFO so that, while she is working on the budgets submitted by all the vice presidents, she knows they cannot change. The budget will be sent to the corporate records center.

Creating a records center

Creating a records center is a straightforward process. Create a new site collection, and select the Records Center template (which is shown in Figure 5-6). Although you could select a team site template and then manually build it up into a records center, it's better to use the Records Center template because a records library is going to be faster and more capable of serving a large volume of documents than if you started with a team site and activated the features, using a team-site document library. Plus, while I recognize that you don't need to use an entire site collection to create a new records center (it can be a subsite within a site collection), you really should use a new site collection to create a new records center.

If you have a large number of records or a wide variety of record types, my thinking is that, from a usability standpoint, it's just easier to use subsites within the same records-center site collection than it is to keep building out multiple records centers to host all the records (assuming you can stay within site quotas). Also, you'll have a more straightforward URL to work with when setting up your Send To connections. Moreover, some companies require strict security and processing isolation for records-oriented repositories, so creating the records center as its own site collection will be mandatory for some readers of this book.

Once the records center has been created, the next step is to create the content type or types at the hub that will be used as the plumbing for routing the documents from the team site to the records center. Although you could manually create the content types twice—one in the source site collection and the other in the records center—it's administratively easier to create it in the hub and syndicate the content type around your tenant. Moreover, if the workflow is such that the same content type will be used in multiple source locations to send documents to the records center, it makes even more sense to create the content types in the hub and syndicate them to your site collections.

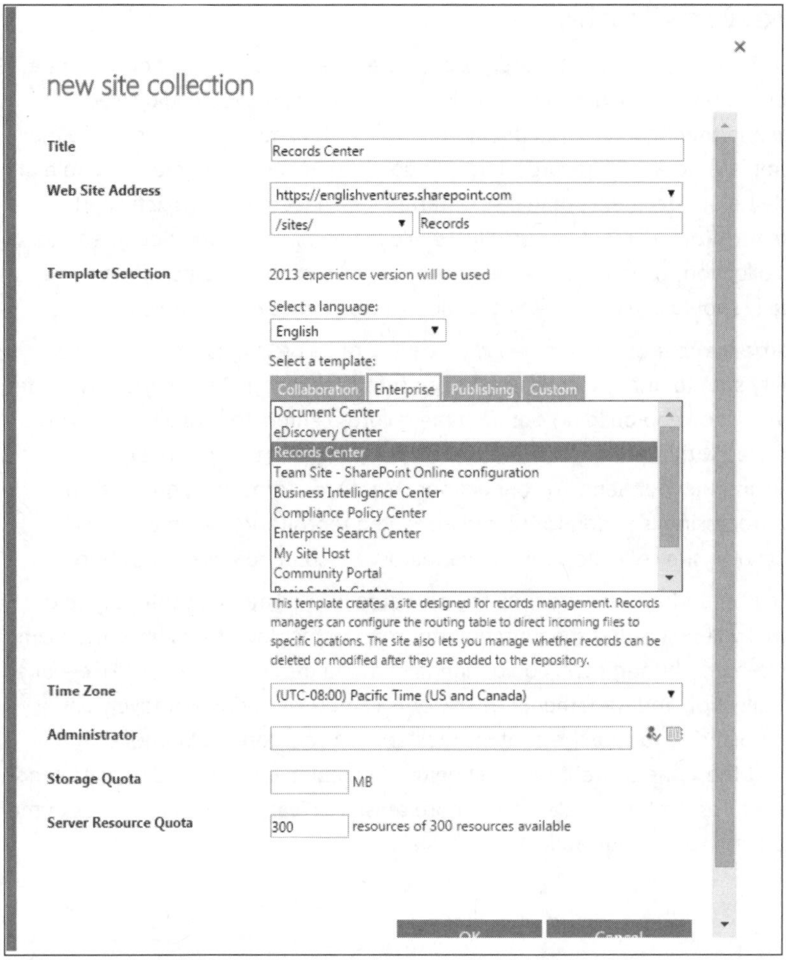

FIGURE 5-6 Selecting the Records Center site template to create a new records center

Create and syndicate content types

This part is not the work for your end users to complete—this is work that you, the system administrator, should be doing. I'll navigate to the content type publishing hub in my SharePoint Online environment. From the Site Content Types page, I'll click Create. On the New Site Content Type page (not illustrated), I'll enter the following:

- **Name:** Annual Budget Request per Division
- **Description:** This is the spreadsheet to be used only by vice presidents to submit their annual budget requests to the CFO.
- **Select Parent Content Type From:** Document Content Types
- **Parent Content Type:** Document
- **Put This Site Content Type Into:** Select New Group, Budget Submission Content Types

After you click OK, the new content type is created. For the sake of time and limiting illustrations, I'll perform minimal configurations on this new content type. How you will configure the new content type in your organization is entirely dependent on the information architecture and structure of what your users want to accomplish. You, the system administrator, cannot perform your duties here in a vacuum. You must be informed via some type of file plan as to what workflows are to be associated with the content type, what template is to be used (if any), what Document Information Panel settings are needed, what Information Management Policy settings are needed, and so forth. The content owners need to take responsibility and make these decisions, and then have you implement their decisions.

For this new content type, I will make one configuration change:

- **Advanced Settings:** I'll upload a simple spreadsheet as the default template by selecting the Upload A New Document Template option (not illustrated).

Now I'll add two new site columns to the content type, with both connected to term sets in the term store. First, I'll add a site column named **Year** and a second column named **Division**. To do this, I'll click the Add From New Site Column link that appears at the bottom of the Site Content Type page.

Once I do this, I'm presented with the Create Column page (shown in Figure 5-7). I'll enter the site column's name **For year**, and select the Managed Metadata option for the column type. I'll accept the default setting of Custom Columns, into which this customized site column will be created. It's important to select the Managed Metadata option as the column type in order to find the term set to which you want to connect this site column.

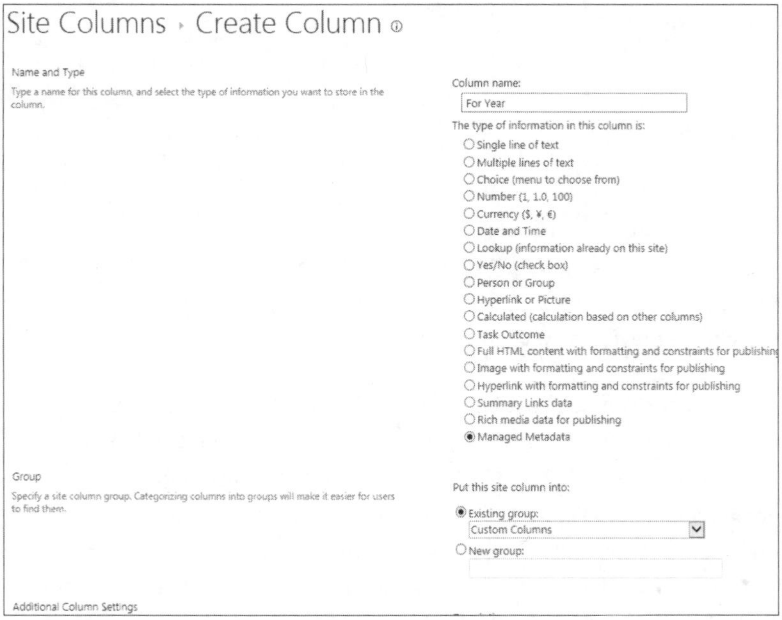

FIGURE 5-7 Creating a new managed metadata site column

If you scroll down, you'll see the lower part of this screen has refreshed. Navigate to the Term Set Settings area of the page and expand the Taxonomy of your term store. When I do this, I'm able to find my term sets named Year and Division. You might notice that I have some term sets in a Standard Term Sets folder. I tend to do this for generic types of data, such as a list of numbers, cities, years, quarters, division names, department names, and so forth. If a particular division or department needs its own term sets, somebody in that department can create them directly in the local term sets or create their own term group in the term store and create their term sets there.

Moving forward, I'll select the Year term set and not allow fill-in choices. Even if the Year term set was an open term set, I wouldn't allow fill-in choices. It wouldn't make sense to allow fill-in choices for a list of years. (See Figure 5-8.)

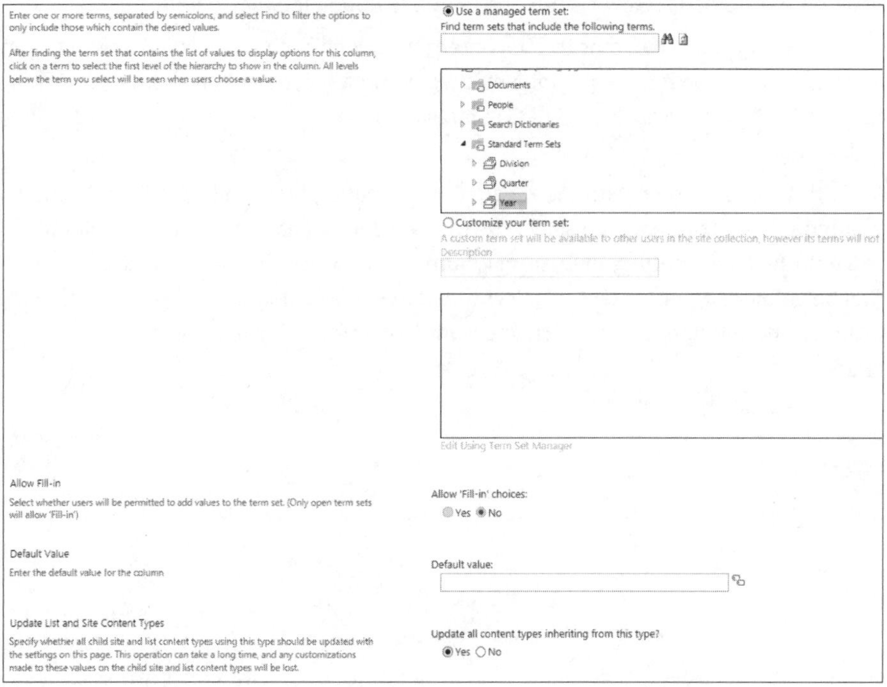

FIGURE 5-8 The lower half of the Create A New Column page

I'll repeat this process to add a new site column for the Division term set. Once that step is completed, I'm ready to syndicate the content type, so I'll click the Manage Publishing For This Content Type link and select OK to publish the content type (not illustrated).

Following the process outlined in Figure 5-4, I'll create a source library and a destination document library. The source library will be where the budget is created. I'll create the destination library in the records center as the intended location for the budget to be moved to and then declare my budget document a record.

Creating a new library is as simple as creating a new app. In the records center, I'll create a new document library called **Year End Budget Requests**. In the source team site, I'll use the default document library that was created when the team site was created.

One of the keys to making this all work is to add the Annual Budget Request Per Division content type to the library. You'll need to enable the management of content types under the Advanced settings of the document library and then find the Content Types section, which will appear below the General settings. You'll click the Add From Existing Content Types link to go through the Add Content Types screen, shown in Figure 5-9, to add the new content type. The reason you're clicking this link is because the syndication functionality from the hub has copied the content type to your site collection and, after syndication, it is a local or existing content type in your site collection.

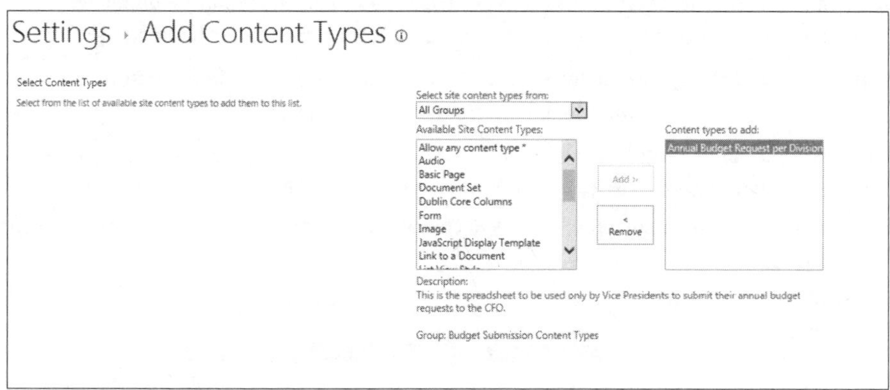

FIGURE 5-9 Add Content Types screen

After the content types are added to the libraries, the site columns will automatically be added at the first use of the content type to create a new content item in the library.

Automatic records declaration

In the library settings of the document library in the records center, you need to configure the Records Declaration settings to automatically declare new documents as records as soon as they arrive in the library. Refer back to the discussion related to Figure 5-3 in the "Automatic declaration" section of this chapter to see how to do this.

Configure the Send To link

In the SharePoint tenant administration area, you'll configure a Send To link that points to the records center. You do this so that anyone can use the link to send any document or content item to the records center. The content organizer will handle the routing of the document or content internally within the records center, so all your users need to know is how to get a document over to the center. The easiest way to give them the ability to do this is to create a Send To link.

To configure this capability, click the Records Management link in the left pane and then enter the URL of the records center along with the */_vti_bin/officialfile.asmx* suffix on the site's URL. (See Figure 5-10.) The interface has instructions on how to do this. (A bit of trivia—*vti* stands for *Vermeer Technologies Incorporated*. This was the company Microsoft purchased in 1996 for its FrontPage technologies. The configuration directories have persisted since 1996.) Be sure to test the validity of the URL by clicking the Click Here To Test link. Don't proceed until you know you have the right link entered into this box. Give the connection a name, and decide how you want SharePoint to handle the movement of the documents to the records center. You have three options:

- **Copy** This makes a copy of the document when it is sent to the records center. Depending on the information architecture, compliance requirements, or both, that might be something you don't want to do. So you might find yourself creating multiple links to the records center—one that copies documents and one that moves the document.
- **Move** This is a "copy then delete" action, but the effect is that the document is moved to the records center and will no longer exist in the source library.
- **Move And Leave A Link** This is the move option with the addition of a link created in the source location to the destination of where the document was moved. This option is a nice convenience if users are accustomed to going to the source location to find the document.

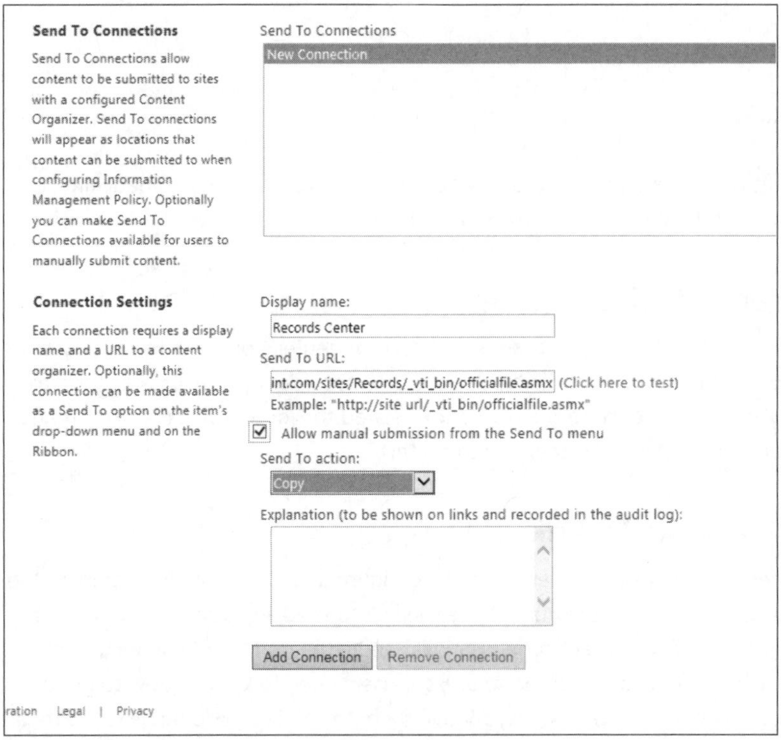

Send To Connections
Send To Connections allow content to be submitted to sites with a configured Content Organizer. Send To connections will appear as locations that content can be submitted to when configuring Information Management Policy. Optionally you can make Send To Connections available for users to manually submit content.
Send To Connections
New Connection
Connection Settings
Each connection requires a display name and a URL to a content organizer. Optionally, this connection can be made available as a Send To option on the item's drop-down menu and on the Ribbon.
Display name:
Records Center
Send To URL:
int.com/sites/Records/_vti_bin/officialfile.asmx (Click here to test)
Example: "http://site url/_vti_bin/officialfile.asmx"
Allow manual submission from the Send To menu
Send To action:
Copy
Explanation (to be shown on links and recorded in the audit log):
Add Connection Remove Connection
ration Legal | Privacy

FIGURE 5-10 Creating a New Send To connection

Content Organizer

To use the Content Organizer function, you must first activate the Content Organizer feature in the site where the document is being sent to. However, in the Records Center site, this feature is already activated by default. Once the feature is activated, a new document library named Drop Off Library becomes available. This library acts as a routing mechanism for incoming documents and using a routing system (Content Organizer Rules) to match the content type and metadata with the correct document library.

For the document to be routed to the appropriate library, a new content organizer rule must be created that defines the content type and the condition of the metadata match so that users know where the document will be routed. The content types must exist as additional content types in the destination library in the records center.

The Content Organizer has some settings you'll want to pay attention to. Click the Content Organizer link under Site Settings to arrive at the Content Organizer: Settings page, as illustrated in Figure 5-11.

First you'll see the Redirect Users To The Drop Off Library setting, which is selected by default. This setting specifies what happens when users try to upload content to libraries that have one or more content organizer rules pointing to them. Unless you have a good reason not to do so, you should leave this setting at the default.

You can use the second setting, Sending To Another Site, to specify another site collection as a target location in one or more of the rules. By default, you'll only be able to route content items within the local site collection itself—in this running example, that is the records center. So, if you need routability from the local site collection to other site collections, select the Allow Rules To Specify Another Site As A Target Location check box.

In the Folder Partitioning area, you'll find settings for configuring how many items go into a folder before a new folder is created and the default naming convention for those folders. These settings are handy if you need to host thousands of documents inside a single library and partition them in some manner using folders.

Next, if documents with duplicate names are submitted, you're given the option of using SharePoint versioning (not recommended) or appending a string of unique characters to the end of the duplicate file name (recommended). The default is to append a unique string of characters to the document name. This functionality was available in SharePoint 2007 and has persisted through to SharePoint Online.

If the submitted document includes the original audit logs and properties, those can be preserved by using settings in the Preserving Content area. In most cases, documenting the change of custody and chain of modifications are essential to preserving the truthfulness of the record. The default is to enable this feature, and I recommend that you leave it that way.

Finally, you can decide how you want notification email messages handled and specify who manages the Content Organizer rules. The defaults are to email rule managers when submissions do not match a rule and when content has been left in the Drop Off Library. Note that distribution lists can be included as a single email address.

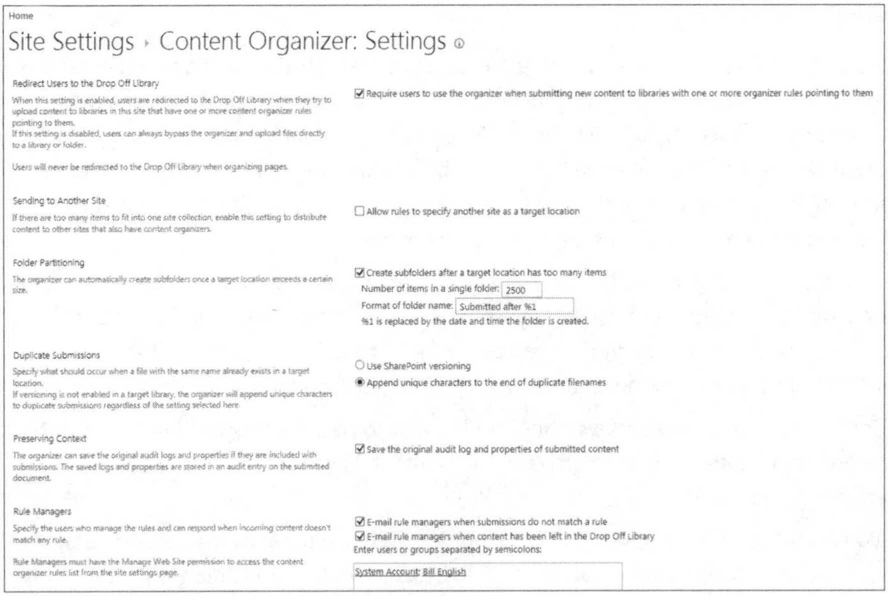

Home

Site Settings › Content Organizer: Settings

Redirect Users to the Drop Off Library

When this setting is enabled, users are redirected to the Drop Off Library when they try to upload content to libraries in this site that have one or more content organizer rules pointing to them.
If this setting is disabled, users can always bypass the organizer and upload files directly to a library or folder.

Users will never be redirected to the Drop Off Library when organizing pages.

☑ Require users to use the organizer when submitting new content to libraries with one or more organizer rules pointing to them

Sending to Another Site

If there are too many items to fit into one site collection, enable this setting to distribute content to other sites that also have content organizers.

☐ Allow rules to specify another site as a target location

Folder Partitioning

The organizer can automatically create subfolders once a target location exceeds a certain size.

☑ Create subfolders after a target location has too many items
Number of items in a single folder: 2500
Format of folder name: Submitted after %1
%1 is replaced by the date and time the folder is created.

Duplicate Submissions

Specify what should occur when a file with the same name already exists in a target location.
If versioning is not enabled in a target library, the organizer will append unique characters to duplicate submissions regardless of the setting selected here.

○ Use SharePoint versioning
◉ Append unique characters to the end of duplicate filenames

Preserving Context

The organizer can save the original audit logs and properties if they are included with submissions. The saved logs and properties are stored in an audit entry on the submitted document.

☑ Save the original audit log and properties of submitted content

Rule Managers

Specify the users who manage the rules and can respond when incoming content doesn't match any rule.

Rule Managers must have the Manage Web Site permission to access the content organizer rules list from the site settings page.

☑ E-mail rule managers when submissions do not match a rule
☑ E-mail rule managers when content has been left in the Drop Off Library
Enter users or groups separated by semicolons:
System Account; Bill English

FIGURE 5-11 Settings screen for the Content Organizer

To create the routing rule, navigate to Site Settings in the records center and click Content Organizer Rules. This will bring up a list with the same name. Click New Item to create a new rule. In my running example, after clicking New Item, I name the item **Annual Budget Requests Routed to Year End Budget Requests Library**. I give it a long, descriptive name so that when I see the name, I know exactly what the routing rule refers to (as you can see in Figure 5-12).

I'll leave the Status settings at their defaults. You can change them if you want one rule to have priority over the running of another rule if documents are submitted at nearly the same time.

The Submission's Content Type area is important. The entire reason I advocate using a syndicated content type is because of this setting. You'll select the syndicated content type, and your submission process will be cleaner because it uses the same content type at the source as it does at the destination. Note that I selected the content type I created at the hub. The reason I was able to select it was because it had been syndicated to the records center site collection by the managed metadata service. The important part to understand here is that you must select the correct content type for the document being submitted as part of this routing rule.

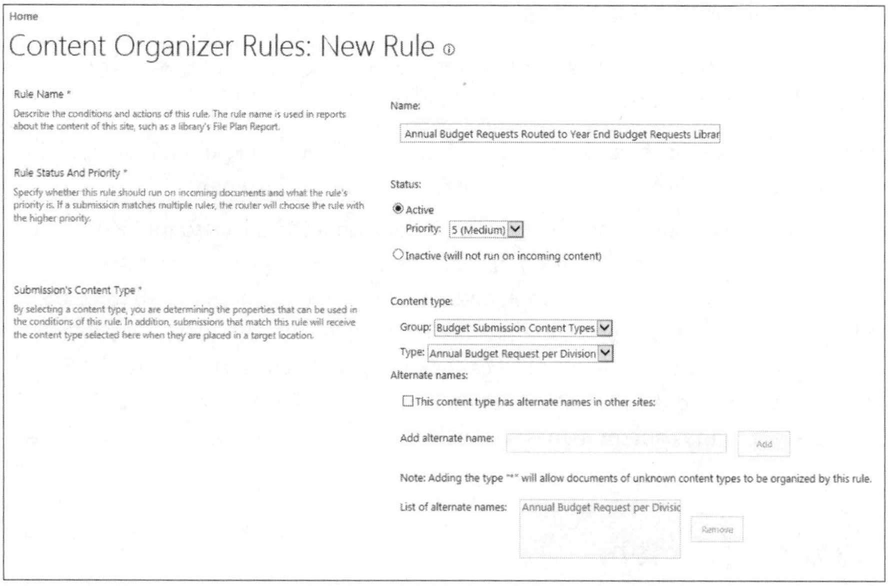

Home

Content Organizer Rules: New Rule

Rule Name *

Describe the conditions and actions of this rule. The rule name is used in reports about the content of this site, such as a library's File Plan Report.

Name:

Annual Budget Requests Routed to Year End Budget Requests Librar

Rule Status And Priority *

Specify whether this rule should run on incoming documents and what the rule's priority is. If a submission matches multiple rules, the router will choose the rule with the higher priority.

Status:

Active

Priority: 5 (Medium)

Inactive (will not run on incoming content)

Submission's Content Type *

By selecting a content type, you are determining the properties that can be used in the conditions of this rule. In addition, submissions that match this rule will receive the content type selected here when they are placed in a target location.

Content type:

Group: Budget Submission Content Types

Type: Annual Budget Request per Division

Alternate names:

This content type has alternate names in other sites:

Add alternate name: Add

Note: Adding the type "*" will allow documents of unknown content types to be organized by this rule.

List of alternate names: Annual Budget Request per Divisic Remove

FIGURE 5-12 Content Organizer routing rule—the upper half of the rule configuration screen

Once the correct content type is selected, the Content Organizer will read the properties and site columns on the content type and then present those options to you under the Conditions section of the rule settings. In this case, we want to route budget submissions for the year 2016 to a folder named "2016." Notice in Figure 5-13 that the condition is a selection of a "property," which in this context means "site column" on the content type. You'll have standard operators you can work with, which you can see if you click the Operator drop-down list.

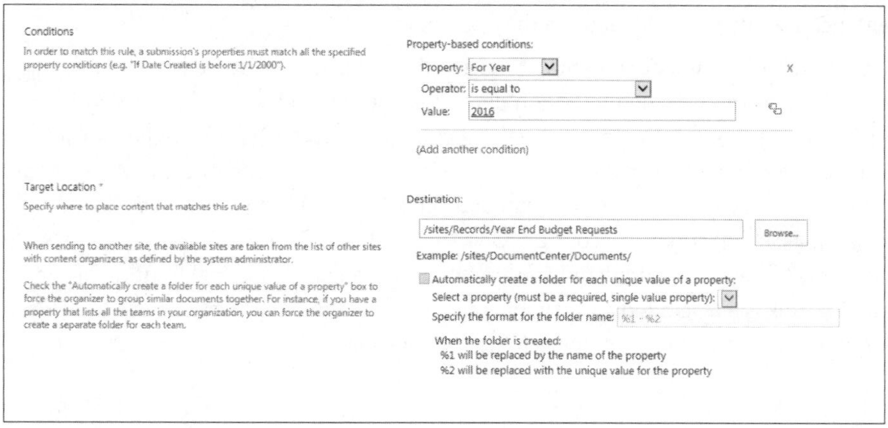

Conditions

In order to match this rule, a submission's properties must match all the specified property conditions (e.g. "If Date Created is before 1/1/2000").

Property-based conditions:

Property: For Year

Operator: is equal to

Value: 2016

(Add another condition)

Target Location *

Specify where to place content that matches this rule.

When sending to another site, the available sites are taken from the list of other sites with content organizers, as defined by the system administrator.

Check the "Automatically create a folder for each unique value of a property" box to force the organizer to group similar documents together. For instance, if you have a property that lists all the teams in your organization, you can force the organizer to create a separate folder for each team.

Destination:

/sites/Records/Year End Budget Requests Browse...

Example: /sites/DocumentCenter/Documents/

Automatically create a folder for each unique value of a property:

Select a property (must be a required, single value property):

Specify the format for the folder name: %1 - %2

When the folder is created:

%1 will be replaced by the name of the property

%2 will be replaced with the unique value for the property

FIGURE 5-13 The Conditions and Target Location sections of a routing rule in the Content Organizer

You can add multiple conditions to a routing rule such as this:

If Property A is equal to 1 and Property B is empty, route to Folder 1. But if Property A is equal to 1 and Property B is not empty, route to Folder 2.

Although you cannot branch your logic within a single rule, you can put multiple rules in place that effectively branches the routing of a particular type of document.

Browse to select the folder in which you want the document to be routed (not illustrated). I chose the library I created for this illustration: Year End Budget Requests. Select the Automatically Create A Folder For Each Unique Value Of A Property check box to force the organizer to group similar documents together. For instance, if you have a property that lists all the teams in your organization, you can force the organizer to create a separate folder for each team. Finish setting the routing rule in the Content Organizer by assigning the conditions under which the content item is routed and the destination to which it should be routed.

Routing the document

Now that the routing rule and required libraries are in place, it is time to move to the second process and see how a user routes a document to the records center. From a document library outside the records center, I created a sample budget spreadsheet. For our purposes, the content of the document is irrelevant. What is relevant is that it was created with the content type specifically for the budget proposal. So I'll create the file from the library using the custom content type and save it back into the library as Contoso Annual Budget Request 2016. Before I save the document, I'll use the Document Information Panel to populate my metadata fields for the budget request. (See Figure 5-14.) The metadata fields you see in the Document Information Panel are produced by the site columns that were applied to the content type at the hub. Populating the metadata fields at the initial point of capture of this document increases its findability later in the document's life cycle.

Now it is time to send the document to the records center. In the source library, I'll select the Contoso budget and then, in the ribbon under the Files tab, select the Send To option. Then I will select the Records Center (Copy) that I configured in the Send To settings. You'll notice that I created two Send To connections: one is a copy action, and one is a Move action. This illustrates how you can create more than one Send To connection to the same location with both a move action and a copy option. Once the budget has been submitted, I'll receive a page that says "Operation Completed Successfully," with a link to the final location of the document. The link is a DocIdRedir.aspx page, meaning that the document went to the Drop Off Library and was redirected from there to its final destination.

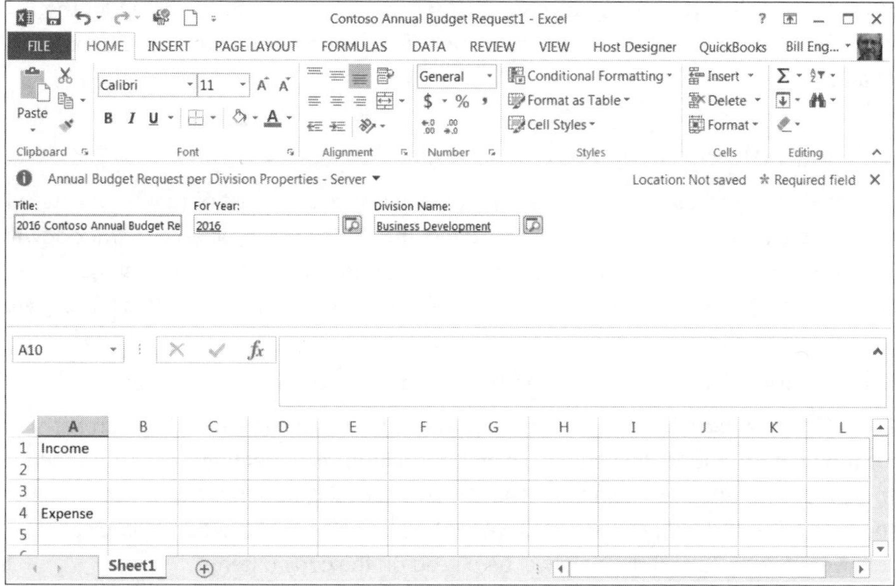

FIGURE 5-14 Saving the Contoso budget request back to the source collaboration site where it is being created

Using workflows to move the document

What I just demonstrated was a manual way to move a document from a source location to the records center. The more preferred way to do this in environments where the electronic recording of the chain of custody and chain of modifications is important is to use workflows—preferably, a single workflow that includes both the approving and sending components. Space does not permit me to dive into how to build this workflow and apply it, but it should be a workflow built by your developers because this functionality is not available with the in-browser workflow features.

The reason you want to use a workflow is because the history of who has done what and when they did it inside the workflow is recorded in a task list. This task list becomes evidence for the chain of custody and chain of modifications for the document in question. From a compliance standpoint, this can be used to show adherence to (or divergence from) a process.

Managing the records center

At some point, legal or regulatory demands might require that you discover and then hold certain documents that were sent to the records center. You'll be happy to know the records center carries the following unique compliancy-management functions to enable you to do this:

- Discover And Hold Records
- Generate A File Plan Report
- Generate An Audit Report

To access these three options, you can use the Manage Records Center page under the SharePoint cog menu or in Site Settings, where you will also find the Hold management group of administration links.

Discover and hold records

In a situation where a company is being called into litigation and, as part of that legal case, all records pertaining to a specific contract are required, it is important to be able to track down all items that match that requirement. With the Discover And Hold settings you can issue a search query to locate the items in question and then issue a hold on those records. There are three configuration options:

- **Search Criteria** Define the URL and the search query context for discovery.
- **Local Hold Or Export** If Local Hold is selected, the items remain in their current location but cannot be deleted even if an information-management policy is defined to delete items after a certain time. The item with Local Hold selected will remain until the hold is lifted. If Export is selected, you can choose another location to copy all the discovered items to and the hold will be placed on the copied items.
- **Relevant Hold** This option specifies what the item on hold is subject to. First you create a hold, and then you can create multiple hold descriptions and attach files if required. The items on hold will have the relevant hold information associated with them. You can also enter the email address of the person responsible for managing the hold so that questions about the hold can be directed to that individual.

The hold process will not change how the document looks at the user end. For example, I placed a hold on the phrase "SIPOC," which is really a query against the index plus (if you're trying to hold email messages as well) a real-time scan against the Microsoft Exchange databases. Once the hold for documents is enforced, you'll be able to see that it is on hold in the Compliance Details dialog of the document. Note that you can add documents to a hold on an individual basis too by simply clicking the Add/Remove From Hold link. (See Figure 5-15.)

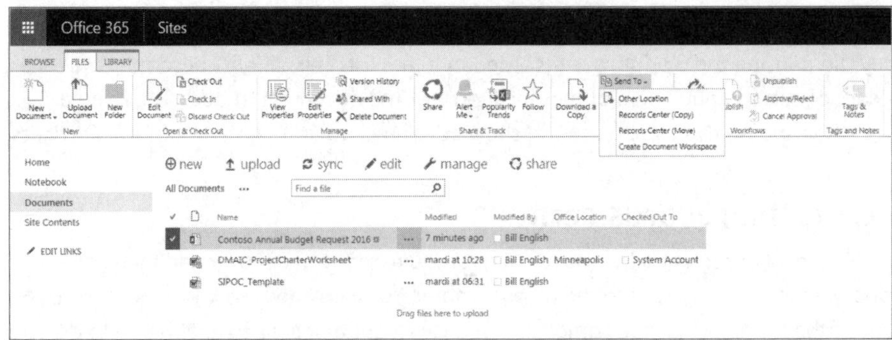

FIGURE 15-15 Compliance Details of a document that has a hold placed on it

An item can be held more than once if it is pertinent to more than one hold process in its current state. In these instances, an item still remains on hold even if one of the holds is lifted.

Generate a file plan report

The Generate A File Plan Report option (found in the library settings) allows you to create an Excel file that outlines your file plan as currently figured on your records center. To create the file plan, you need to specify a location to store it. Note that how Microsoft defines a "file plan" is different than how I defined it earlier in this chapter. The file plan (not illustrated) is more of a vitals report on the record center than a process that was outlined in the table shown earlier in the chapter. Once the file plan is generated, you can obtain detailed information, such as the following:

- Site details such as declaration settings and the number of items on hold
- Content types used in the policies
- Policy names associated with the content types
- Policy description details
- Retention details (you can drill down into more information on this secondary sheet)
- Folder details (you can drill down for information on folders such as item total and security)

Each new report will be stored separately in the folder you specify when the file plan is created.

Generate an audit report

In the records center, you can generate an audit report, which will give you detailed information about what has happened in the records center. These reports do not automatically report activity. You first need to enable auditing at the site-collection layer by selecting the needed check boxes on the Configure Audit Settings page, which can be accessed by clicking the Site Collection Audit Settings link in the Site Collection Administration area of Site Settings.

The reports are Excel based and use the Globally Unique Identifiers (GUIDs) to report the who and the what. So, for user names, you'll see GUIDs, not user names. You'll need a third-party tool or custom code to turn the GUIDs into user names, folder names, and so forth. A number of third-party tools can generate better-looking, more meaningful reports, but all of them will depend on the initial auditing being set up at the site-collection layer and use the auditing information in the databases to populate their reports. You'll need to look for vendors who have written their tool to specifically work in the Microsoft Office 365 tenant.

As time progresses and more information is generated, the reports will be a vital piece of information for auditors and legal counsel. Consider using custom reports for a more detailed picture of specific events.

Document IDs

While not specifically part of the records center *per se*, the Document ID feature is automatically activated when the Records Center site is created. The feature is scoped to the site collection itself. It is populated with a random string of characters, which is hardly helpful with the findability of a document. Document IDs are intended to be an elementary document-numbering system, with the configurable portion of the ID being applied to all documents in the site collection and the latter part—the numbers—being autogenerated by SharePoint Online when the document is initially created or uploaded in the document library.

Best practice is to change the Document ID prefix—the configurable portion of the ID (4 to 12 characters)—as soon as the records center is created to conform to your information design. From a governance standpoint, if you want to uniquely identify the site collection that is hosting the document, you should have a naming-convention plan for document IDs across all your site collections.

Summary

In this chapter, we looked at the records center more from a process and usability standpoint than from a bland "here's what you potentially can do" viewpoint. The chapter was divided into two major sections—first discussing In-Place Records Management and then illustrating how to set up a simple process to manually move documents from a team site into a records center.

In the process, I discussed content types (which were more fully discussed in Chapter 4, "Managing a term store in SharePoint Online"), how to syndicate them, and how to create routing rules in the Content Organizer based on the properties of the content type. I also discussed some basic governance regarding the process and included two Visio process diagrams you can download and use to help you get a records center up and running.

I also noted that the manual movement of documents between life-cycle stages should be accomplished through workflows rather than manual intervention, even though the illustration used was manual in nature.

In this chapter and in Chapter 4, we looked at the putability side of the equation—how information goes into the information-retrieval system. In the next chapter on search, I'll dive into how information is pulled out of the information-retrieval system. It is a concept called *findability*. You'll know it better as "search and indexing." It is to this topic to which we now turn our attention.

CHAPTER 6

Configuring search

In a very real sense, the last two chapters on the term store and records management focused on the portability side of the information-management equation. Both chapters dealt with how to input information into Microsoft SharePoint Online and how to organize it. Entire books could be written on those two topics. In fact, hundreds of books have been written on them.

So when we come to search, we're really talking about the findability aspect of information management. If information goes into an information-retrieval system, it needs to come out. And search is the main way you pull information out of the information-retrieval system. This makes search a very important topic for you, the system administrator of a SharePoint Online environment. Users are going to put information into SharePoint Online, and naturally they will want to pull it back out quickly and easily.

You can do a lot right in your SharePoint Online implementation and it might still fail if you don't figure out how to help people get information out of SharePoint Online in the form and manner that they need to support their daily job duties. Unfortunately, search is often viewed as an application-specific solution for findability. Scores of companies believe that if they just have enough Google boxes or search servers they'll be able to find the information that they want, when they want it. The problem is that search focuses on matching keywords with the content. Many companies assume that if their users have the right keyword, they can match that keyword correctly to the content item they need. But generating syntactically correct result sets is only a part of what search is about in SharePoint Online.

What most people don't realize is that as the size of the corpus grows, the ability to find the right document using a simple keyword search diminishes. Research based on analyzing large bodies of text shows that the two words we use most frequently in the American version of the English language account for 10 percent of all the words we use. Moreover, 50 words account for 50 percent of all the words we use. And because people tend to use the same word to mean different things instead of learning new words, which would be more difficult, the meaning of many words becomes more diverse and generalized over time. Hence, language naturally trends toward the use of fewer words to refer to a wider range of concepts, objects, and elements, with the range of meanings becoming both more diverse and disparate.

Let me illustrate this. A word as simple as "horn" can have vastly different meanings: a car horn, a musical instrument, or the horn on an animal, such as a ram. So, is it a horn, horn, or horn? Is it resume or resumé? As you can see in the English language, we use the same word to refer to vastly different things. People tend to use the easiest word or phrase to express what they mean instead of thinking through to use more descriptive terms. It's just how we are.

Committing a search using the humble keyword will get your users only so far in finding the content they want. The keyword really represents meaning, and meaning can often be expressed in phrases, idioms, and the unique use of individual words. For example "good grief," can be an expression of several different emotions. "Give it a go" is often an expression of hope and optimism in trying to do something new.

This is why your search solution must include the use of refiners and filters. They can improve meaning in a keyword query. For example, if I search on the word "horn" and use the filter "musical instruments," I've added meaning to the keyword that makes the system more likely to return documents that contain the word "horn" as well as the word "trumpet." Perhaps after getting the generated results, I might then use a refiner that shows me only documents generated by a particular trumpet manufacturer. So you can add meaning to the keyword query through the use of filters and refiners both at the time of the initial query and when refining the result set you receive from the index.

Relevance, precision, and recall

Relevance, precision, and recall are three concepts you need to keep in the back of your mind as you're configuring Search in SharePoint Online.

Relevance refers to the idea that the content items in the result set are useful to the person viewing them. This is a highly subjective standard to meet, and it's really based on figuring out what the user wants to know versus what they already know. For each user and each query, the relevance standard is different, and for the same user and query, what is "relevant" will change over time. As the user learns new information or as the user changes her interest over time, a result set that was relevant six months ago might not be relevant to the user today.

Precision measures how well the system retrieves only the relevant documents the user is after. The more syntactically accurate documents that the system retrieves that are irrelevant to the user, the more it is said that the system is generating false positives and lacks precision. Part of the goal of implementing a robust Search solution in SharePoint Online is to reduce the number of false positives as much as possible.

Recall measures how well the system retrieves all the relevant documents. Although it is good to retrieve only relevant documents, it is much better if the system retrieves all the relevant documents or content items the user is after in her query.

Generally speaking, people will not seek information that makes their jobs harder and they will not work hard to find the information they really need to do their jobs. Hence, to provide a robust findability solution using Search, you have to work hard at building good result sets, result types, and query transforms. It won't be easy, but the payoff will be profound for those who are dumping millions of documents into SharePoint Online.

Analytics processing

SharePoint Online uses the same analytics processing engine as SharePoint 2013. Because the administration of multiple analytics servers and databases is removed from SharePoint Online administration, I won't get into the nuts and bolts of how that all works. But you'll find it helpful to know that the analytics component analyzes both the content itself and how users interact with that content. Over time, search relevance will increase as the component learns how users interact with the content.

The content analytics component extracts information such as links and anchor text from the content as it is being crawled and processed for the index. The extracted information is stored together with information about clicks on the search results. The analytics component includes the following elements:

- **Anchor text processing** Analyzes how corpus content is interlinked. You can manually affect relevance here through authoritative pages, a feature in SharePoint Online search settings you can use to change relevance based on a URL.
- **Click distance** Analyzes the number of clicks between authoritative pages and items in the index.
- **Search clicks** Uses historical information about which items users click in the search results to promote or demote content items in the index.
- **Social tags** Analyzes the words and phrases users apply to content in the Tag and Notes dialog boxes.
- **Social distance** Analyzes the relationship between the users who use the Follow Person feature and then calculates first-level and second-level followings.
- **Search reports** Shows the results of some analysis in Microsoft Excel–based reports to help you, the system administrator, refine and improve the search experience for your users.

- **Deep links** Analyzes the information about what people really click in the search results to calculate the more important subpages on a site.
- **Usage counts** Retains the number of clicked and viewed items, and includes how many times an item is opened overall, not just from the search results. This information is written to the analytics database every 15 minutes.
- **Recommendations** Creates recommendations for items based on how users have interacted with the items on a site. This produces the "People who viewed this also viewed . . ." functionality.
- **Activity ranking** Analyzes the usage events to influence search relevancy. Items with high usage activity (clicks or views) are usually ranked higher than other, similar content, all other things being equal. It also looks for trends in item activity. So a time element is applied so that older content that will typically have more clicks overall doesn't "win" against new content that is being heavily accessed.

Managing the search schema

At its core, the search index is made up of keywords that are tied to a number of properties, including their URL location, their location in the document, the number of times the keyword occurs in the document, as well as a host of other types of properties that have been applied to the term store or individual site columns within the list or the library. All the properties for all the content items in SharePoint Online are held in the search schema. The schema can be found within the search administration area by clicking the Manage Search Schema link (not illustrated).

When your tenant is first created, SharePoint Online creates well over 600 properties along with the plethora of system-generated content types. Recall the content type is nothing more than a data element with one or more metadata fields wrapped up into a template you use to create content items. The metadata on these content types are represented in the search schema as *crawled properties*. Crawled properties are then grouped into *managed properties*, and those are the managed properties you work with to build result sets, result types, advanced searches, and query transforms.

When you arrive at the Manage Search Schema page, it will be focused on the Managed Properties view. If you want to see the crawled properties, simply click the Crawled Properties link. Once you do that, you'll see a single-page list of crawled properties. When you click into one of the crawled properties, you'll see the base information associated with this property, including the managed property to which it is mapped, if applicable. Some crawled properties will not be included in the full-text index, which means that values entered for this property will not be indexed unless the crawled property is mapped to a managed property that has the Searching attribute selected or has the Full-Text Index check box selected. Selecting the Included In Full-Text Index check box, shown in Figure 6-1, will enable users to find content based on the values entered for this property. However, you do not need to associate this property with a managed property for this findability to work.

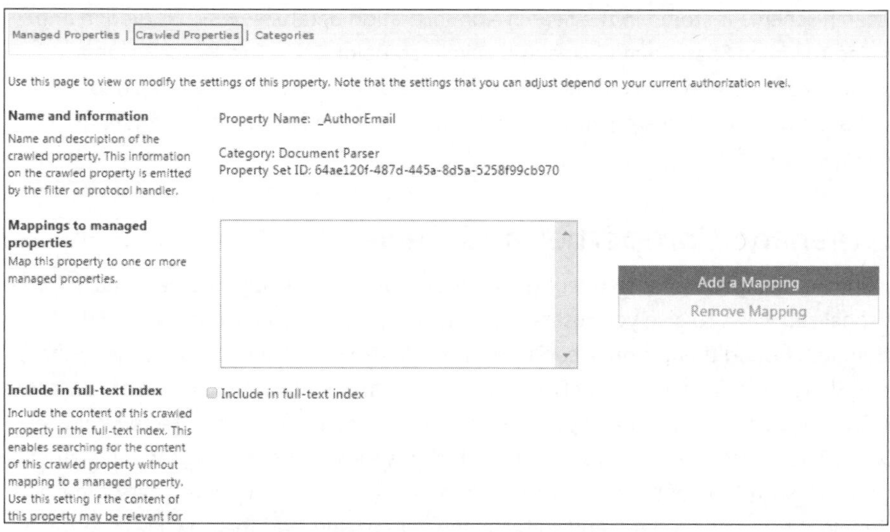

FIGURE 6-1 Crawled properties base information

The search engine will automatically pick up a new site column that is used, whether this site column is created in the site or site collection via a new content type or manually, within a list or library. In my research here, I decided to create a new site column in the Documents library in my test site. The site column is titled "Colors," and for the documents in the library, I've entered "green" for one document (not illustrated). After search completes its next incremental crawl, there will be two crawled properties in this case: "colors" and "ows_colors." The latter is for Office Web Services, whereas the former is for the local SharePoint Online schema. By default, "colors" is not included in the full-text index, but "ows_colors" is included there.

Users can search only on managed properties, not on crawled properties—unless you make the crawled property indexable and don't map it to a managed property. You can map multiple crawled properties to a single managed property or map a single crawled property to multiple managed properties. With managed properties, you have the ability to treat multiple crawled properties as a single unit.

Referring back to Figure 6-1, you'll notice a Categories link to the right of the Crawled Properties link. Categories are based on the IFilter or protocol handler of the item. Example categories are Office (crawled properties from Microsoft Office Word documents, Excel worksheets, and so on), Business Data (crawled properties from, for example, databases), and Web (crawled properties from websites). The IFilter is what you use to tell the crawler what kind of content is being crawled so that it knows how to read out the content and metadata. In SharePoint 2013, when you set up a content source, you specify the type of content source it is—file, web, SharePoint, and so forth. The type of content sources determines the IFilter that the crawler will use. In SharePoint Online, you have no ability to create content sources, so you'll be trusting Microsoft and Office 365 to load all the appropriate IFilters so that content in your tenant is successfully crawled.

The search schema is stored in the Search Administration database, which is hidden and not revealed to you in SharePoint Online as it is in SharePoint 2013. The search schema contains the mappings between crawled and managed properties, how the managed properties are stored in the search index, and the various settings you can configure on a given managed property.

Using managed properties and Delve

Delve uses managed properties to query the Office graph and to display content cards. Delve uses personalized views to give your users access to all the files they have used recently, what's trending around them (from a social technology viewpoint), and what has been shared with them. SharePoint Online and OneDrive for Business are the primary sources of content in Delve. How you and users manage permissions on documents and sites affects what users see in Delve. The content cards, an example of which is shown in Figure 6-2, contain elements like a graphical illustration of the item, who it is shared with, the last modified date/time, a button to add it to another board, and so forth. Individual users add their own tags to the content, thereby organically growing their own taxonomy of information as well as the larger taxonomy related to the specific content item.

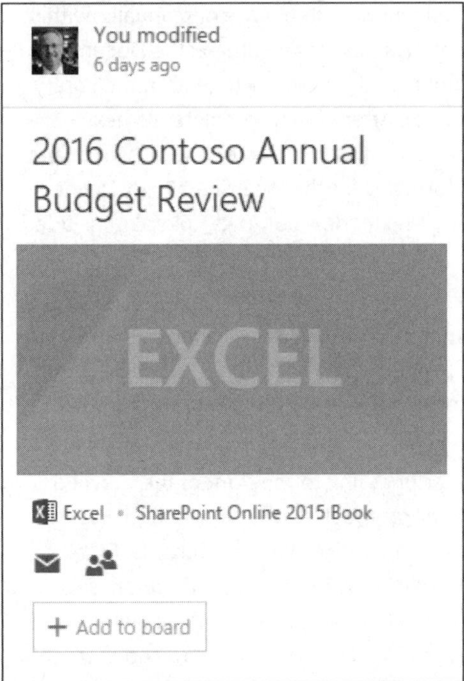

FIGURE 6-2 An example of a Delve card

MORE INFO At the time of this writing, Microsoft has placed a nifty video about Delve within the SharePoint Online tenant that shows how it works with OneDrive and promotes better collaboration. I suggest you watch it.

Users can use the HideFromDelve managed property to hide a document from Delve. You can keep storing the document in Office 365, and people can still find it through search—it just won't show up in Delve anymore.

For Delve to work, you need to activate the SharePoint Online service and assign users a SharePoint Online license. You also have to set up Microsoft Exchange Online if you want attachments to show up on users' Home pages in Delve. If you set up Lync Online, users can start Lync conversations directly from Delve.

TIP If you want to receive new functionality in Delve before it's made available in standard releases, you can opt in to the First Release program. You'll receive new feature updates a minimum of two weeks before customers in the Standard Release program. To learn more, see the Office 365 release programs at http://tinyurl.com/kzee552. The First Release program is available for Office 365 Enterprise and Office 365 Education.

Delve uses information from user profiles in SharePoint Online to determine who users in your organization work with most closely. Ensuring that people populate their user profiles and work with OneDrive for Business is the best way to ensure that your users have a positive Delve experience.

Configuring managed properties

Managed properties have certain configurations that are available for you to manage to enhance the search experience of your users in a SharePoint 2013 implementation. In SharePoint Online, these configurations are set by the tenant administrators. Although you can view the settings of managed properties, for the most part, you cannot change the configurations. The exception to this is when you create a new managed property.

A *managed property* is little more than a grouping of one or more crawled properties with some settings that affect how the managed property is used. Managed properties, in and of themselves, contain no data *per se*. Instead, they contain crawled properties. Recall that a metadata field—more commonly known as a *site column*—is where the user inputs the values for the metadata. In schema terminology, this is the *crawled property*. To reiterate: although the TechNet articles and such discuss the content of a managed property as being included in the full-text index, bear in mind that the managed property contains no information—it is the crawled properties that are mapped to the managed property that give the appearance and feel that the managed property contains data.

When it comes to ranking, you can change the *context* of a managed property (in this context, "context" means the weight-to-ranking ratio) to influence the ranking of content items that are described by the crawled properties mapped to that managed property.

The settings you'll see in a managed property's properties are outlined in Table 6-1.

TABLE 6-1 Managed property settings

Managed Property settings	What it means	Example
Searchable	Values entered into the metadata fields are indexed. Content can be found by querying on the metadata values of the crawled properties mapped to the managed property.	If the managed property is "author" and the crawled property is "book author", a simple query for "English" will return content items whose managed property contains "English" as well as content items that contain the word "English".
Advanced Searchable Settings	Enables you to change the full-text index to which the managed property is written. You can also change the weighting (also known as the context) of the property for relevance ranking. It is not recommended that you change the weighting for any default managed properties.	
Queryable	This setting enables querying against a specific managed property.	For example, you can include the name of the property in the search query string, such as "Author:English" and the query will then be executed only against the managed property "Author".
Retrievable	This setting turns on or off the inclusion of the content respresented by this managed property in the result sets. It's either enabled or disabled.	
Allow Multiple Values	Allows the user to enter multiple values of the same type into a crawled property that is mapped to the managed property.	If this is the "author" managed property, a document with multiple authors assigned in the "Book Author" crawled property will be stored and reported out as a separate value in the managed property.
Refinable	There are three settings for the managed property that appear in the drop-down list. If either Yes – Active or Yes – Latent is selected, you'll find that Queryable will be selected as well. The selections are defined as follows: ■ **Yes – Active:** This setting enables the use of the managed property as a refiner for search results. You'll need to manually configure the Refinement web part to display this managed property. ■ **Yes – Latent:** This setting enables switching this managed property to an active refiner later without having to conduct a full crawl after the change in configuration. ■ **No:** This setting removes the managed property from the possibility of it being used as a refiner in the result set.	

Managed Property settings	What it means	Example
Sortable	This setting also has three options—the same options as Refinable: ■ **Yes – Active:** This setting enables the managed property to be used as a sorting agent on the result set. ■ **Yes – Latent:** This setting allows the managed property to be switched to Yes – Active at a later date without having to conduct a full crawl when the switch is made. ■ **No:** This setting removes the managaed property from the possibility of it being used to sort the result set.	
Safe for Anonymous	This setting allows values contained within this managed property to be returned to those who are logged in to SharePoint Online using the Anonymous account.	
Alias	Defines an alias name you can use for the managed property if you don't want to use the real managed property in queries and result sets. Note that you must use the original managed property name when mapping a crawled property to a managed property.	
Token Normalization	Enables SharePoint Online to return results to the user without considering the casing of the letter and diacritical marks that might have been used in the query.	For example, the keyword query "resumé" also will return "resume".
Complete Matching	Only content with an exact match will be returned in the result sets.	For example, a keyword query on "English" will not return content with "english".
Mappings to Crawled Properties	This dialog box shows all the crawled properties that are mapped to this managed property. You can use this interface to remove or add crawled property mappings.	
Company Name Extraction	This setting enables the system to extract company-name entities from the crawled properties when crawling new or updated items. The extracted terms are later used as refiners. You can edit the company-name dictionary from the term store.	For example, if a company name is found in the body of a document, company-name extraction is enabled on the managed property "Body," and a full crawl has been run, the company name is extracted and mapped to the managed property companies. You can then use the Companies managed property to create refiners based on the extracted company name in the Refinement web part on the search results page.
Custom Entity Extraction	This setting enables one or more custom entity extractors to be associated with this managed property. During the crawl operation, Search will extract the entities from the managed property. They will be available for use later as refiners. (At the time of this writing, this setting is in the UI but not available in SharePoint Online.)	To use custom entities as refiners, you first create a custom-entity extraction dictionary in the term store. Then you configure a managed property to use a custom-entity extractor. After that, you can configure the Refinement web part on the search results page to use the custom entity as a refiner.

> ***MORE INFO*** There is a real art to executing a great search query. The more your users utilize SharePoint Online to find intelligence, not just information, the more likely it is they will need to understand how to construct a great query. I refer you to the following two resources for learning more about how to construct queries that produce great result sets. The first is the Keyword Query Language (KQL) syntax reference guide at *https://msdn.microsoft.com/en-us/library/office/ee558911.aspx*. The second is the FAST Query Language (FQL) syntax reference guide at *https://msdn.microsoft.com/EN-US/library/office/ff394606.aspx*.

Custom-entity extraction is not available to SharePoint Online customers. SharePoint Server 2013 administrators can create and deploy custom-entity-extraction dictionaries to configure the search system to look for specific words or phrases (entities) in unstructured content. The extracted entities are stored in separate managed properties, and you can use them to improve your organization's search experience—for example, by creating refiners.

> ***MORE INFO*** Custom-entity extractions, at the time of this writing, are not available to SharePoint Online customers. Company-name extractions can be a bit tricky to set up. There are a couple of articles that will explain in step-by-step form how to do this. For custom-entity extractions, see this TechNet article: *https://technet.microsoft.com/en-us/library/jj219480.aspx*. For the company-name extractions, see this TechNet article: *https://technet.microsoft.com/en-us/library/jj591605.aspx*.

Creating a new managed property

When a new site column is created in SharePoint Online, a new crawled property is created using the column's name. If the column was created as part of a new content type, search doesn't pick up its existence until it is used in a list or library to create a new content item. Search doesn't index the content types *per se.* But once it is picked up by search, the values entered into the metadata field are indexed and content items can be found. The crawled property is automatically added to the index, so there is no real need to create a managed property for that crawled property unless the configurations noted previously in this chapter regarding managed properties are needed.

> ***IMPORTANT*** From a governance perspective, the creation of a managed property should be handled by the system administrator, whether it is created at the tenant or site-collection level. Most site-collection administrators do not have the training or experience with search that is sufficient for properly creating a new managed property. This is a reminder that will come in handy often in SharePoint: just because the interface allows a particular role to perform a particular action doesn't mean that role *should be* performing that task or making that decision.

Let's now focus on how to create a managed property manually. Navigate to the Manage Search Schema section in the SharePoint Online admin area. Once you are there, click the New Property link that appears on the page (*listmanagedproperties.aspx*). When you click New Managed Property, use Table 6-1 as a reference guide on how you'll configure the managed property. Even though this is a new managed property, you'll not be able to configure the following:

- Allow multiple values
- Refinable
- Sortable

Moreover, when you create a new managed property, it will need to be either a property type of Text or Yes/No. The other property types—Integer, Decimal, Date and Time, Double Precision Float, and Binary—are not available to you. However, all is not lost. If you need a property of a type other than Text or Yes/No or one that has different characteristics than what is available, you can just rename an existing managed property and use it for your own purposes. You'll rename the property by giving it an Alias name, not by renaming the property itself.

Any managed property that is not mapped to a crawled property can be reused for your purposes, as long as it is the type of managed property you need. The default "empty" managed properties are outlined in Table 6-2. Note this table is taken directly from the Microsoft TechNet article "Manage the Search Schema in SharePoint Server 2013" at *https://technet.microsoft.com/en-us/library/jj219667.aspx.*

TABLE 6-2 Empty managed properties that can be reused in SharePoint Online

Managed Property Type	Count	Managed Property Characteristics	Managed Property Name Range
Date	10	Queryable	Date00 to date09
Date	20	Multivalued, queryable, refinable, sortable, retrievable	RefinableDate00 to RefinableDate19
Decimal	10	Queryable	Decimal00 to Decimal09
Decimal	10	Multivalued, queryable, refinable, sortable, retrievable	RefinableDecimal00 to RefinableDecimal09
Double	10	Queryable	Double00 to Double09
Double	10	Multivalued, queryable, refinable, sortable, retrievable	RefinableDouble00 to RefinableDouble09
Integer	50	Queryable	Int00 to Int49
Integer	50	Multivalued, queryable, refinable, sortable, retrievable	RefinableInt00 to RefinableInt49
String	100	Multivalued, queryable, refinable, sortable, retrievable	RefinableString00 to RefinableString99

Managing search dictionaries and query suggestions

Search dictionaries are used to include or exclude company names that are extracted from the content of your index. These words can then become refiners for search results. They are also used to include or exclude words for query spelling correction. The essential difference between the two dictionaries is this: If there are words you never want to have suggested with the Did You Mean functionality, enter them into the Query Spelling Exclusions dictionary. For words you would like SharePoint to suggest using the Did You Mean functionality, enter them into the Query Spelling Inclusions dictionary.

In short, to set this up, you'll want the name of the company that you want to extract entered into the Company dictionary in the term store. Once you have done this, you can then use the managed property "companies" to create refiners based on the extracted company name in the Refinement web part, on the search results page. You'll add the Companies refiner in the properties of the Refinement web part. See the upcoming section "Search Refinement web part" for more information.

Managing query spelling correction

SharePoint Online has the "Did you mean?" functionality. If a word is misspelled when a keyword is entered into the query string, the results page will display query spelling corrections and basically ask the question, "Did you mean to enter this word?" In other words, is it spelled correctly?

For example, if you enter a query that contains the word "chrysanthenum" (as shown in Figure 6-3), the query spelling correction would show "chrysanthemum" if this term is in your indexed documents and you entered both the correct spelling and the incorrect spellings into the inclusions dictionary in the term store. You can add terms such as the one just shown to the Query Spelling Inclusions list, or to the Query Spelling Exclusions list, to influence how you want query spelling corrections to be applied (or not applied). It takes up to 10 minutes for any changes to the Query Spelling Inclusions list or Query Spelling Exclusions list to take effect.

> ***MORE INFO*** **In working with SharePoint Online, you might experience some frustration at the amount of time required for new content to appear in the index of your tenant. Although Microsoft has turned on continuous crawling to make sure that changes to content appear in the search results as soon as possible, its target timeframe to update the index is between 15 minutes and one hour. However, by the company's own admission, heavy environment use can result in as long as six hours of wait time before content changes appear in your index.**
>
> **You can think of continuous crawls as a 15-minute sliding window. At the beginning of the crawl period, the change log is interrogated and all changes form the list that the crawler will touch to update the index. At the next 15-minute interval, the change log is again interrogated and everything new in the change log since the last log check is queued up for the crawler to touch as it updates the index. The challenge comes when too much**

information is uploaded or modified for the crawler to touch and index within a single 15-minute window. It basically means that the change log is large enough that crawling takes longer for the items than what can be finished within the 15-minute window. When this happens, nothing is discarded and the next continuous crawl engages on time regardless of whether the first one has finished.

You can force a pickup on your site by clicking the Index This Site Now button in the admin pages. This forces a full crawl of your site on the very next 15-minute window. Again, though, if everyone did that, it would slow down everyone. So there are no guarantees.

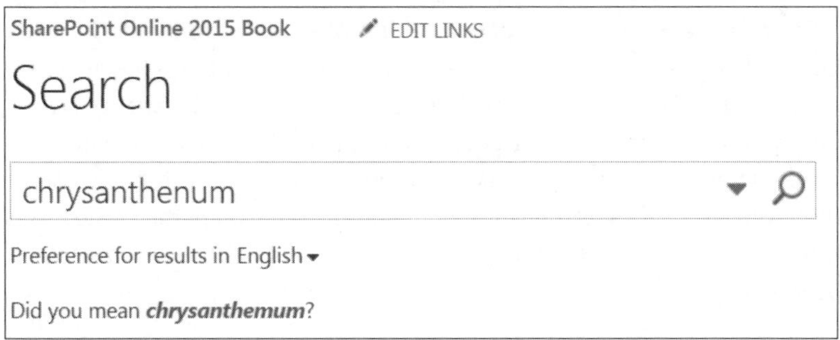

FIGURE 6-3 The Did You Mean? feature of SharePoint's Online search functionality

If you worked with SharePoint 2001, 2003, and 2007, you can think of these exclusion and inclusion dictionaries as replacing the old XML Thesaurus files in which you manually created expansion and inclusion sets.

If a word occurs more than 50 times when there is a minimum of 1000 documents in the SharePoint Online index, it becomes part of the dynamic query spelling dictionary and the Did You Mean functionality will automatically kick in without you needing to manually populate the dictionaries. For words that occur less than 50 times in the index, if you want Did You Mean functionality, you'll need to manually enter these words into the dictionaries.

Query suggestion settings

By default, search suggestions are turned on. You can turn them off by navigating to the Query Suggestion settings and clearing the Show Search Suggestions check box. If you choose to leave that functionality on and you work in a multilingual tenant, you can select the language in which you want suggestions to appear. The default setting is the initial language of the tenant.

In the Always Suggest Phrases and Never Suggest Phrases (not illustrated) areas, you can import and export terms to and from a text file. If you're moving from an on-premises version of SharePoint to SharePoint Online, it will be easier for you to export and then import your search dictionaries.

Managing authoritative pages

Authoritative pages are those that link to the most relevant information your users find through search. By using authoritative pages, you can influence the ranking of content items in the result set such that pages more closely linked to the most authoritative pages will rank higher in the results than pages that are further way from the authoritative pages, as measured by click distance.

Click-distance measurement is straightforward: the more number of clicks required to get from one page to another, the farther away those two pages are from each other. Hence, the closer a document or content item is to an authoritative page, the higher its static rank is in the index.

By default, SharePoint Online sets each root page in a site collection to be the most authoritative, as illustrated in Figure 6-4. As you can see, this Most Authoritative Pages list was automatically generated by SharePoint Online. This default setting makes sense only when all your site collections are equal in importance. In many deployments, this will not be the case. So you want to ask yourself the question, "Where do my users host their most important information within my Office 365 environment?" If you can stratify their tendencies into primary, secondary, and tertiary levels, you'll have your three sets of URLs to input into these three input boxes.

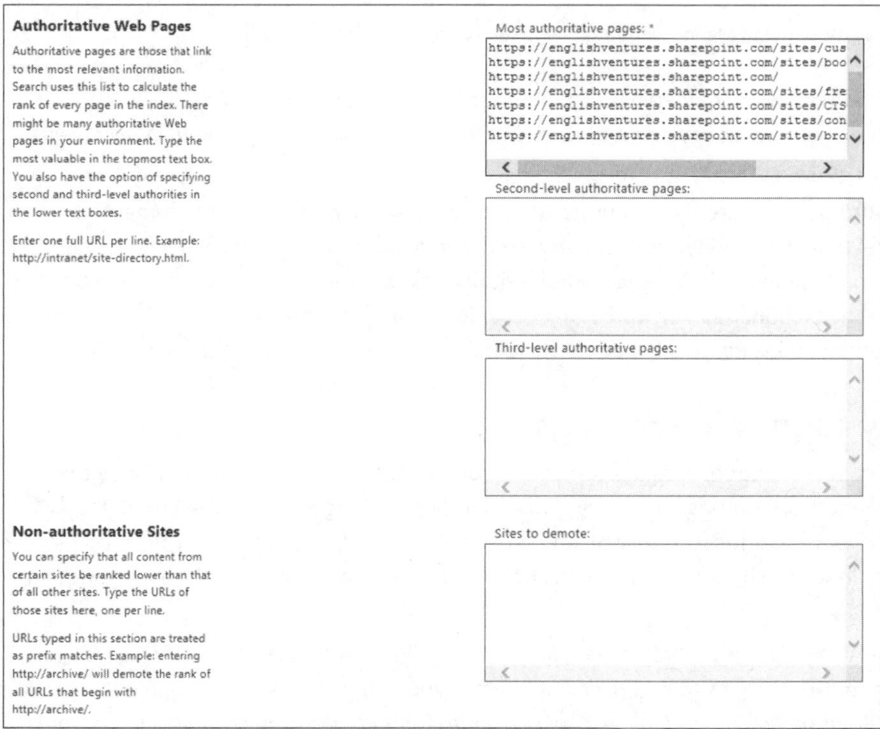

FIGURE 6-4 Default setting for Authoritative Pages in which all site collections are added to the Most Authoritative Pages section

For example, if you have a records center at *https://tenantname.sharepoint.com/sites/records* where mission-critical documents are stored and an archive center at *https://tenantname.sharepoint.com/sites/archive* where outdated, reference documents are stored, you'll want to put *https://tenantname.sharepoint.com/sites/records* in the Most Authoritative Pages section and *https://tenantname.sharepoint.com/sites/archive* in the Sites To Demote section.

You can drag and drop existing URLs between the four input boxes, saving you time and headaches from typing and correcting misspelled URLs. However, it is easy to grab only a portion of the URL in the interface when highlighting and copying the URL. So be sure you copy the entire URL before trying to drag and drop it.

Your content hub site collection, which is automatically generated by SharePoint Online, does not need to be given the highest level of authority in authoritative pages. Consider demoting this site collection to that of tertiary or place it in Sites To Demote, especially if you're not going to use it to host anything other than your content type hub. The URL is *https://<sitename>.sharepoint.com/sites/contentTypeHub*.

Managing result sources

With the advent of Search Server 2008, whose functionality was later folded into SharePoint Server 2010, we gained the ability to create search scopes on indexed content that didn't reside in our local index. Moreover, we gained the ability to send queries to external indexes and have the results from those external indexes appear on the same webpage as the results from our local index. In effect, we gained the ability to execute one query to multiple indexes and organize the various result sets on a single webpage. Add to this search scopes—which we've had since SharePoint Portal Server 2003—and put it all together. In SharePoint Server 2013, result sources provide all this functionality.

You create and use a result source to specify a location from which to receive search results and to specify the connection protocol for getting those results. In a result source, you can also restrict queries to a subset of content by using a query transform—literally, a transformation of the query *after* it is submitted by the user in the search box and *before* it is used to build the result set from the index. Query transforms give you a nearly unlimited way of finding information. They can be used like search scopes. For example, the predefined Local Video Results result source uses a query transform to return only video results from the local SharePoint index. Or, you can change the query based on the user. For example, a query on the word "governance" will take people in the organization to a set of training videos on governance, whereas those with titles that start with "President" or "Chief" are taken to the Board of Director's internal governance website.

You can create your own result sources or use one of the 16 predefined result sources. If you create your own result source, you'll need to configure Search Web Parts and query-rule actions to use it. Results sources can be created by the tenant administrator or the site-collection administrator. Result sources created at the tenant level are available to all site collections in the tenant. Result sources created at the site-collection level are available only within that site collection.

To create a new result source, go to the Manage Result Sources page for the level you want to work at. Second, on the Manage Result Sources page, click New Result Source (not illustrated). In the General Information section, type a name and a description for the new result source. In the Protocol section, choose one of the following protocols to retrieve search results. (Note that, at the time of this writing, the interface has all four of these options even though you can only connect to the Local SharePoint option.)

- **Local SharePoint** This protocol will return results from the search index of the tenant in which you're working.
- **Remote SharePoint** This protocol will return results from the index of a search service that resides in a different SharePoint tenant or farm. In the Remote Service URL input box, type the address of the root site collection of the remote SharePoint farm.
- **OpenSearch 1.0/1.1** This protocol connects SharePoint with a search engine that uses or is compliant with the OpenSearch 1.0/1.1 protocol.
- **Exchange** This protocol will return results from a Microsoft Exchange Server. Click AutoDiscover to have the search system find an Exchange Server endpoint automatically, or type the URL of the Exchange web service to retrieve results from—for example, *https://contoso.com/ews/exchange.asmx*.

If you choose Local SharePoint as the protocol, you'll have to select between the SharePoint Search Results (which is the entire index) or the People Search Results (which is that portion of the index that hosts the user-profile information and My Site information. The People search will return user profiles in the result set.

In the Query Transform section, you can modify or transform the queries by either leaving the default query transform (*searchTerms*) as is or typing in a different query transform into the box.

> ***MORE INFO*** **I know from experience that reading standards can be boring and sleep-inducing. Yet, taking the time to read through the OpenSearch standards will help you a great deal in terms of understanding how query transforms are constructed. To learn more, you can visit *www.opensearch.org* or read the chapter I wrote on OpenSearch in *Microsoft Office SharePoint Server 2007 Best Practices* (Microsoft Press, 2008).**

If you want to further transform the query, click the Launch Query Builder button to build your own query. When you do this, it will present you with the Build Your Query dialog box. (See Figure 6-5.)

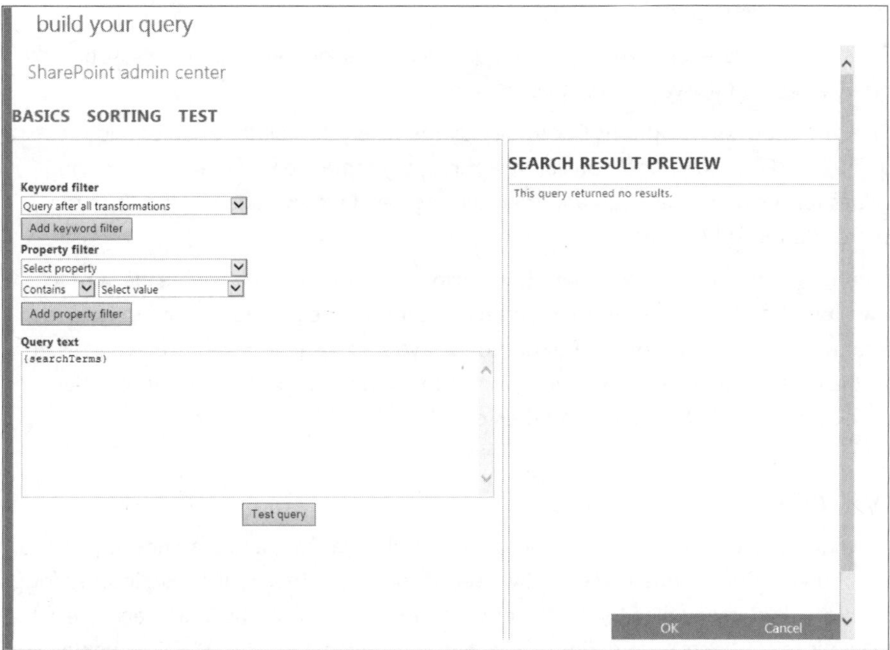

FIGURE 6-5 Build Your Query dialog box

Notice that the default *{searchTerms}* (yes, capitalization is important, and these OpenSearch variables are case sensitive) is the initial query transform in the Query Text input box. On the Basics tab, you can select one of the following:

- **Keyword Filter** Use this to add predefined query variables to the query transform. Select query variables from the list, and add them to the query by clicking Add Keyword Filter. For example, you can transform the query by specifying that only sites that contain the content items you're looking for are returned in the result set.
- **Property Filter** Use property filters to query the content of managed properties that are set to Queryable in the search schema. For example, you might decide you want to see only files that have a FileType of *Excel*.

On the Sorting tab, you can do the following:

- Sort the results based on one or more managed properties that have the sorting element activated. For example, you could sort the result set based on the last time the documents were modified and then subsorted based on the author's name. To sort by relevance, select Rank.
- If you selected Rank from the Sort By list, choose the ranking model to use for sorting. SharePoint Online contains a number of default ranking models. If you select a ranking model, you'll be able to add a Dynamic Ordering Rule that will override the defaults in the ranking model. For example, if the title contains certain keywords, you can promote those items within the ranking model.

On the Test tab, you can do the following:

- See the final query text, which is based on the original query template, the applicable query rules, and the variable values.
- Click the Show More Options link to display the Query Template variables and the query text. From this page, you can test the query template you built by specifying values for the query variables and then clicking Test Query to see the results in the Search Results Preview pane.

Coming back to the main page, in which you can create a new result source, be sure to scroll down into the Credentials Information section and choose an authentication type for users to connect to the result source. Be sure to save your work. If you want to save a result source as the default for users to use, simply point to the result source you want to set as the default, click the arrow that appears, and then click Set As Default.

Query rules

You can use query rules to enter additional configurations that can help searches respond to the intent of users. A query rule is essentially a set of conditions that, when met, indicate one or more actions that are invoked by the system. Essentially, when you build a query rule, what you're saying is this: "When X (condition) is present or is met, do Y (action)." For example, when a user queries on the word "Microsoft" (condition), promote the link to Microsoft's home page (action).

So, when a query meets the conditions in a query rule, the search system performs the actions specified in the rule to improve the relevance of the search results. For example, you might build a query rule that is specific to the person executing the query. You might choose to return generic results for a particular keyword query, except when the user's department in the user's profile is equal to a specified department name. Then the results would show a defined set of results for users in a result block. You can configure query rules for one or more result sources, and you can specify the time period during which the query rule is active (publishing).

Query rules are used to create promoted results. Promoted results are the new way to think of the old Best Bets. Promoted results appear above the result set and below the keyword query input box and the Did You Mean information.

You can create new query rules just by clicking the Create New Query Rule link from the Manage Query Rules page. The default page to create a New Query Rule is illustrated in Figure 6-6.

You'll notice that as part of this page, you need to specify the conditions under which the rule will be invoked. There are six conditions you need to understand, and they are outlined in Table 6-3.

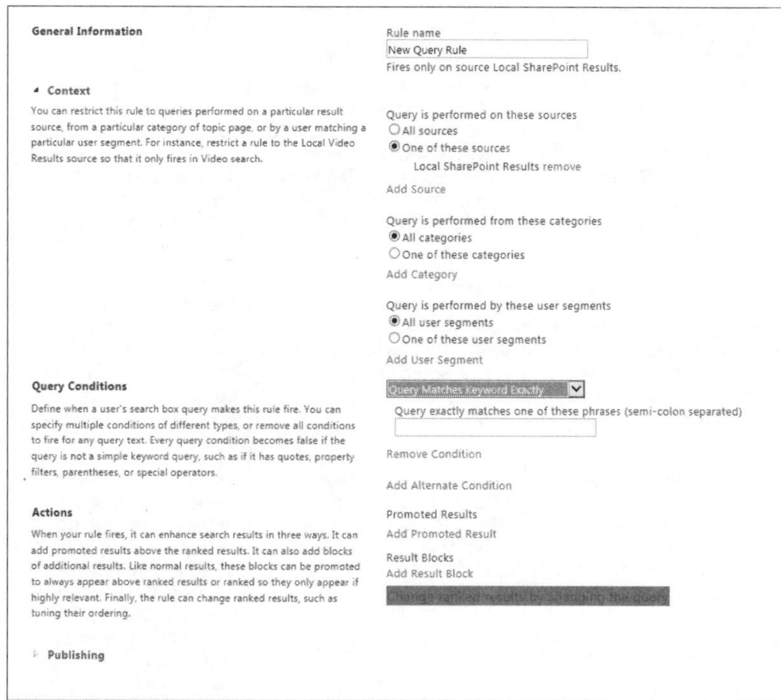

General Information
Rule name
New Query Rule
Fires only on source Local SharePoint Results.
Context
You can restrict this rule to queries performed on a particular result source, from a particular category of topic page, or by a user matching a particular user segment. For instance, restrict a rule to the Local Video Results source so that it only fires in Video search.
Query is performed on these sources
All sources
One of these sources
Local SharePoint Results remove
Add Source
Query is performed from these categories
All categories
One of these categories
Add Category
Query is performed by these user segments
All user segments
One of these user segments
Add User Segment
Query Conditions
Define when a user's search box query makes this rule fire. You can specify multiple conditions of different types, or remove all conditions to fire for any query text. Every query condition becomes false if the query is not a simple keyword query, such as if it has quotes, property filters, parentheses, or special operators.
Query Matches Keyword Exactly
Query exactly matches one of these phrases (semi-colon separated)
Remove Condition
Add Alternate Condition
Actions
When your rule fires, it can enhance search results in three ways. It can add promoted results above the ranked results. It can also add blocks of additional results. Like normal results, these blocks can be promoted to always appear above ranked results or ranked so they only appear if highly relevant. Finally, the rule can change ranked results, such as tuning their ordering.
Promoted Results
Add Promoted Result
Result Blocks
Add Result Block
Change ranked results by changing the query
Publishing

FIGURE 6-6 The Create New Query Rule page

TABLE 6-3 Query conditions

Query Condition	When to Select This Option	Configuration	Notes
Query Matches Keyword Exactly	The query rule will be invoked when the keyword query exactly matches a word or phrase that you specify.	In the Query Exactly Matches One Of These Phrases input box, enter the words and/or phrases you want to be part of the condition. Separate multiple entries with semicolons.	For example, "car" is input as a condition, so the rule will be invoked when "car" is part of a keyword query, but the rule will not be invoked for "cars", "carried", or "automobile".
Query Contains Action Term	The query rule will be invoked when the keyword query contains an action word that is at the beginning or end of the query string. The point is that the action word is probably not something the user is looking for, but instead, is something the user wants to do with the content he hopes to find.	In Action Term Is One Of The Phrases or Action Term Is An Entry In This Dictionary, specify the action term or terms, such as "Download" or "Create".	If the user types in the search box "create new annual budget" (without the quotation marks), the user probably isn't looking for instructions on how to create the annual budget. Instead, he is likely to be looking for the template to create a new annual budget. If "Create" is specified as an action word, it will *not* be passed to the search engine, while the remaining words New, Annual, and Budget will be passed to the search engine.

Query Condition	When to Select This Option	Configuration	Notes
Query Matches Dictionary Exactly	This option will invoke the query rule when a keyword query exactly matches a term in a specified dictionary.	From the Query Contains An Entry In This Dictionary menu, select a dictionary. To specify a different dictionary, click Import From Term Store, select a term from a term set, and then click Save.	For example, if you have a term set named "Customers" that contains all your customer names, the rule is invoked when a user types a name that matches a customer name from the Customers term set.
Query More Common in Source	This option will invoke the Query rule when the query is frequently issued by users on a different result source than you specified in the query rule.	From the Query Is More Likely To Be Used In This Source drop-down box, select a result source for this rule.	The query rule will fire if a user types the word "training" in a search box and that word was frequently typed in a search box in the Videos vertical.
Result Type Commonly Clicked	This option will invoke the query rule when other users frequently clicked a particular result type after they typed in the same query.	In the Commonly Clicked Results Match Result Type drop-down box, select a result type.	An example of this is when users commonly click a particular blog post after typing in a query and you notice this from the log reports. So you create a query rule of this type, select "SharePoint Blog", and then add a promoted result that points to the commonly accessed blog post.
Advanced Query Text Match	This option will invoke the query rule when there is a pattern that can be expressed as a regular expression, a phrase, or a dictionary entry.	Enter the expression needed for creating the pattern that will be matched to the keyword query.	An example of this is when you want to match all phone numbers in a certain format, so you enter a regular expression.

MORE INFO Regular Expressions, or "RegEx" has its own syntax as a way to find text or positions within a body of text. RegEx is used to find, validate, replace, or split content, based on the instructions included in the expression. There are a couple of sites that might interest you if you want to learn more about RegEx: *http://www.regular-expressions.info/reference.html and http://regexone.com/.*

When building query rules, you'll be able to add alternate query conditions, such that these six different conditions can be included in the same query rule. The additional query conditions are connected with an OR statement, not AND.

The query rule can also have a rich context setup for it within the rule. By default, when you navigate to the page in which a new query rule is created, the Context area is not expanded, so you'll need to manually do this by clicking the Context link on the left side of the page. Referring back to Figure 6-3 this is an illustration of the page already having the Context area expanded. You use the context area to narrow or better focus when the query rule is invoked:

- **Query is performed on these sources** This means that you specify which result sources the query will associate with. For example, you might want the query rule to fire only on microblog content items, not on documents or SharePoint blog posts.
- **Query is performed from the categories** In this instance, *categories* really refers to one or more term sets in the term store.
- **Query is performed by these user segments** Here, you'll create your own user segment and then add terms from the term store (from any term set where the terms are configured as being available for tagging) to build your own, customized user "segment." For example, a user who is a project manager in the Minneapolis office will find a query rule will be invoked, whereas a project manager in the Barcelona office will not find the same query rule invoked. Both might find their job titles coming from the same "category," but because the user segment didn't include the term *Barcelona*, it doesn't fire for the Barcelona project manager.

Along with the context and conditions are *actions* that you want to have taken when the context and conditions are met within the rule. The actions that can be invoked are to promote certain results, add a result block, or both. The Promoted Result dialog page (not illustrated) is merely a title with a URL entry box that will render a link to the promoted result above the result set. (See Figure 6-7.)

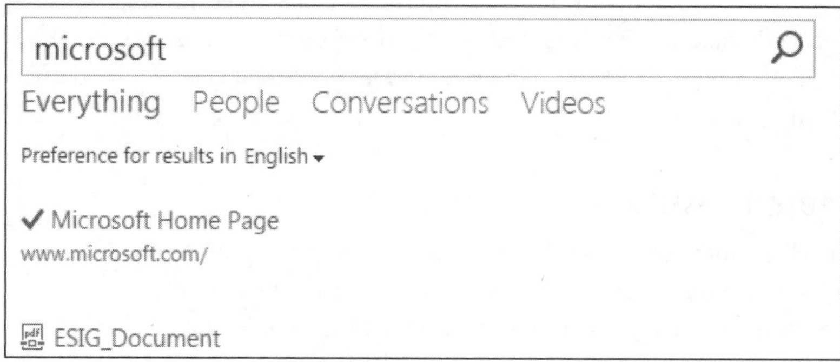

FIGURE 6-7 The Microsoft website as a promoted result

Adding a result block is similar in concept to adding a promoted result, except that within the block, you can display another set of results that comes from using the Query Builder. This gives you added flexibility in displaying the results that users intended to receive from their queries. You can think of a result block as an automatic query that is generated based on the original query with the results displayed in a quarantined block—similar to how results from a Federated Search were displayed in a web part in SharePoint Search Server 2008 and SharePoint Server 2010.

The ranked results also can be changed by modifying the query itself that is embedded within the query rule. Click the Change Ranked Results By Changing The Query link.

The last part of creating a query rule is the publishing area—you can decide when or if the rule is active, determine the rule's start and end dates, and specify a person to contact about the rule. The advantage here is that you can build the rule and test it well in advance of when you'll need it or, if it is used on an annual basis (such as giving specific results to the company users for the annual company giving campaign), it can be activated and deactivated and dates can be specified for when it will be available and not available.

Query client types

Not only can you configure result sources that tightly define from where search results are generated and build query rules that further refine how search results are returned to the user, you also can define client types that define how important a query is based on the type of client making the request. For example, a client might tell you it is an automated query, at which point, you can configure those types of requests to be lower in priority than, say, a user query of people and their profiles. Query client types are really about throttling queries to protect the search system resources. The goal is to ensure lower-priority clients like automated queries don't squeeze out higher-priority clients like real users submitting queries to the search engine. Query client types are also used for things like logging, reports, and determining relevance.

You can't turn query throttling on or off. It comes on automatically when the search resources limit is reached as determined by the tenant thresholds that Microsoft manages. If those limits are reached, the throttling is turned on to process queries in the priority set by you, the SharePoint administrator. Once throttling is no longer needed, it will be turned off until it is needed again.

Removing search results

Sometimes content will get into your index that you don't want, or someone in your organization doesn't want, in the index. This is most often the case when secret or confidential information is mismanaged and the content gets indexed. Happily, the content can be removed by entering the URL of the content item. It is removed immediately.

You cannot enter URLs of containers. For example, you cannot enter a single URL to a document library to remove all the documents within the library. Only URLs that point to specific content items can be removed. The removal is temporary until the next crawl (every 15 minutes), so you'll need to remove the content item from your tenant or set the list/library in which it resides to not be indexed if you want to permanently remove the item from the index.

Viewing usage and search reports

Usage reports for search are helpful if you want to extend your administrator responsibilities to finely tuning the search experience for your end users. There are nine default reports in SharePoint Online, though there are only five different types of reports. I'll cover each type in the following sections. There is no way to customize the reports from Search within the user interface.

Number of queries

This report shows the number of queries your users executed against the index. It just shows the raw number of queries by all result sources combined and then by individual result sources. It does not indicate what keywords were queried or what URLs appeared in the result set. Use this report to see if, overall, your users are using search more, less, or about the same as in previous time periods. A trend downward might indicate that users are losing faith in the SharePoint Online search, which means you'll need to do additional research with your users to find out why.

Top queries by day and month

This report shows the most popular search queries and should be used to understand what type of information your users are looking for. The information provided will include the following:

- Result source
- Query text
- Total queries for each unique query text
- % of all queries each unique query text comprised

The report will be generated for a 14-day period, starting with the present day and moving backward in time.

Similar to the Top Queries By Day report, the Top Queries By Month report shows the most popular search queries on a monthly basis. It too can be used to understand what type of information users are looking for. It provides the same information set as the Top Queries By Day, but it divides up the time by month.

Abandoned queries by day and month

This report is somewhat misnamed because it shows queries that received low click-through rates, not just those queries that produce result sets and no content items are clicked on to follow through to the content. A high number of abandoned queries indicates dissatisfaction with the result set and likely means that your users are not finding the content they want to find with the keyword queries they are entering. Information included in this report is

- Result Source

- Query Text
- Total Queries
- % with No Clicks

Now, the problem could be that your users are entering poor queries—those that are not specific enough (for example, a user enters "horn" when she is looking for "trumpet") or contain the wrong set of keywords (for example, a user enters "meeting room" when he is looking for "hotels"). But the problem is more likely that your information is not properly tagged, is set to not be indexed, or exists in a different information-hosting system than SharePoint Online and the users misunderstand where to look for specific information.

In addition, many times, people think they are using the right keywords to find a document when, in fact, the document does not contain those words. For example, a user might be looking for a document on governance, so she enters the words "Governance Non-Profit Boards" for a document named "Standards for running an approved IRS 501C3 Organization." It could be that the document discusses governance for nonprofit boards in general terms but never uses those terms. This is a common problem, so ensuring that your metadata is highly descriptive and that your users have been educated on how to use your metadata structures to find information is paramount to a good findability solution.

Also, if this metric is increasing, it is also likely that the Number Of Queries metric is decreasing. It stands to reason that there would be an inverse relationship—at least temporarily—between the metrics in these two reports. As users try to find information and then abandon their result sets, their dissatisfaction increases. As part of that increase, users will naturally turn to other methods to find information—even if it means copying to their desktops.

No result queries by day and month

Even more problematic for your organization is when users commit queries and receive an empty result set. This report—by day and by month—can be used to identify search queries that will likely result in user dissatisfaction. Here are the report parameters:

- Result Source
- Query Text
- Total Queries
- % with no Results

Unlike SharePoint 2013 where you several tools at your disposal to improve the discoverability of content—such as creating new content sources—you'll need to work with Result Sources (think Query Builder here for Federated Search) to find content outside your tenant or ensure that the content users are looking for really exists in your tenant. But the larger point is that if they are looking for content and receiving an empty result set, this is a problem that should be proactively managed by you, the system administrator.

Query rule usage by day and month

This report shows how often query rules fire, how many dictionary terms they use, and how often users click their promoted results. You'll use this report to see how effective your query rules and promoted results are to your users. The content contained in the report includes the following:

- Result source
- Query rule
- Owner of the rules
- Owner type
- Dictionary term
- Number of times the rule has fired
- The promoted result

This is especially helpful if you create a promoted result that is not heavily used. It probably means you have the wrong result promoted for a given keyword. In addition, if a query rule you created is rarely used, it's good to know this so that you can revisit the reason you created it in the first place and work with your users to modify the rule to give them a more meaningful result set. An example of this report is illustrated in Figure 6-8. The other search reports have a similar look and feel to them. All of them are Excel based.

Query Rule Usage by Day: 3/31/2015

Tenant: Tenant Administration

This report shows how often query rules fire, how many dictionary terms they use, and how often users click their promoted results. Use this report to see how useful your query rules and promoted results are to users.

Result Source	Query Rule	Owner	Owner type	Dictionary term	Times fired	Promoted resul	Promoted resul	% Promoted re
All Sources	Adobe PDF		Service	0	0			
All Sources	Conversations		Service	0	0			
All Sources	Excel		Service	0	0			
All Sources	Fill In Results		Service	0	0			
All Sources	Image		Service	0	0			
All Sources	Location in People Search		Service	1658	0			
All Sources	Location in Sharepoint Search		Service	1658	0			
All Sources	OneNote		Service	0	0			
All Sources	People Expertise Search		Service	0	0			
All Sources	People Name in Conversations Search		Service	0	0			
All Sources	People Name in People Search		Service	0	0			
All Sources	People Name in Sharepoint Search		Service	0	0			
All Sources	Phone Number in People Search		Service	0	0			
All Sources	Phone Number in Sharepoint Search		Service	0	0			
All Sources	PowerPoint		Service	0	0			
All Sources	Queries commonly performed in People Sea		Service	0	0			
All Sources	SharePoint Blog		Service	0	0			
All Sources	SharePoint Wiki		Service	0	0			
All Sources	Site		Service	0	0			
All Sources	Tags in Conversations Search		Service	0	0			
All Sources	Tags in Sharepoint Search		Service	0	0			
All Sources	Visio		Service	0	0			
All Sources	Word		Service	0	0			
All Sources	Zip		Service	0	0			
All Sources	Microsoft External		Tenant	0	0			

FIGURE 6-8 Query Rule Usage By Day report

Search center settings

The one setting you can configure here is the URL for the global search center. This setting instructs the search system where to send user queries by default. The URL entered is the search center that is automatically created when SharePoint Online is initially instantiated. The default URL is *https://<tenant_name>.sharepoint.com/search/Pages.*

Exporting and importing search configurations

When you click the Export Search Configuration link, you are not taken to a page. Instead, an XML file is generated that includes all customized query rules, result sources, result types, ranking models, and site search settings that didn't get created with the default installation of SharePoint Online. Settings that SharePoint Online creates when it is first installed by the tenant is not included in this configuration file.

Included are all exportable, customized search configuration settings at the tenant, site collection, or site level from where you start the export. For example, a search configuration file for a site collection doesn't contain search-configuration settings from the individual sites within the site collection. Being able to export a search configuration at the site-collection level allows you to create the configuration once and then apply it to multiple site collections in your tenant. When you import a search-configuration file, SharePoint Online creates and enables each customized search-configuration setting in the tenant, site collection, or site from where you start the import.

Table 6-4 shows the settings you can export or import. There are dependencies that must exist for each customized search-configuration setting. If the customized configuration settings depend on a customized search-configuration setting at a different level—for example, if a site query rule depends on a result source at the site-collection level—you must export and import settings at all the relevant levels.

TABLE 6-4 Export customization settings

Configuration Setting	Dependency
Query rules	Result sources, result types, search schema, ranking model
Result sources	Search schema
Result types	Search schema, result sources, display templates
Search schema	No dependencies
Ranking model	Search schema

There are times when the import will fail. Most failures have to do with naming issues:

- If the exported settings and the target settings have the same name, the import will fail, with the following exceptions:
  - If you are reimporting the configuration file to the same location, the same names will not cause the import to fail.
  - If the properties on a managed property are the same in the import file and the target property.
  - If the mapped crawled properties, the aliases, or both are different, the import action will add the aliases and mappings to the target managed property.
- If there are invalid characters in the names of a managed property or alias.
- The names of the managed properties and aliases of the schema must be unique for a site and its parent site collection.

When an import fails, the failure, in and of itself, does not disable the settings that have already been applied to the search service for the site, site collection, or tenant.

Search Navigation web parts

The Search Navigation web part shows links that help users move between the different search pages. These search pages are known as *search verticals*. They are predesigned to give users different search experiences depending on what they are looking for. For example, the People link will take your users to the people search page (vertical) where they can view information about people about whom they search. The four default verticals are Everything, People, Conversations, and Videos.

You can change how the Search Navigation web part is set up by specifying a different web part from which to get the results, change how many links to show, and change the appearance and layout of the web part. You make these changes by editing the properties in the Web Part tool pane.

Changing the settings for the Search Navigation web part

To edit this web part, you need to execute a query and then, from the search results page, edit the page. Once the page is in edit mode, click the down arrow in the upper-right portion of the Search Navigation web part that appears when you hover your cursor over it. It doesn't appear unless you hover the cursor over it, as shown in Figure 6-9.

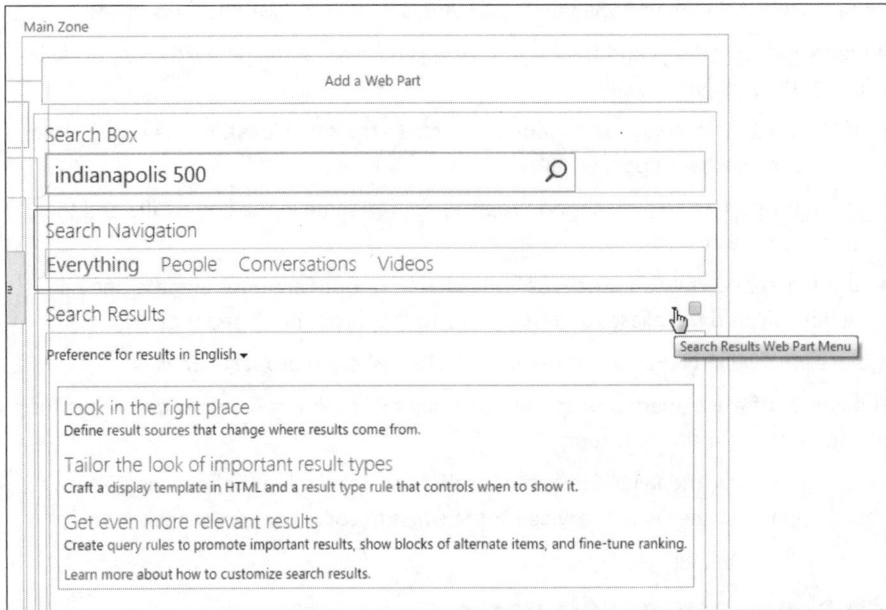

FIGURE 6-9 Clicking the down arrow to edit the web part

Once you have the web part Properties box open (as shown in Figure 6-10), you can select which web part this web part will receive search results from and how many links must exist before overflowing begins in the Control section of the web part properties.

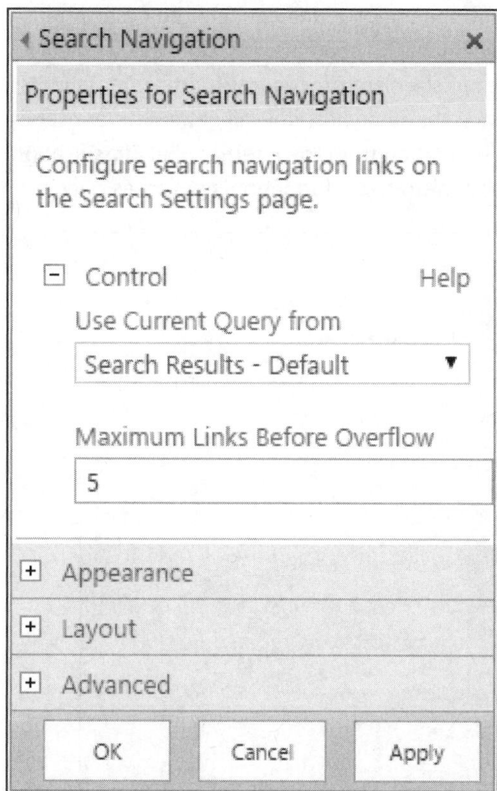

FIGURE 6-10 Control section of the web part properties

Changing the display name or the URL of a search vertical

If you want to change the display name or the URL of a search vertical, all you need to do is open the site settings in the search center (or any other site collection), click Search Settings and then, in the Configure Search Navigation (refer forward to Figure 6-13) area, highlight the vertical name and click the Edit link to edit the name.

Once you're in edit mode (as shown in Figure 6-11), you'll be able to change the name of the vertical, specify the page you want to use as the results page for this vertical, and specify whether or not you want the page to open a new window. Happily, you can also assign an Audience to the vertical, meaning that the vertical itself will appear only in the interface if the user is a member of a specific audience. Through the use of audiences, you can customize the search experience so that users in one department (for example, nurses) would get one set of verticals in which to commit queries (such as standard procedures for moving patients within the hospital) and a doctor or psychiatrist in the same hospital will get a different set of verticals in which to commit queries (such as information from the International Classification of Diseases). The description field is there for administrative informational purposes only.

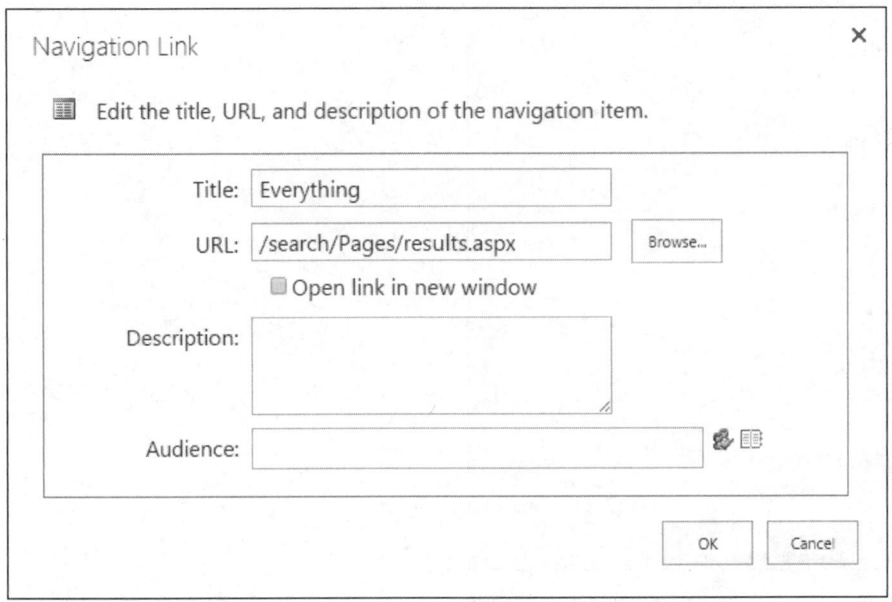

FIGURE 6-11 Editing the search vertical's name, results URL, and audience associations

In the same Configure Search Navigation area, you can change the order in which the verticals appear just by selecting one vertical and then using the Move Up and Move Down links. (See Figure 6-12.) Also, you can use the Add Link to add another vertical to the group. You can use the same query and results pages if you'd like, but the real power is in building a specialized set of pages that will enhance and refine the search experience. If you use the standard search pages, I see little reason to add another vertical.

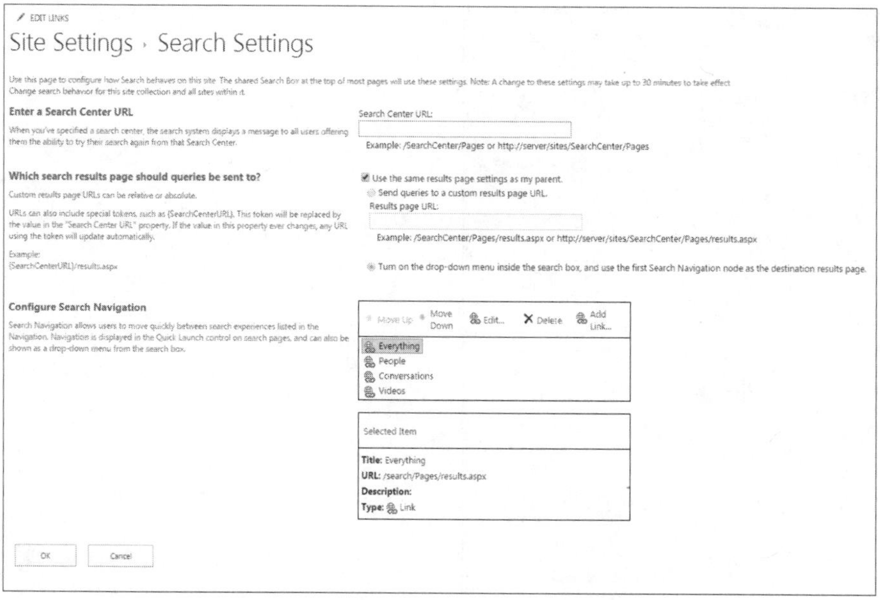

FIGURE 6-12 Configure Search Navigation on the Search Settings page

Search Refinement web part

The Refinement web part filters search results into categories called *refiners*. Users can click these refiners to narrow search results to find what they're looking for more easily. It is added to the left pane of the search results page. By default, it is used on all default search result pages.

The Search Refinement web part, as you might expect, is customizable. You can do the following:

- Filter search results from a different Search Results web part.
- Specify which refiners to show.
- Change the display template for a refiner.
- Change display names for refiners.
- Add counts to refiners.

To customize the Refinement web part, open a search results page and then go into Edit mode on the page. In the left pane, you'll see a web part named Refinement. Select the down arrow for that web part in the upper-right portion of the web part. Select Edit Web Part, and the Refinement properties will appear on the right side of your screen (as shown in Figure 6-13).

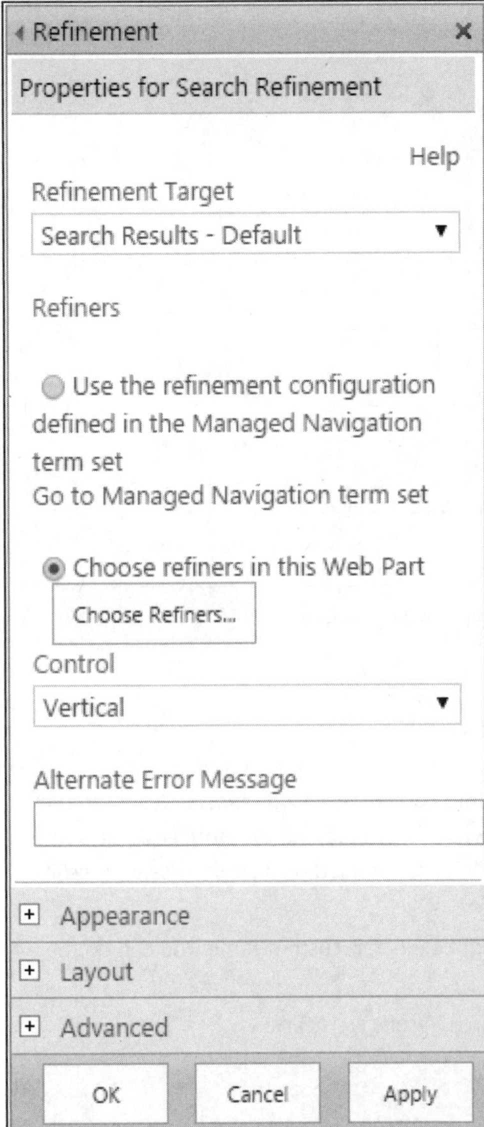

FIGURE 6-13 Refinement web part properties

If you attempt to choose an available refiner whose managed property isn't set to Refinable And Queryable, you will not be successful in adding the refiner to the web part. Moreoever, the content that contains the managed properties will need to have been crawled before the properties can be used as refiners.

By default, the name of the managed property will be used as a display name for the refiner. However, many managed property names are less than ideal when it comes to usability. You can fix this problem by changing the name of the refiner in a JavaScript file.

Open the CustomStrings.js file from the Language Files page in the Master Page Gallery in your site collection. For each managed property for which you want to change the display name, use this syntax:

```
"rf_RefinementTitle_ManagedPropertyName": "Sample Refinement Title for
ManagedPropertyName"
```

If you want to show how many content items in the result set are associated with each refiner, you need to modify the Filter_Default.html file, located in the Filters folder under the Display Templates in the Master Page Gallery. Set the value for ShowCounts to TRUE.

Basic Search Center information

The Search Center is where users enter search queries and view the search results. In SharePoint Online, a Search Center site is automatically available at <*host_name*>/search/. There are a set of default pages and web parts you'll want to be aware of, as outlined in Table 6-5. You'll find the pages in the Pages library.

TABLE 6-5 Default pages and web parts

Search Center Page	Description	Result Source
Default.aspx	This is the home page for the Search Center.	
Results.aspx	This is the default results page for the Search Center and the default page when users select the Everything vertical from a site-level search.	Default
Peopleresults.aspx	This is the results page for the People search vertical.	Local People Results
Conversationresults.aspx	This is the results page for the Conversations search vertical.	Conversations
Videoresults.aspx	This is the results page for the Videos search vertical.	Local Video Results
Advanced.aspx	This is the Advanced search page where additional rules can be applied to the query before it is submitted to the index for processing.	

Summary

In this chapter, I discussed the tasks and decision points involved in managing search in SharePoint Online. We went through the various administration screens that will help you understand how to perform day-to-day search administration tasks.

Even though search is a big area, it's not the only important management function in SharePoint Online. For example, learning how to implement what was once known as Single Sign-on—now called the Secure Store Server—can significantly improve your user's experience of SharePoint Online. It is to this topic to which we now turn our attention.

CHAPTER 7

Securing information

Though it is not popular to discuss, several of the largest data breaches in recent memory—Edward Snowden and the NSA/PRISM leak and the earlier PRISM leak by WikiLeaks—involved the use of Microsoft SharePoint by both organizations and the attackers. In both cases, SharePoint was used to compromise the confidentiality of the information hosted therein.

Enterprises often fear hackers as their number-one security threat. Their focus is misplaced. According to Ponemon's 2013 Data Breach Report, human or system error is still the cause of 64 percent of data breaches. Moreover, according to recent Cryptzone research, 36 percent of users breach their own SharePoint security policies—when such policies exist, which it turns out is rather rare. InfoSecurity has revealed that 65 percent of SharePoint users have no security policy that they routinely follow. In addition, the Cryptzone research found that even though some organizations do not allow sensitive information to be stored within SharePoint environments, nearly a quarter of respondents were ignoring this directive and putting such information in SharePoint anyway. It appears the organizations have no way to track where their mission-critical information is being stored. Cryptzone, I'm sad to say, also found that a majority of SharePoint administrators perceive their "permission" to be unrestricted, leading Cryptzone to conclude that, "Many SharePoint administrators are abusing their access capabilities, which leads to putting confidential data at risk."

> ***MORE INFO*** You can read about Cryptzone's research here: *http://www.cryptzone.com/company/news-events/press-releases/cryptzone-survey-reveals-sharepoint-users-are-breaching-security-policies*. You can review Ponemon's report here: *http://www.ponemon.org/library/2013-cost-of-data-breach-global-analysis*. You can review the InfoSecurity report here: *http://www.infosecurity-magazine.com/news/a-hackers-dream-two-thirds-of-sharepoint-users/*.

Back in the old days, I used to teach classes on Microsoft Exchange Server 2000 and Exchange Server 2003. I would tell my students that even though they *can* read the CEO's emails, they *shouldn't*. Sometimes, this open admission that platform administrators can get to everything hosted by the platform would lead to a discussion about two undeniable truths that most organizations want to ignore:

- No one can build a software platform that can guard against an untrustworthy administrator.
- No one can build a software platform that can guard against an unwise administrator.

SharePoint Online doesn't change those realities.

Recently, Microsoft released new security measures for Microsoft Office 365, including

- Compliance with ISO 27018 and HITRUST
- Sign-in page customizations
- Self-service password reset

However, these measures will do little to solve the human problem of security. Whether they perform their actions intentionally or unwittingly, employees themselves are the major security concern when it comes to the loss or exposure of critical data. The ease with which users bypass IT departments and security teams when using cloud-based services is common and well known. Yet, getting managers and users to agree on how to implement an IT policy that curbs the potential for loss of data due to compromised security is a conundrum for many IT professionals, which contributes to the problem.

The stark reality is that many decision-makers don't take seriously the human factor when it comes to security. They prefer to see it as a technology problem instead of a cultural and process problem. "Don't slow me down" and "Don't mess up my stuff" are common themes that cause significant push-back against increasing security measures.

It doesn't take a starburst of insight to realize that the more secure a document is, the harder it is to get to it and to use it within a process. Those charged with delivering profits and on-time projects will respect security to a point, but they will also accept more risk than perhaps they should because they are not measured on and rewarded for how well they keep information secure. Instead, they are measured on and rewarded for on-time performance and profits generated. People focus on what their performance is measured by. If security becomes a hindrance, it is set aside or ignored. No one likes annual reviews where they don't attain all of their goals and receive their bonuses.

One solution that some organizations have attempted to implement to balance security with collaboration is to clearly identify sensitive information using classifications. Yet research shows that the vast majority of users are not tagging their data, nor do they want to. Moreover, less than 10 percent are protectively marking all emails, and the same percentage said they do the same for all documents. Only 17 percent of respondents said they mark all email and documents.

REAL WORLD I use an encryption solution for all my email messages. My solution checks for public keys of those to whom I'm sending messages before I send the email message. If a public key is found, the message is encrypted and sent to the recipient. If a public key is not found, the message is sent anyway, but at least the default is to attempt sending the message encrypted. In the two years that I've used this solution and for the thousands of email messages I've sent, less than 20 of those messages were sent in encrypted format.

In talking with people about this, the two common themes I've heard as to why people don't use a Public Key Infrastructure (PKI) solution for encrypting email messages are these:

- I have nothing to hide, so why bother?
- I don't really think anyone is listening to or reading what I send, so why incur the additional cost?

In both instances, there is a common, nonchalant attitude. So people send critical, confidential information unencrypted across the Internet. They send payroll files, applications for patents, proprietary research, and so forth across the Internet backbone with nearly nonexistent knowledge about who could be listening in on their transmissions and nearly complete trust that their information won't be compromised. I recently had a colleague send me their Visa information—the entire credit card number, expiration date, name and back-of-the-card-numeric codes in a single email, unencrypted. I'm confident it didn't occur to this individual that someone might copy the credit card number while the email was in transit and use it for their own purposes.

In this day and age—when organizations can be attacked directly by foreign governments, when sensitive customer information is leaked in massive amounts, and when well-documented eavesdropping by various governments occurs on all electronic communications—you would think that encrypting email messages would be a natural action for people to take. But this is not the case, illustrating the point that our greatest security issues are not technology related, they are human related.

Company data on employee hardware

The human factor's affect on security is increased with the advent of the Bring-Your-Own-Device age. The potential for data loss is heightened. With Office 365, many organizations receive five Office licenses for each user so that the Office suite can be installed legally on five different devices, *most of which are owned by the end user, not the organization.* Although this feature is great for collaboration and using any type of device for work-related tasks, it creates a security nightmare because the organization can't control the endpoints of where their data is stored or how it is secured in transit. Consider this hypothetical scenario:

> *Katrina is the Vice President of Product Development for a $180-million company with 300 employees. She travels between offices in different cities and countries, meeting with customers, partners, and employees to stay on top of new customer preferences as well as industry trends. Her position requires her to have access to nearly all confidential information the company has.*
>
> *She has a desktop computer in her office, a laptop she uses on the road, plus her own Microsoft Surface tablet and smartphone. All of her data is stored in her OneDrive for Business account. She accesses her data from all four devices.*
>
> *On one particular trip, she was using her Surface (because she likes to "mark up" her documents using the pen and ink technologies offered with the Surface) to read highly sensitive information about a key competitor related to a new, innovative product her company would soon be releasing. She placed the Surface in the seat-back holder for magazines on the seat in front of her. During her flight, she took a short nap and then forgot to retrieve the Surface before she de-planed. It wasn't until later in the day, hours after she had left the airport, that she remembered where she left her Surface.*
>
> *Several weeks later, her company's mission-critical information was sold to the competitor and some of her internal email messages about her competitor, as well as her private thoughts about her CEO that were intended only for her close friend, were leaked to the press. The data loss embarrassed the company, embarrassed her, made public an ongoing interpersonal conflict between herself and the CEO, and resulted in her loss of employment.*
>
> *After a thorough investigation, the company's board of directors terminated the CEO and CIO, citing negligence in the creation and enforcement of information-security policies, encryption technologies, and endpoint swiping technologies. Thereafter, the board mandated that all employees attend additional security training and use only company-owned hardware with biometric, encryption, and swiping technologies to ensure their own data would never be leveraged against them in the future, even if the physical hardware was lost or stolen.*

When it comes to employees accessing and storing company-owned data on personal hardware, it seems obvious that the company should require them to comply with company information-security policies and to accept the possibility that the company will combine automated swiping technologies with employee education to enforce governance policies.

By using technology that does not interfere with daily activity, companies can give themselves the means to monitor content for potential compliance issues and take action to prevent unauthorized distribution and sharing. Of course, employees must fully understand why these guidelines exist and what it means to the whole organization should they be violated.

Overly trusting bosses also need education and re-alignment in their thinking. The Bring-Your-Own-Device environment has less to do with whether or not you trust employees and much more with how devices are lost and employee choices that inadvertently make critical information available through unencrypted email and lack of security enforcement. Mistakes can and will be made by employees.

You also cannot rule out malicious intent. According to Ponemon, half of employees admit to taking corporate data with them when they left their jobs or were fired, and 40 percent planned to use that data in their new positions at other organizations. Unlimited access to internal information can create considerable opportunities for data loss. Trusting bosses need to be more concerned about data integrity than whether or not they appear to trust those whom they lead.

Introduction to Microsoft Intune

Microsoft Intune is a suite of technology solutions designed to help overcome the human factor I just discussed. Microsoft Intune helps you manage computers and mobile devices and secure your company's information on those devices. It's a good step forward in balancing the Bring-Your-Own-Device needs and information-security management. You can use Microsoft Intune to manage Microsoft Windows computers and mobile devices, including iOS, Android, Windows RT, and Windows Phone devices. You can use Microsoft Intune alone or integrate it with Microsoft System Center 2012 R2 Configuration Manager to extend its management capabilities.

MORE INFO This chapter will focus only on the cloud-based, stand-alone version of Microsoft Intune. For more information on how to use Microsoft Intune with System Center 2012 R2, reference the following article: *https://technet.microsoft.com/en-us/library/dn646980.aspx*.

NOTE You do not need an Office 365 tenant or account to use Microsoft Intune. You can subscribe to Microsoft Intune separately from Office 365.

NOTE The installation of Silverlight will be required on the computer used to manage Microsoft Intune.

In short, you can enforce policies for device security, app management, resource access, and inventory and reporting. Let's review these aspects of Microsoft Intune.

> ***TIP*** **Microsoft Intune is constantly changing, so as this book ages, this information will become more and more out of date. However, you can keep up with the changes to Microsoft Intune by referencing this page:** ***https://technet.microsoft.com/en-us/library/dn292747.aspx.***

If your users connect to Microsoft Intune from your network, you'll need to open up ports 80 and 443 for a number of domain names, which are listed in this TechNet article: *https://technet.microsoft.com/en-us/library/dn646950.aspx#BKMK_InfrastructureReqs.* Moreover, there are connectors you can install for on-premises Exchange and Windows Active Directory. You can read about those connectors in the aforementioned article.

When it comes to mobile devices, the different types of mobile devices will result in different requirements for direct management of those devices. For example, to manage iOS devices, you need an Apple Push Notification service certificate, and to manage apps for a Windows RT 8.1 device, you need side-loading keys and a code-signing certificate.

Microsoft Intune can manage the following devices with mobile device management:

- Apple iOS 6.0 and later
- Google Android 4.0 and later (includes Samsung KNOX)
- Windows Phone 8.0 and later
- Windows RT and Windows 8.1 RT
- Windows 8.1 computers

Microsoft Intune has its own management console that is not integrated (at the time of this writing) with the Office 365 Administration back end. The dashboard will contain buttons or links to the following elements:

- Start managing mobile devices
- Start managing computers
- General information on getting started
- What's new
- Forums
- System overview
- Mobile device management

In all these areas, Microsoft has written extensive product documentation that should help you learn how to manage and secure corporate information that is hosted on mobile devices. Microsoft Intune is larger than just endpoint security, but because this section of this chapter is focused on mobile devices and endpoint security, I'll limit our Microsoft Intune discussion to these aspects.

Before you can directly manage mobile devices, you must make Microsoft Intune the mobile-device-management authority. You will do this by selecting the needed mobile-device-management-authority setting on the Mobile Device Management page of the Administration workspace. The mobile-device-management-authority setting determines whether you manage mobile devices with Microsoft Intune or System Center Configuration Manager with Microsoft Intune integration.

You can find the Mobile Device Management page by performing the following actions.

First, click the (very large) Start Managing Mobile Devices button (as illustrated in Figure 7-1).

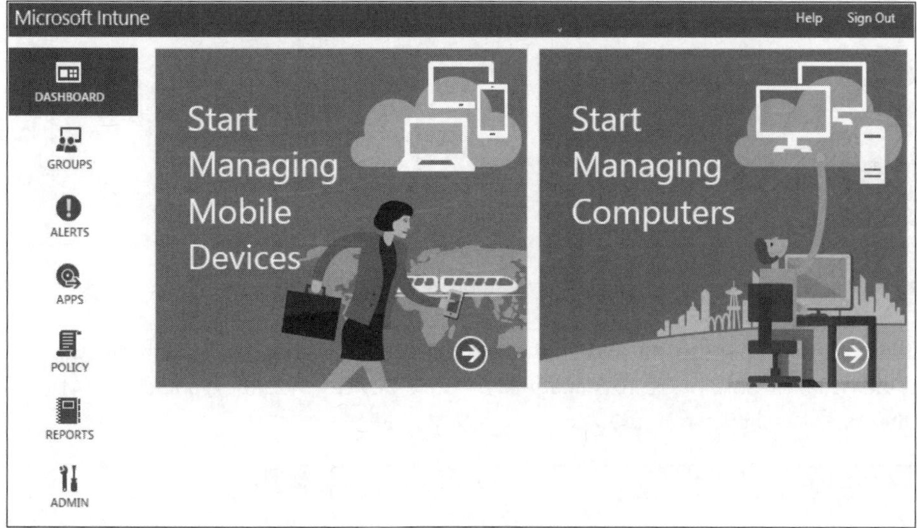

FIGURE 7-1 Microsoft Intune Dashboard, which shows the Start Managing Mobile Devices button

Clicking the button will not only take you to the Administration area of Microsoft Intune, it will also focus you on the exact administrative activity in which you need to engage. Notice in the right pane that there is a wizard-type interface that will walk you through the rest of the steps.

Click the Set Mobile Device Management Authority link (as shown in Figure 7-2).

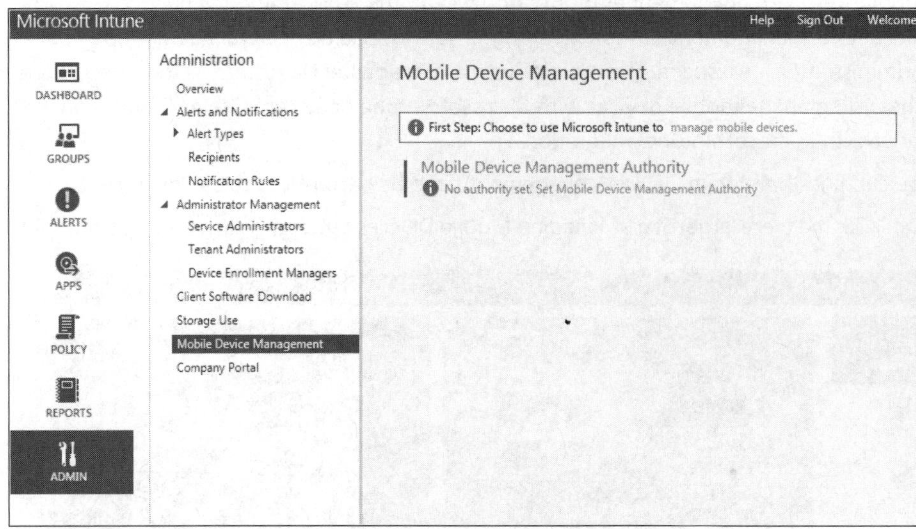

FIGURE 7-2 The Set Mobile Device Management Authority link in the right pane

Clicking the link opens the first page of the Mobile Device Management Authority wizard. Select the Use Microsoft Intune To Manage My Mobile Devices check box, and click OK to start the wizard as shown in Figure 7-3.

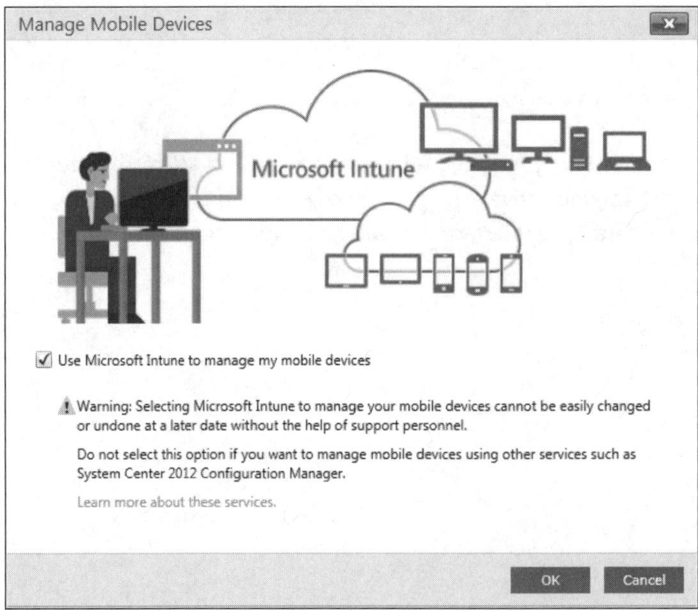

FIGURE 7-3 Selecting the Use Microsoft Intune To Manage My Mobile Devices check box

After you click OK, you'll be presented with the wizard page shown in Figure 7-4. Notice that the platforms available for enrollment are listed along with links to make specific configuration choices for most of the platforms. It is outside the scope of this book to go through how to set up each of these platforms. However, there is ample written instruction to the right of this page (not illustrated) with a link for each platform that will take you to step-by-step instructions on how to configure the enrollment processes for each platform.

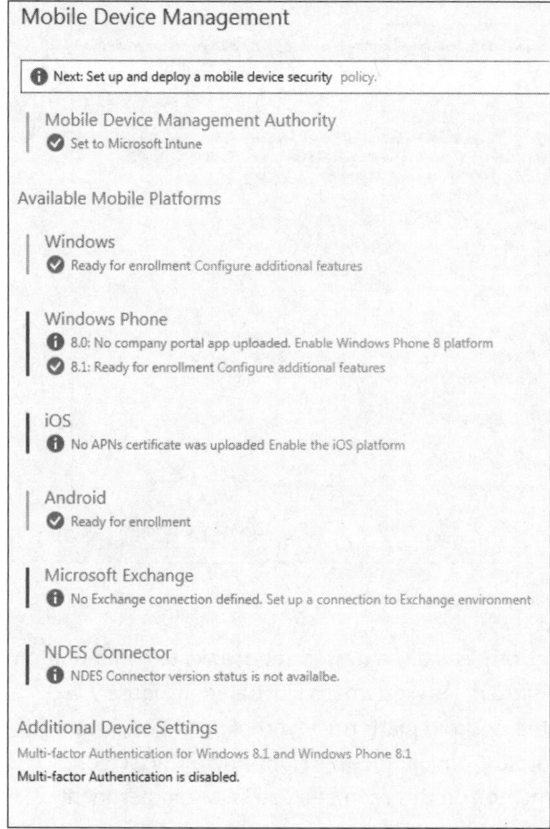

FIGURE 7-4 The Mobile Device Management page

Your next step is to create configuration policy templates that can be applied to the various mobile devices when they are being enrolled. While the previous step concerned itself with the *process* of enrollment (such as DNS settings, certificate considerations, signing company apps, and so forth), policies relate to the *security* of the device once it is enrolled. These settings control features on the mobile devices such as software updates, endpoint protection, firewall settings, and the end-user experience of Microsoft Intune. You create policies using templates that contain recommended or customized settings and then deploy them to device or user groups. Policies are applied during the enrollment process, but they are not concerned with *how* enrollment takes place. Instead, they are concerned with device configuration and compliance once the device has been enrolled.

To create a new policy, click the Policy link (shown earlier in Figure 7-4). Then, on the Policies page (not illustrated), click the Add link. Another way to get to the Policies page is to click the Policy icon in the left pane and then click Configuration Policies in the left pane. Both approaches will get you to the Configuration Policies page within Microsoft Intune. When you click the Add link, it will invoke a short wizard, as illustrated in Figure 7-5.

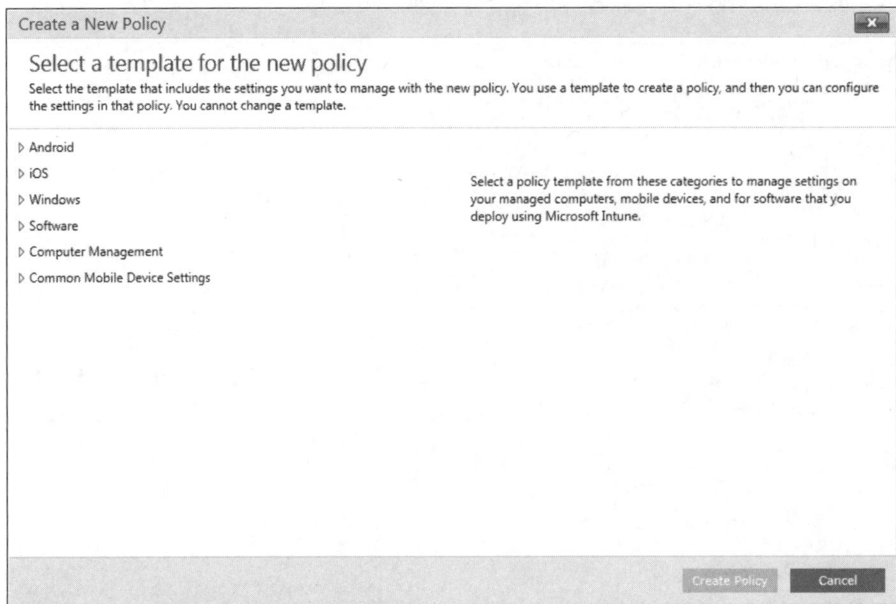

FIGURE 7-5 Create A New Policy wizard

In Figure 7-5, you can see that each platform is really a nested set of links to configuration options. For example, if you expand the Android, you see what's illustrated in Figure 7-6—configuration options that are unique to the Android platform. If you highlight one of the options—the SCEP Certificate Profile (Android 4 and later)—the right side of the screen changes to display context-sensitive information. In this example, you can read pertinent information about this enrollment protocol and then choose to create and deploy a custom policy for the SCEP protocol.

If you click the Create Policy button shown at the bottom of Figure 7-6, a webpage is displayed that you can use to configure the policy for your users. In this instance, you should read up on the SCEP protocol so that you understand how to configure the SCEP Certificate settings (not illustrated).

Each of these links within each nest will have option buttons for creating and deploying a policy. But the pages you're taken to when creating these policies will be unique to each policy setting. Obviously, this will become a complicated area. From a training and staffing viewpoint, if you look through the various configuration options, you'll see more than 30 choices, each with varying levels of similarity and dissimilarity with other options within the same or other platforms.

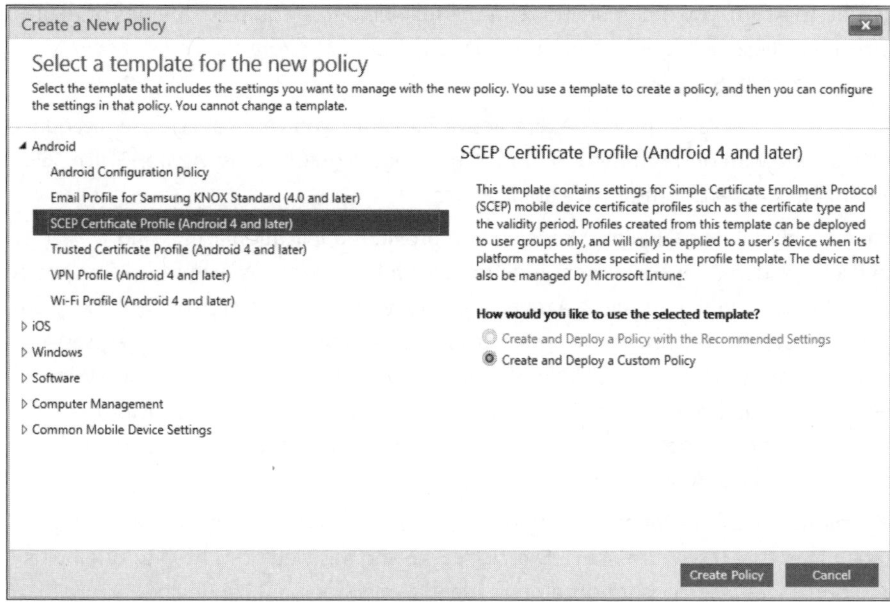

FIGURE 7-6 Selecting a template from which to create a new policy

For example, the SCEP certificate settings page will be the same whether you're focused on the SCEP Certificate Profile for the Android platform or the SCEP Certificate Profile for the Windows Phone 8.1 and later. But the General page for both profiles will be different. In an environment where you have tens of thousands of devices being enrolled across all these mobile platforms, it will likely require a half-time to full-time position to manage the enrollment processes and policies and to troubleshoot enrollment issues. This is a more complicated area than you might initially think. And it is a new technology, so having an experienced administrative individual with a track record of successfully implementing a new technology corporate-wide would be some of the elements I'd look for when hiring a person for the Microsoft Intune management role for a larger corporation or government entity.

Microsoft Intune isn't the only security aspect you need to consider. There's Azure Active Directory, which I'll discuss in the next section.

A brief overview of Azure Active Directory

Azure Active Directory is the online version of Windows Active Directory. Azure combines directory services, advanced identity governance, and application-access management. There are different versions of Azure that can be purchased with your Office 365 tenant. When you subscribe to Azure, you get your choice of the following free and paid editions of Azure Active Directory (these bullet points are taken directly from *https://msdn.microsoft.com/en-us/library/azure/dn532272.aspx*):

- **Free** With the Free edition of Azure Active Directory, you can manage user accounts, synchronize with on-premises directories, get single sign on across Azure, Office 365, and many Software-as-a-Service applications.
- **Basic** Azure Active Directory Basic edition provides application access and self-service identity management requirements for task workers with cloud-first needs. With the Basic edition of Azure Active Directory, you get all the capabilities that Azure Active Directory Free has to offer, plus group-based access management, self-service password reset for cloud applications, Azure Active Directory application proxy (to publish on-premises web applications using Azure Active Directory), a customizable environment for launching enterprise and consumer cloud applications, and an enterprise-level SLA of 99.9 percent uptime.
- **Premium** With the Premium edition of Azure Active Directory, you get all of the capabilities that the Azure Active Directory Free and Basic editions have to offer, plus additional feature-rich, enterprise-level, identity-management capabilities. Azure Active Directory Premium and Azure Active Directory Basic are not supported in China at the time of this writing.

NOTE **Microsoft guarantees at least 99.9 percent availability of the Azure Active Directory Basic service.**

NOTE **Because this book is focused on SharePoint Online administration, I won't dive into how to manage the various parts of Azure Active Directory. There are a number of articles that can help you do this. A good starting point is *https://msdn.microsoft.com/en-us/library/azure/dn532272.aspx*.**

The reason I brought up Azure is because a common task in managing security for SharePoint Online is understanding how Azure Active Directory and Windows Active Directory connect. Almost everyone synchronizes with on-premises Active Directory via Azure Active Directory Connect using Azure Active Directory Synchronization. They also have to make the decision to authenticate against a synchronized password hash stored in Azure or use Active Directory Federation Services to proxy the authentication on-premises. In any case, the idea is to decide between *single* sign-on and *same* sign-on. With single sign-on, the authentication in the cloud is sent back to the Windows Active Directory service for authentication, meaning there is only one directory used to authenticate the user. Same sign-on means that when a user traverses from on-premises to cloud, the user must authenticate again, but she uses the same credentials (same user name and password).

Setting up a single-sign-on system requires more effort and requires Active Directory Federation Services to be installed and properly configured in Windows Active Directory. Some organizations will not concern themselves with multiple login prompts—others will decide that getting to a single-sign-on configuration is one of their highest priorities when implementing Office 365, SharePoint Online, or both. Microsoft supports both configurations.

Let's go over how to install and configure the Azure Active Directory Connect tool. You'll first need to download the tool. At the time of this writing, there is a public preview of it that can be downloaded from here: *http://connect.microsoft.com/site1164/program8612*.

Once you download the tool, you'll run it to perform the installation. You'll run this tool on your domain controller. On the opening screen (not illustrated), you'll read and then agree to the licensing agreement. After this, you'll click Continue, and the tool will want to install the following prerequisites on the next screen (not illustrated):

- Microsoft Online Services Sign-In Assistant for IT Professionals
- Windows Azure Active Directory Module for Windows PowerShell
- Microsoft Visual C++ 2013 Redistributable Package

You'll click the Install button and, rather swiftly, the bits will be installed. After installation, you'll be presented with the Install Synchronization Services screen, as shown in Figure 7-7. You can optionally choose to configure a SQL Server name, a service account, permissions, and import settings.

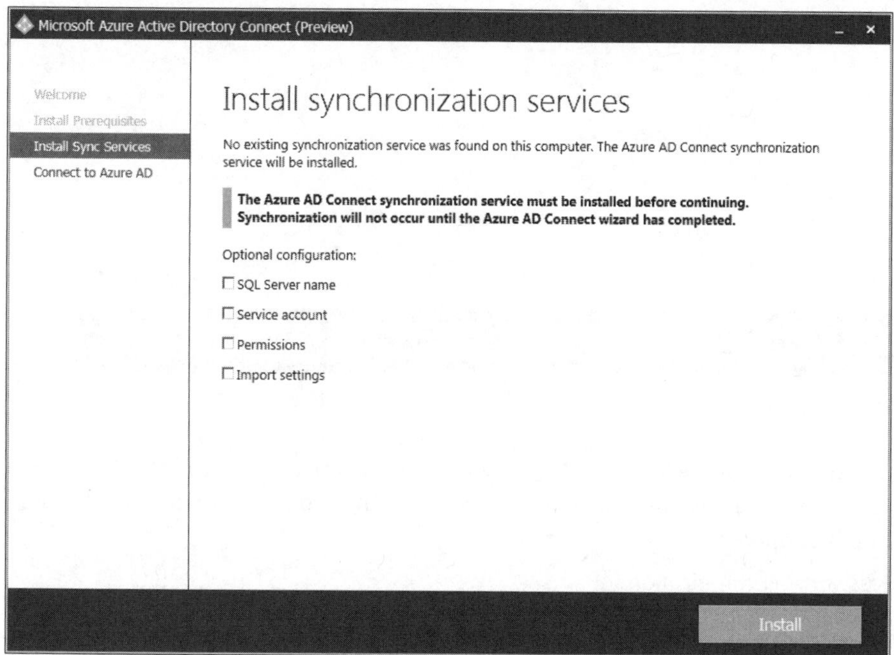

FIGURE 7-7 Install Synchronization Services screen

Selecting the SQL Server name will allow you to specify the SQL instance you want to use for the synchronization services. The wizard will create a database called *ADSync*. It is this database that will host the synchronization account information. Entering the service account name and password will allow you to specify which account Azure should use when logging in to Windows Active Directory for synchronization services. This account should be an enterprise admin account.

After you install the synchronization services, the next screen (not illustrated) will ask you for log-in credentials to your tenant. After you enter your credentials and log in, the wizard will give you the option of performing an Express or Customized installation. If your on-premises environment is a single Windows Active Directory Forest, you can move forward with the Express installation. However, if you want to customize your installation, you can do so by clicking the Customize button. (See Figure 7-8.)

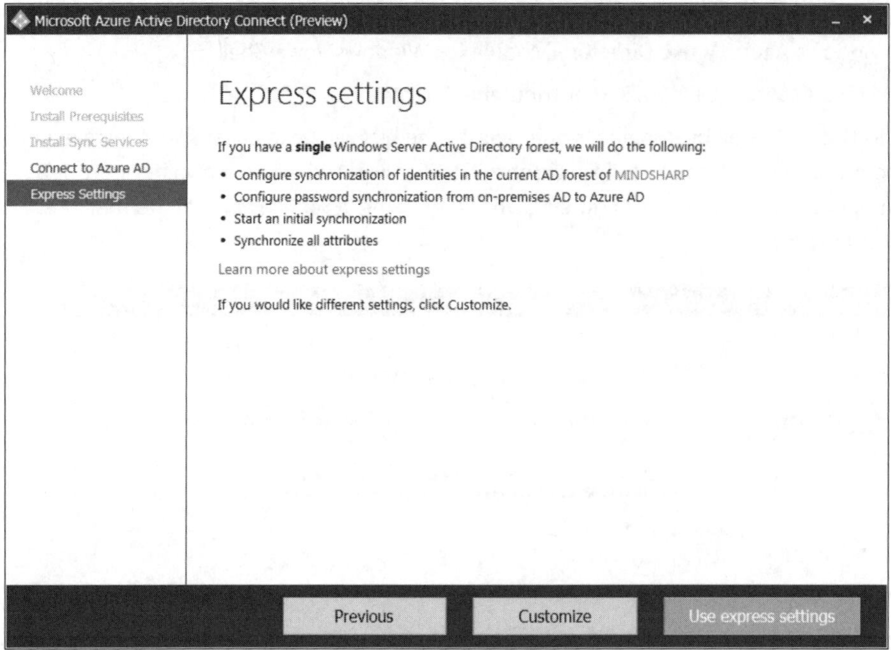

FIGURE 7-8 Express Settings screen

If you click the Customize button, the User Sign-in page is displayed (as shown in Figure 7-9). On this page, you can select the type of single-sign-on method your organization should have. You'll have three options:

- Password Synchronization
- Federation With AD FS
- Do Not Configure

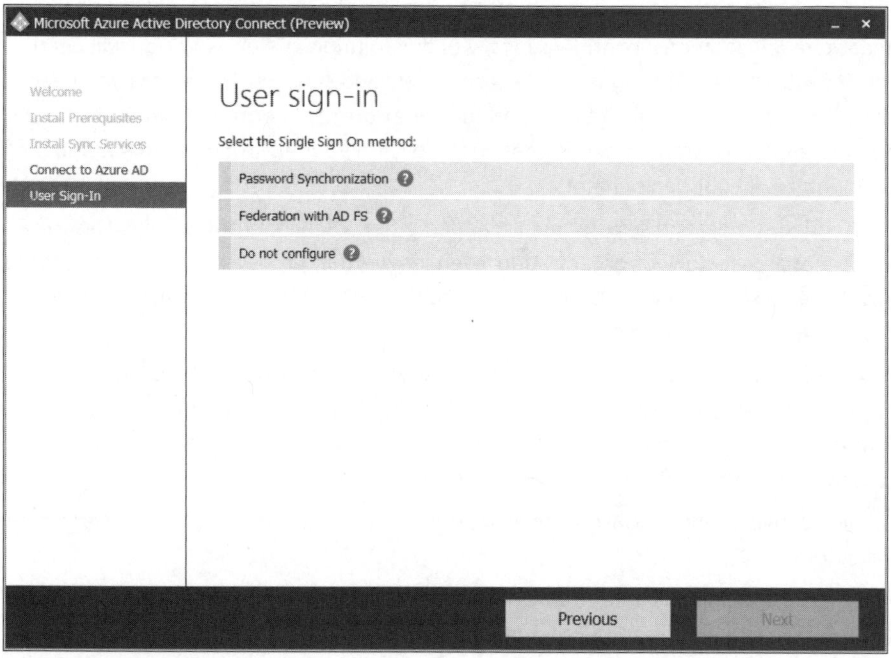

FIGURE 7-9 User Sign-in screen

The obvious advantage of using Active Directory Federation Services is that users log in once to the local domain and then traverse to cloud services without additional log-in prompts. This gives you true single sign-on because the re-entry of user credentials is not required. With password synchronization, a user must still re-enter his password, although it will be the same password he uses on-premises.

Active Directory Federation Services allows for client-access filtering, which restricts access to Exchange Online to users based on their IP address. Customers frequently use this control to limit hourly workers to checking mail only while onsite. In addition, any log-in time restrictions set for users in Active Directory will be enforced.

Another advantage of using Active Directory Federation Services is that a customized webpage can be used for users to change their passwords while they are outside the corporate network. And with Active Directory Federation Services, the authentication decision is always made on-premises by your Windows Active Directory servers, and no password hashes are synchronized to the cloud. In some cases, this will be a security policy requirement.

In addition, when you use Active Directory Federation Services, you can immediately block a user from further activity on either your on-premises or cloud platforms. And if needed, multifactor authentication products can be employed. It is true that Azure supports multifactor products, but most of them require some type of on-premises configuration and confirmation that works in conjunction with Azure Active Directory.

Now that I've sung the praises of Active Directory Federation Services, you should be aware that there are additional considerations with this solution as well. First, you will need additional infrastructure to deploy the necessary servers and services. This means you need additional administrator effort to set it up and further effort to support it. Whether this translates into additional staffing needs depends wholly on your environment, the number of users, and the size of your deployment.

Second, added servers and services means added points of failure (potentially). This *will* result in additional costs to your organization, even if everything runs as smoothly as possible. Third, you'll need a specific SSL certificate from a public Certificate Authority (CA) that will need to be renewed on a periodic basis.

With password synchronization, a hash of the password is passed over the connection between your on-premises servers and your cloud environment. This hasn't proven to be a problem for most organizations, but if the passage of the hash itself is seen as a security threat, password synchronization will not be the option to select.

The choice between single sign-on and same sign-on seems to come down to several core decisions points:

- **User experience** Will your users tolerate multiple log-in prompts or not?
- **Password security** Do you want user passwords stored in multiple places or in a single location? Do you want the hash of these passwords sent over the Internet connections?
- **Password changes** With same sign-on, a password change in the cloud can be written back to the Windows Active Directory. Do you want to write back password changes, or do you want password changes to be committed in only one location?
- **Access revocation** The more swiftly you need to implement access revocation, the more likely it is you'll need to implement single sign-on.
- **Configuration complexity** How complex of an implementation are you willing to support?

Additional security features for SharePoint Online

Beyond Microsoft Intune and single-sign-on technologies, you have additional tools at your disposal that will help you secure your SharePoint Online environment. These tools are already in the Microsoft ecosystem. This overview is intended to help you architect a larger security solution. By the way, I'll assume that you trust Microsoft to provide consistent uptime and that its datacenters are secured against physical and Internet-based attacks as well as providing reliability and data integrity should there be natural disasters. Also, bear in mind that security (as an applied science) is an ongoing process, not a steady state. It is constantly maintained, enhanced, and verified by you, the system administrator.

Data integrity and encryption

Microsoft offers various security technologies you can implement in Office 365 and SharePoint Online. These technologies offer various ways to encrypt data whether the data is at rest or in transit. These technologies are as follows:

- Rights Management Service
- Secure Multipurpose Internet Mail Extension (S/MIME)
- Office 365 Message Encryption
- Transport Layer Security (TLS) for SMTP messages to partners

Rights Management Service

Rights Management Service is a privacy-oriented technology that works at the file level. With Rights Management Service, you can not only encrypt (128-bit AES) data but also apply policies on the data to restrict what the recipient of the file can do with the data in the file. The policies applied to the file are hosted within the file, so whether the file is sitting in SharePoint or an email client, the policies will still apply.

The types of restrictions are as follows:

- **Do not forward (email)/Restricted Access (Office Apps)** Only the recipients of the email or file will be able to view and reply. They cannot forward or share with other people, and they cannot print the file.
- ***CompanyName* Confidential** Only people inside your organization (logically, not physically) can access the content of the file. For example, if your company name is Contoso, only people with an Office 365 account @contoso.com can access the content, make edits to it, and share it with others inside your company.
- ***CompanyName* Confidential View Only** Only people inside your organization can view this file, but they cannot edit or change it in any manner. They can print and share (electronically) with other people in your organization.

You can implement Rights Management Services through Azure Active Directory in your Office 365 tenant. SharePoint Online is agnostic when it comes to Rights Management Services. It doesn't really care or notice if Rights Management Services are turned on or off for different documents. But it will work well with a robust Rights Management Services implementation.

> ***TIP*** **To learn more about how to deploy Rights Management Services with Azure Active Directory, reference this TechNet article:** ***http://technet.microsoft.com/en-us/library/jj585016.aspx.***

Secure/Multipurpose Internet Mail Extension

Secure/Multipurpose Internet Mail Extensions is a standard for public key encryption and digital signing of email. This technology applies to cryptographic security services for email applications. Those services include the following:

- Authentication
- Message integrity
- Nonrepudiation of origin (using digital signatures)
- Privacy and data security (using encryption)

If you implement this technology internally, you'll be able to use the Certificate Services of your Active Directory to generate the public and private certificates. Public certificates are distributed to your Windows Active Directory and stored in two attributes, which can then be replicated to your tenant in Office 365. Private certificates are distributed to end users and can be stored on their various devices. You'll maintain control of the master key in your PKI infrastructure.

This technology will work with the standard Outlook client, Outlook Web App (OWA), or Exchange ActiveSync (EAS) clients.

Because of the public/private key architecture, an email message encrypted with another user's public key can be decrypted only by the user with their private key. This means that an email message cannot be decrypted by anybody other than the recipient of the email if such an email is intercepted in transit or at rest.

> ***TIP*** **You can learn more about how to implement Secure/Multipurpose Internet Mail Extensions by referencing this TechNet article:** ***http://technet.microsoft.com/library/dn626158.***

Office 365 Message Encryption

Office 365 Message Encryption is intended to be used to transmit secure email to users outside your organization. In this respect, it competes with third-party products built on standard encryption technologies, such as Pretty Good Privacy. Office 365 Message Encryption is an online service that's built on Microsoft's Azure Rights Management Service.

Office 365 Message Encryption works a bit differently than you might expect. When a user sends an email message in Exchange Online that matches an encryption rule, the message is sent out with an HTML attachment. The recipient of the email message will open the HTML attachment and (hopefully) follow the embedded instructions to view the encrypted message on the Office 365 Message Encryption portal. The recipient can choose to view the message by signing in with a Microsoft account or a work account associated with Office 365, or by using a one-time passcode. Both options help ensure that only the intended recipient can view the encrypted message. Note that the recipient can reply using encryption as well. Figure 7-10 illustrates how this works. (This illustration is taken directly from this TechNet article: *https://technet.microsoft.com/library/dn569286.aspx.*)

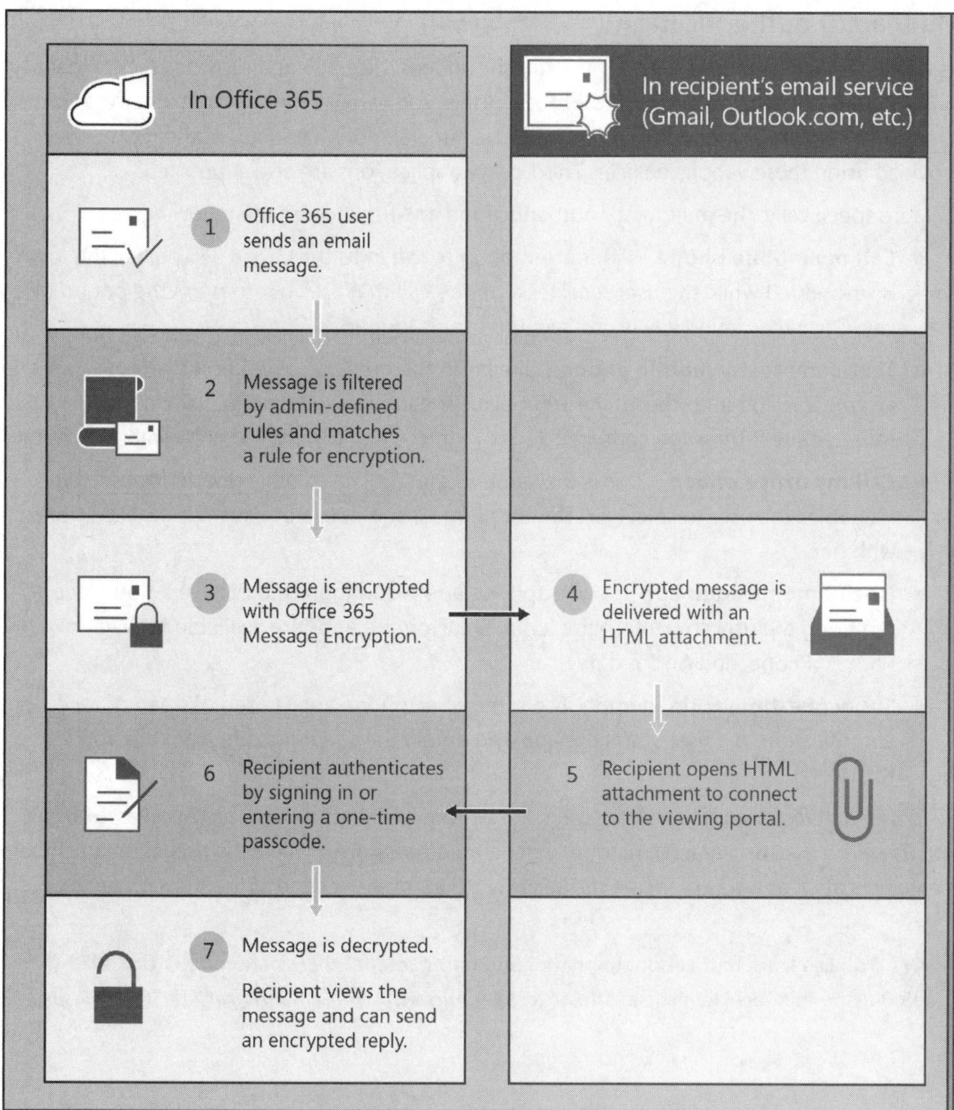

In Office 365
In recipient's email service
(Gmail, Outlook.com, etc.)
1 Office 365 user sends an email message.
2 Message is filtered by admin-defined rules and matches a rule for encryption.
3 Message is encrypted with Office 365 Message Encryption.
4 Encrypted message is delivered with an HTML attachment.
5 Recipient opens HTML attachment to connect to the viewing portal.
6 Recipient authenticates by signing in or entering a one-time passcode.
7 Message is decrypted.
Recipient views the message and can send an encrypted reply.

FIGURE 7-10 Process for how Office 365 Message Encryption works

Anti-malware/anti-spam controls

Anti-malware/anti-spam controls are embedded in Office 365 Exchange Online Services. If you prefer, you can choose to route your Office 365 email through your own anti-malware service. You can configure anti-malware, anti-spam connection filter and anti-spam content filter policies. Although you'll be working in the Exchange Admin Center to implement these controls, bear in mind that many documents are sent via email, so content controls and multi-engine malware scanning will help eliminate documents containing malicious code.

Multifactor authentication

As I discussed earlier, Azure Active Directory sits under Office 365 and provides secure identity management of your user accounts. Because of this, you can use multifactor authentication to enhance security in a multidevice and cloud-centric world. Multifactor authentication is provided using these various devices. Third-party applications are also supported.

More specifically, the multifactor authentication abilities include the following:

- **Call my mobile phone** After attempting to log in to the Office 365 portal, the login is suspended while the user receives a phone call that asks her to press the pound (#) key. Once the pound key is pressed, the user is logged in.
- **Text code to my mobile phone** Similar to the previous bullet point, after the user attempts to log in to the Office 365 portal, the login is suspended while the user receives a text message containing a six-digit code that she must enter into the portal.
- **Call my office phone** This is the same as the "Call my mobile phone" option, but it enables the user to select a different phone if she does not have her mobile phone with her.
- **Notify me through app** A smartphone app is configured to receive a notification requiring the user to confirm the login. Smartphone apps are available for Windows Phone, iPhone, and Android devices.
- **Show one-time code in app** The same smartphone app is used. Instead of receiving a notification, the user starts the app and enters the six-digit code from the app into the portal.

To use multifactor authentication, users will be required first to configure App Passwords. An App Password is a 16-character, randomly generated password that can be used with an Office client application as a way of increasing security in lieu of the second authentication factor.

> ***TIP*** **You can learn more about implementing multifactor authentication for Office 365 by referencing this TechNet article:** ***https://technet.microsoft.com/en-us/library/dn383636.aspx.***

Data Loss Prevention

Data Loss Prevention (part of the Compliance Management features in Exchange Online) identifies information patterns in email messages and documents thought to represent sensitive information and then helps users understand how to manage and guard that information carefully. Because so many documents that are hosted in SharePoint Online are transmitted to those outside your tenant through email, it makes sense to understand, at a high level, how Data Loss Prevention works.

A standard example is that a Data Loss Prevention policy can be developed that looks for credit card numbers. When the pattern is recognized within the content, rules are enforced that are meant to guard that data.

You'll have a full range of controls and can customize the level of restrictions for your organization. For example, users can simply be warned about sensitive data before sending the email. Or the sending of the sensitive data can require authorization, or the user can be blocked entirely from sending that data. Rights Management Services can be applied to content when triggered by a Data Loss Prevention rule.

In the future, you'll see this Data Loss Prevention capability more directly baked into SharePoint Online as the technology matures.

Document Deletion Policy Center

At the time of this writing, the Office 365 Compliance Center is just getting started. Part of this center is the Document Deletion Policy Center, a place where document-deletion policies can be created and enforced. If your organization is required to retain documents for a fixed period of time because of compliance, legal, or other business requirements, you'll want to pay attention to the document-deletion policies. These policies can be applied to SharePoint Online as well as OneDrive for Business.

The Document Deletion Policy Center will help you ensure that old, outdated documents are not retained in your SharePoint Online tenant. It is a top-down approach to weeding out old documents, but it is also effective. What's important to remember in this discussion is that you'll use this to build maximum thresholds for how long content can survive in your SharePoint Online tenant before being deleted. Within these maximum thresholds, processes and workflows should be used to apply a life cycle to your documents so that these deletion policies are rarely used.

You can find the Document Deletion Policy Center under Retention in the Office 365 Compliance Center. (See Figure 7-11.) Alternatively, you can create the policy center manually by creating the site collection and choosing Compliance Policy Center on the Enterprise tab. Each tenant can have only one Document Deletion Policy Center, and it'll be created automatically if you start from the Compliance Center.

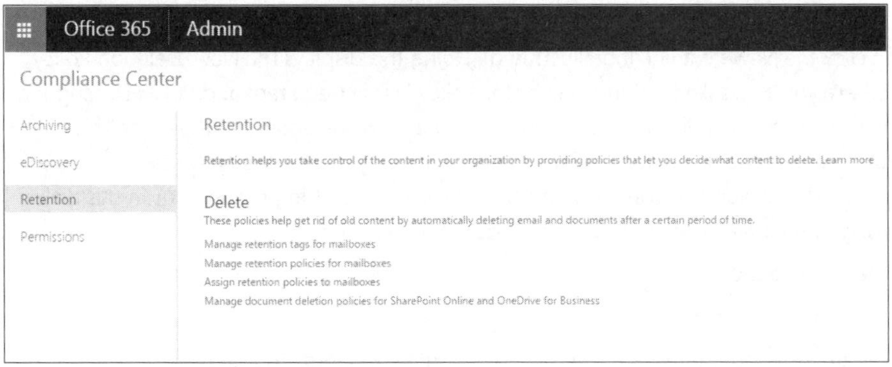

FIGURE 7-11 Compliance Center in Office 365

Figure 7-12 illustrates the Compliance Center when it is created within a Site Collection. Notice that you'll have Deletion Policies, Policy Assignments For Templates, and Policy Assignments For Site Collections areas in your center.

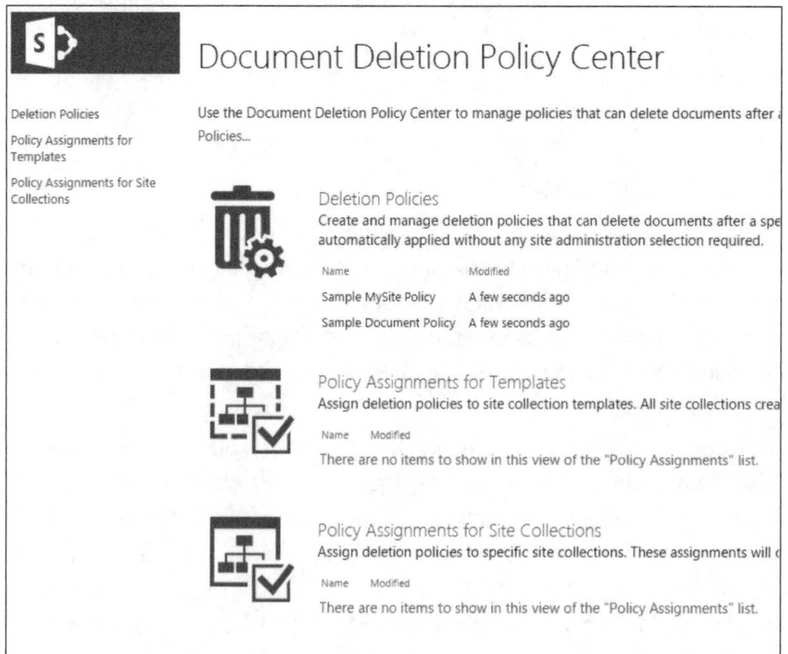

FIGURE 7-12 Document Deletion Policy Center

You can create and manage document deletion policies after the document reaches a certain age based on a configured trigger. The policies are then assigned to one or more site collections, to a site-collection template, or to both. They are applied at the site-collection layer, not the SharePoint Online tenant layer.

To create a new deletion policy, first click the Deletion Policies link (shown in Figure 7-12), and then click the New Item link (not illustrated). Doing this displays the New: Deletion Policy screen, where you'll be asked to input values for Policy Name (required) and Policy Description (not required). After entering this information, click the New link under the Rules For This Policy and begin to define the deletion rules for this policy. When you click the New link, the New Deletion Rule dialog box is displayed (as shown in Figure 7-13). Using the settings in this dialog box, you'll give the rule a name and then configure the following:

- The delete action
- The triggering date
- The time period after which the document will be deleted
- Whether or not the rule is the default rule

Figure 7-13, as configured, shows the default rule that would delete any document once it reaches 10 years of age based on the created date. The deletion action would move the document to the Recycle Bin. Of course, the document could be recovered if needed.

New deletion rule

Name: * Delete after 10 years cre

Delete action:

Delete to Recycle Bin

Permanently Delete

Date from when the document deletion date will be calculated:

Created Date

Time period after which the document will be deleted: *

10 Years

Set as default rule

Save Cancel

FIGURE 7-13 The deletion rule creation dialog box

You use the Policy Assignments For Templates area to assign deletion policies to site-collection templates as well as OneDrive for Business. Click the Policy Assignments For Templates link in the left pane (not illustrated) to get to this section of the Compliance Center. Any subsequent site collections created from the template that has been assigned a deletion policy will inherit the deletion policy, unless there is a policy assigned to a specific site collection that will override this policy template assignment.

To assign a new policy to a site-collection template, click the New Item link (not illustrated). You will be taken to the New: Template Assignment page (shown in Figure 7-14).

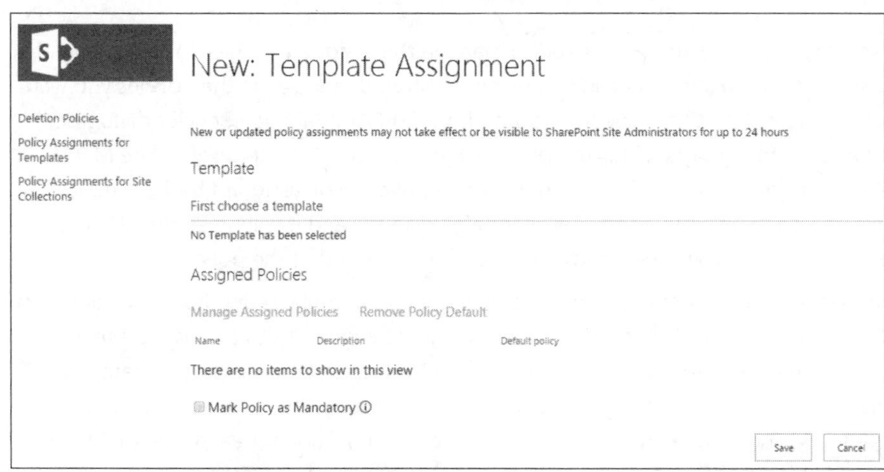

FIGURE 7-14 New: Template Assignment page

Note that the first thing you'll need to do is choose a site-collection template. Click this link and you'll see a dialog box that allows you to assign the deletion policy to either OneDrive for Business or to a particular type of site collection template. The interface does not change when you choose the Assign To OneDrive For Business Template option. (See Figure 7-15.) In this context, you'll need to equate My Sites with OneDrive for Business because, at the time of this writing, My Sites are being rebranded as OneDrive for Business.

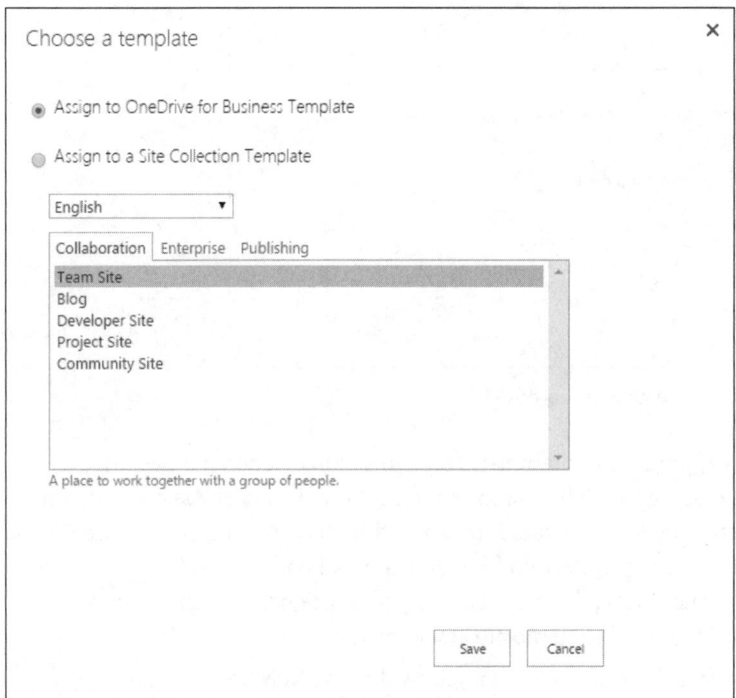

FIGURE 7-15 Choose A Template dialog box

After you select a template, you'll need to manage the assigned policies for that template. Just click the Assigned Managed Policies link (not illustrated) and select the policies you want to assign to the template. Click Save to get out of the Add And Manage Policies dialog box (not illustrated). Before you save this template assignment, you'll need to select the Mark Policy As Mandatory check box if you want only one policy to be assigned to the template. If you do this, the policy must be marked as the default policy, and it will be applied to all sites within the site collection. Site owners will not be able to opt out of the policy.

The only difference between the Policy Assignments For Templates and Policy Assignments For Site Collections settings is that the latter will assign deletion policies to existing site collections, whereas the form assigns deletion policies to the templates used to create new site collections. For the latter, you can input any URL for any existing site collection. Remember, a OneDrive for Business (think "My Site") is a separate site collection for each user that has a OneDrive for Business, so you can assign deletion policies to their documents as well.

From a governance perspective, it's important to understand that the time period specified for a document deletion policy means the time since the document was created or modified, not the time since the policy was assigned. For example, if you create a deletion policy that permanently deletes documents two years after they were created, and then assign that policy to a site-collection template from which several site collections were created four or five years ago, those older documents will be permanently deleted. Be careful how you build and assign these policies.

After the policy is assigned for the first time, all documents in the site are evaluated and, if they meet the criteria, they will be deleted. This applies to all existing documents, not just new documents created since the policy was assigned. In other words, these document-deletion policies are retroactively applied to all documents.

Of course, you should communicate the new policy to site owners before assigning it. Doing this gives them time to assess the possible impact and work with you to ensure that your policy is meeting their needs, not destroying the information they need to do their jobs.

NOTE **The Document Deletion Policies link in the Site Settings area can take up to 24 hours to appear after policies are initially assigned to the site collection.**

Summary

In this chapter, I discussed security in SharePoint Online from a business viewpoint, not the typical role-based security viewpoint. I argued that the human factor is your largest security concern, but it can be curbed substantially through the use of Microsoft Intune and other ambient security technologies. I also pointed out that you can use the new Compliance Center to help you manage the proliferation of documents in SharePoint Online, forcing dead wood out of your tenant.

In the next chapter, we'll turn to a lighter subject—the use of apps in SharePoint Online.

CHAPTER 8

Working with apps

Extending the functionality of Microsoft SharePoint Online is accomplished in different ways than doing so in SharePoint 2013. SharePoint Online gets updated with new features on a regular basis, and these updates can affect certain types of customizations. Conversely, SharePoint 2013's underlying platform has fewer updates, making it easier to install customizations on. The software updates that Microsoft makes to SharePoint Online happen much faster than for SharePoint 2013. Methods for customization that work in SharePoint 2013 won't necessarily work in SharePoint Online. Some of the methods used for customizing and extending SharePoint Server, for example, rely on the fact that the underlying platform is not constantly being updated—as is the case with SharePoint Online.

There is a gradation of SharePoint Online customizations. Similar to SharePoint 2013, these customizations range from nontechnical changes you can apply quickly through the browser—what I call *in-browser customizations*—to using development tools to modify or extend the underlying platform. In the latter stage, you're working in Microsoft Visual Studio. Generally speaking, the gradations are as follows:

- **Customizations using the browser** This includes things like changing the title and logo or a site or updating navigation links and so forth. You can commit hundreds of nontechnical changes like this in SharePoint Online.
- **Customizations using supported tools and applications** Here I am referring to making changes using Microsoft Office applications such as Access 2013, which you can use to create a SharePoint 2013 app as a no-code solution.

- **Customizations using remote provisioning** In SharePoint Online, you can use custom CSOM (client-side object model) code in apps for SharePoint to provision SharePoint site collections, sites, and subsites with branding elements. This site-provisioning pattern is called *remote provisioning*.
- **Customizations using apps for SharePoint** Using the Cloud App Model in SharePoint Online gives you the ability to add apps to your sites, and it is the replacement for sandboxed solutions. The functionality of the apps can be simple and limited or complex and extensive.

Considering the last bullet point, you'll find third-party apps in the SharePoint Store, which is an Office.com-hosted marketplace accessible from SharePoint Online sites. Select the apps that you want to be available in your tenant. You'll have the ability to purchase licenses for specific apps for all users in your organization.

> ***MORE INFO*** **In SharePoint Online, you can develop your own apps and make them available to users through the App Catalog site. If you know how to build a web application, you know how to build an app for SharePoint. You can use any language—such as HTML, JavaScript, PHP, or .NET—and common development tools, including Microsoft Visual Studio and Office 365 Development Tools. Developing apps is outside the scope of this book, so refer to this article for more information: *https://msdn.microsoft.com/en-us/library/fp179930.aspx*.**

When it comes to managing apps in SharePoint Online, you'll have the following responsibilities:

- Making apps available to your organization and managing requests for new apps
- Purchasing apps
- Managing the licenses for purchased apps
- Configuring the app store settings
- Tracking the usage of applications and errors
- Managing app permissions in your tenant

I'll discuss each of these bullet points individually in the following sections, showing you how to build your app catalog and use the apps in your tenant in SharePoint Online.

Creating an app catalog site

The first thing you'll need to do is to create an app catalog site. As you can see in Figure 8-1, when you first click the App Catalog link (from the Apps portion of SharePoint Online administration), you're informed that there is no app catalog for your tenant. You're given the opportunity to create a new app catalog site by leaving the default Create A New App Catalog Site option selected.

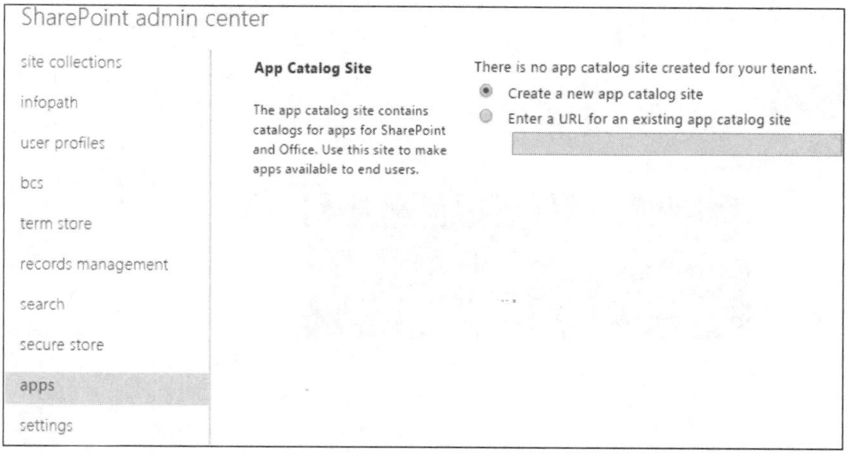

FIGURE 8-1 Creating an app catalog site

When you click the OK button (not illustrated), you're presented with the Create App Catalog Site Collection screen, as shown in Figure 8-2. On this screen, you'll input the necessary information and then click OK.

FIGURE 8-2 Creating a new app catalog site collection

When you click OK after entering the necessary information, the SharePoint Admin Center is displayed, This is where you'll see a list of all the site collections in your tenant. You'll also see that your app catalog site collection is being created. Once the app catalog site collection has been created, you can move forward with this process of bringing apps into your SharePoint Online environment. To be sure it has been created, click on the Apps link in the left pane within your SharePoint Admin Center, and then click on the App Catalog link again. When you do so, you'll be taken to the App Catalog site collection, as illustrated in Figure 8-3.

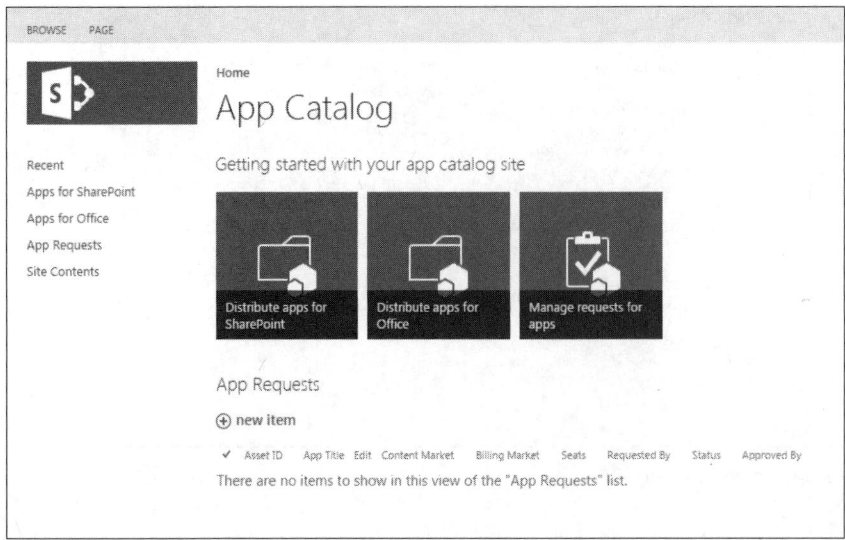

FIGURE 8-3 The App Catalog site collection

Once the app catalog has been built, it will be time to populate it with apps.

Purchase apps from the SharePoint Store

When you click the Purchase Apps link inside the Apps area of SharePoint Online administration, you're presented with a list of apps from the SharePoint Store that is managed by Microsoft. The store will contain apps with different types of functionality. Some will be free, and some will cost money. There will be a set of Featured Apps presented in a web part that appears to be a modified Getting Started web part. You'll be able to sort the apps by clicking on the sorting links:

- Most Relevant
- Highest Rating
- Lowest Price
- Name
- Newest

In the left pane are the app categories that, when selected, refine the list of apps you'll see in the content pane. These refiners are subject to change, but at the time of this writing, there were nearly 30 refiners in the left pane. I call them *refiners* because, even though they are listed as categories, the entire page acts like a search result set where the result set is the apps and depending on which link you select, you can filter the apps (results) by category and then sort the apps as well. All of this is illustrated in Figure 8-4.

NOTE The contents of the app catalog will continually change. Figure 8-4 shows what was in the Store at the time of this writing and might not be what you see in the Store when you log in while following the directions in this chapter.

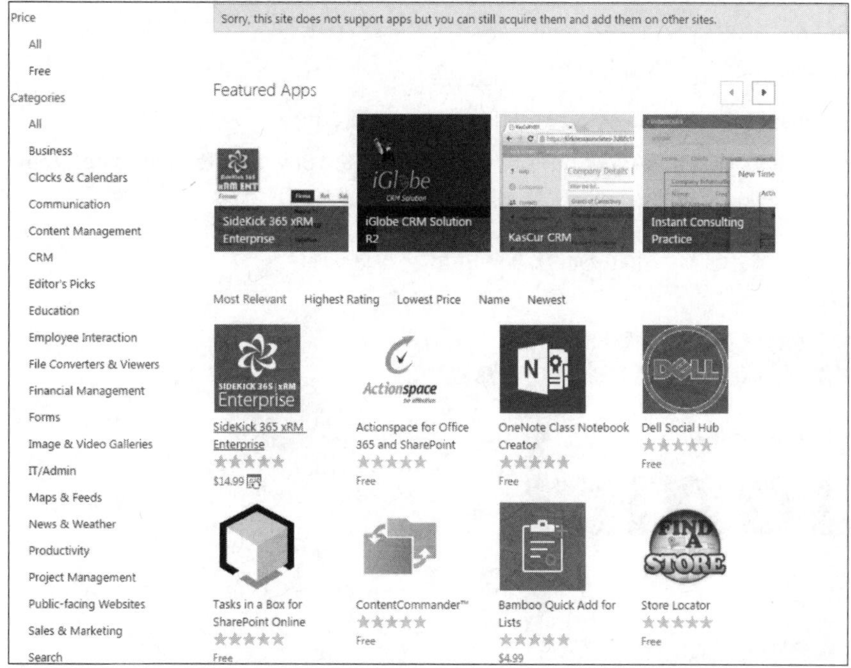

FIGURE 8-4 The Microsoft App Store for SharePoint Online

NOTE The yellow message box with the text "Sorry, this site does not support apps but you can still acquire them and add them on other sites" is not something you need to worry about. All it means is that you can't add apps to the App Catalog site collection.

Unfortunately, the sorting features don't always work as expected. At the time of this writing, for example, when I clicked the Free price and attempt to sort the applications by Highest Rating, the first few applications had two or fewer stars, while higher rated apps appeared further down the page.

When you select an app you want to purchase, you are presented with a screen, as shown in Figure 8-5, which includes the following information:

- Version
- Agreement with the app's permissions
- Cost

- One or more screenshots of what the app's user interface looks like
- Rating
- Release date
- Category
- Link to the support website
- Description
- Supported languages
- Reviews that can be sorted by Newest, Favorable, and Critical

To procure the app, click the Add It button (if it is free) or the Buy It button (if it is not free).

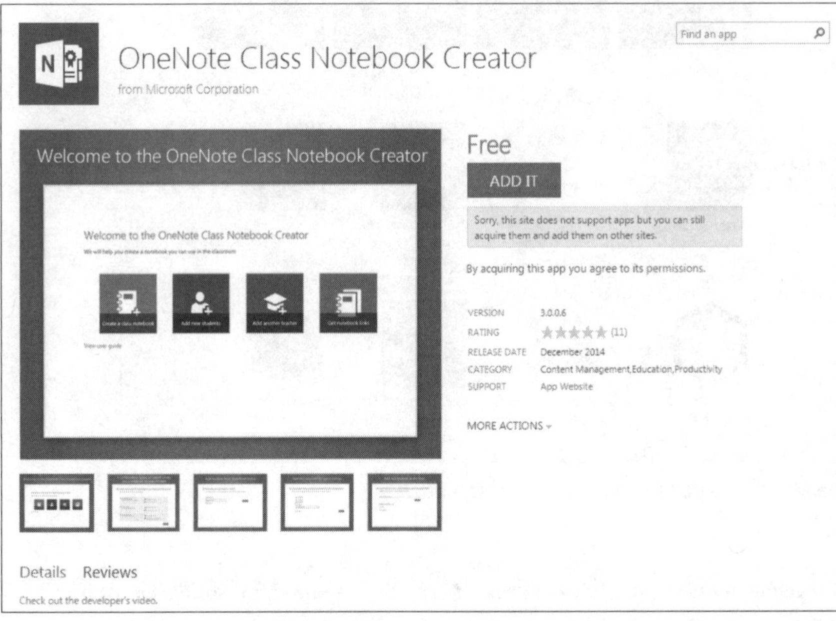

FIGURE 8-5 An app's page in the app catalog

> ***TIP*** **Referring back to Figure 8-5, in the upper-right corner is a search box you use to search for an app through a keyword query. You can search using keywords that might appear in the apps name, its description, or other keywords associated with the app. You can get a good idea about the taxonomy Microsoft has implemented for the apps in its app store by looking at the category headings in the root of the app store.**

When you click the Add It (or Buy It) button, you get a confirmation screen (not illustrated). This is actually a security-oriented screen, with the following text displayed:

For your security, before we add your app, we need to confirm that you came from your organization or team SharePoint site. Click Continue to go back to your SharePoint site at https://<tentant_Name>-admin.sharepoint.com/_layouts/15/storefront.aspx?task=OfficeRedirect and finish installing the app. If you don't recognize this site, please go back to your organization's site and try to add the app again.

When you click the Continue button, you're presented with a confirmation screen (titled You Just Got This App For Everyone In Your Organization) with a Return To Site button. If you click that button, it takes you to your SharePoint Admin Center in your tenant.

To see the newly downloaded app, navigate to a site collection that isn't the app catalog and, from the cog icon, click Add An App. From this menu, you'll see the apps you've downloaded are ready for installation and use in the site collection, as shown in Figure 8-6.

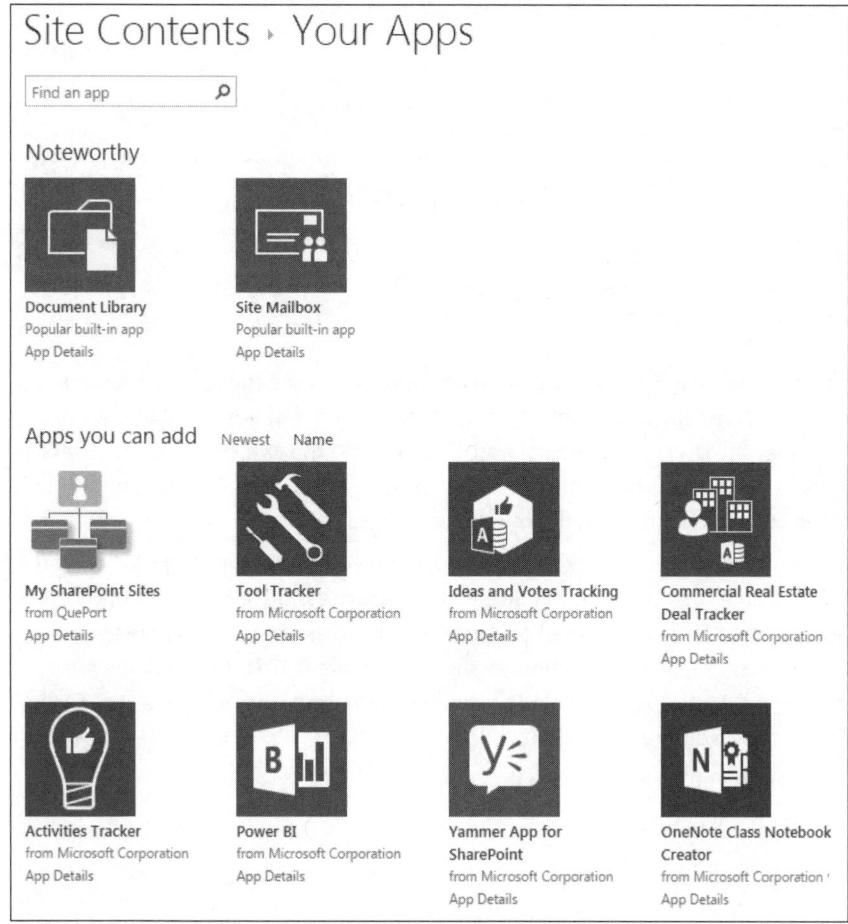

FIGURE 8-6 Add An App page

Managing app licenses

When you purchase an app, unless it is free, you will have purchased a number of licenses with the app that can be assigned, recovered, and removed within the SharePoint interface. In addition, you can assign different user accounts to manage different app licenses so that those who use the apps manage the licenses.

Within the Apps management area of the SharePoint Admin Center, click the Manage Licenses link and you'll see a screen populated with apps from the SharePoint App Store, as shown in Figure 8-7.

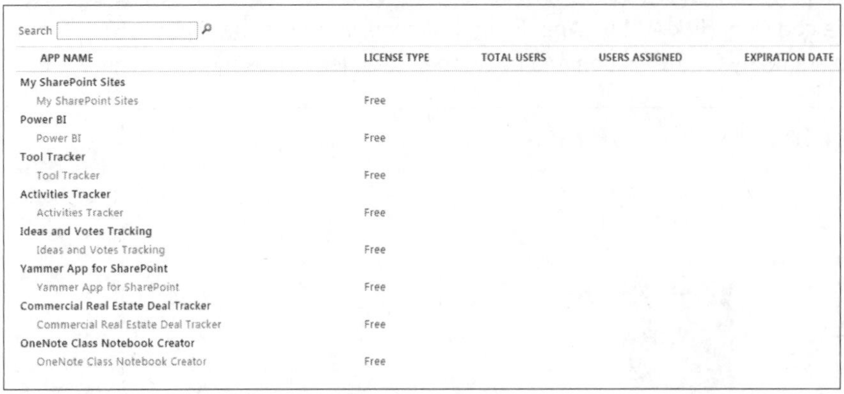

Search

APP NAME	LICENSE TYPE	TOTAL USERS	USERS ASSIGNED	EXPIRATION DATE
My SharePoint Sites				
My SharePoint Sites	Free			
Power BI				
Power BI	Free			
Tool Tracker				
Tool Tracker	Free			
Activities Tracker				
Activities Tracker	Free			
Ideas and Votes Tracking				
Ideas and Votes Tracking	Free			
Yammer App for SharePoint				
Yammer App for SharePoint	Free			
Commercial Real Estate Deal Tracker				
Commercial Real Estate Deal Tracker	Free			
OneNote Class Notebook Creator				
OneNote Class Notebook Creator	Free			

FIGURE 8-7 Manage licenses screen in SharePoint Admin Center

Referring back to Figure 8-7, if you purchased any apps, you'll see the total number of licenses for that app under the Total User column and the number of licenses that have been assigned under the Users Assigned column. So don't add the two columns. The Users Assigned column is a subset of the Total User column such that the User Assigned total should never exceed the Total Users total, but the reverse can be true.

To manage the licenses directly, click the link of the app you want to manage. When you do this, you'll be taken to a screen that will give you a place to assign and recover the licenses under the People With A License section. You'll also be able to assign users to manage licenses under the License Managers section, as shown in Figure 8-8. Under the View A Purchase drop-down list you'll also be able to view the purchase history with this app. Each purchase will appear as a different line item.

Under the Actions menu, you'll be to do the following:

- View In The SharePoint Store
- Recover This License
- Remove This License

The actions menu is helpful when you want to learn more about the app by viewing its details, finding the support page for the app from its presentation in the SharePoint Store, or both. Moreover, when someone leaves your team or organization, you can remove that person's license and assign it to another user, presumably someone who has taken the original user's place. The Recover This License option is used when you need to reacquire the license from the SharePoint Store, such as when you are using the licenses in a new tenant or your licenses have become out of sync with the SharePoint Store.

FIGURE 8-8 Screen from which you'll manage licenses and managers

By contrast, if you purchased licenses for the app (instead of downloading a free app, which is what Figure 8-8 illustrates), you'll see a more detailed view of the users who have a license assigned and a *people picker* to find other user accounts to whom you can assign a license. This is illustrated in Figure 8-9. By the way, if you want to purchase more licenses for this app, you can do so by clicking the Buy link (not illustrated). Doing that will take you to the SharePoint Store link. At the SharePoint Store site, you can purchase more licenses, especially if you need to assign the app to more users than what you have in available licenses.

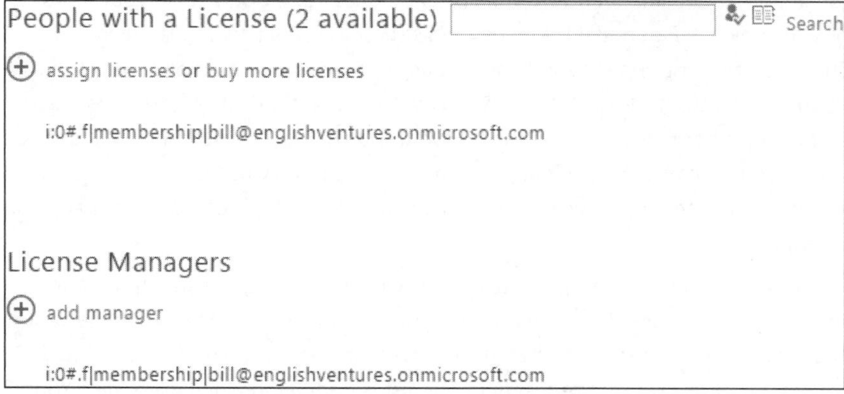

FIGURE 8-9 License information for a purchased app in SharePoint Admin Center

This license page also can be accessed by the users with appropriate permissions directly from the Site Contents page. When you click the ellipses button (...) next to a purchased app, one of the shortcut menu options will be Licenses. When you click on that link, it will take you to the same page illustrated in Figure 8-9, from which you can work with licenses and license managers. It is a different way of arriving at the same administration page.

Configure the Store settings

There are three settings you should pay attention to in this section. Although they are simple, they are important. In a nutshell, these settings refer to App Purchases, App Requests, and Apps For Office From The Store. The settings are illustrated in Figure 8-10.

App Purchases Specify whether end users can get free, trial or paid apps from the SharePoint Store.	Should end users be able to get apps from the marketplace? Yes	No
App Requests View the list of app requests. Users can request apps if they are unable or choose not to get apps directly from the SharePoint Store.	Click here to view app requests	
Apps for Office from the Store Documents stored on the sites of this tenant may contain Apps for Office from several sources. This option determines whether Apps for Office from the store can be started when an end user opens a document in the browser. This will not affect Apps for Office from this tenant's app catalog.	Should Apps for Office from the store be able to start when documents are opened in the browser? Yes	No

FIGURE 8-10 Configuring the Store settings

The first setting configures your users' ability to go directly to the SharePoint Store to purchase apps. The default is Yes. Select No if you want to turn this off. By doing so, you'll remove the SharePoint Store link on the Your Apps page under Site Contents in your users' site collections, as shown in Figure 8-11. Most administrators of SharePoint 2013 turn this off because they don't want users randomly downloading apps and installing them without some type of quality-control testing. But in SharePoint Online, with Microsoft responsible for the integrity of your platform, it's an advantage leave this turned on. Presumably, Microsoft has thoroughly tested each app before it appears in the Store to ensure that an app won't harm the integrity of your tenant. However, you might want to turn this off for governance or cost-control reasons.

The second setting is a link to the App Catalog site, which has a list that shows the app requests from your users. It's best to set an alert for yourself (or for whomever manages apps in your organization) on this list so that when new requests come in, you're notified of it and are aware of what your users are requesting. This list is populated when users click Your Requests on the Your Apps page (which was shown in Figure 8-11) within their site collection (not illustrated).

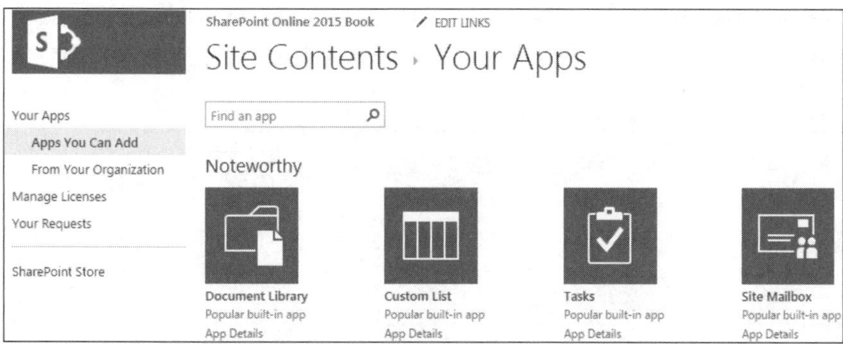

FIGURE 8-11 SharePoint Store link on the Your Apps page

With the Apps For Office setting, you can specify whether apps that have been installed from the Office Store can start when a user opens a file that invokes a Microsoft Office application within the browser that has an Office app installed to work within it. Office apps are installed in Office applications. For example, when a user opens a Word document from within the browser, do you also want any Office apps that work with Word Online to start as well? That is the focus of this question. Your choice is either Yes or No.

> ***MORE INFO*** **The SharePoint Store and the Office Store should not be confused, even though they both have the word "SharePoint" at the top of their respective pages. For example, when you click on the SharePoint Store link on the Your Apps page within your site collection, the ensuing page is produced by the storefront.aspx page in your tenant, which appears to be a result set produced by a custom result source that queries Microsoft's online store. However, the apps for Office are located at *https://store.office.com*, but the title of the page is Apps For SharePoint.**
>
> **I couldn't find confirmation of this, but it appears to me that the intention of Microsoft is to build the SharePoint Store such that it contains apps that are specific to working in a SharePoint site collection, whereas Office apps are designed specifically to work within the Office productivity applications, such as Word or PowerPoint. It would not surprise me if, behind the scenes, it is the same store with different filtered result sets for different clients. But the naming of both sets of pages with "SharePoint" can be confusing, so just understand the difference between these pages.**

Monitor apps

You'll monitor the health status of your apps in the Monitor Apps area, as shown in Figure 8-12. You'll see that each of your apps is listed on this page with a status message, the source from which the application was purchased, and information about how many of the licenses are in use. What is not illustrated in Figure 8-12 are the columns that extend to the right of the page, including the number of installed locations and runtime errors the app has produced in the last four days.

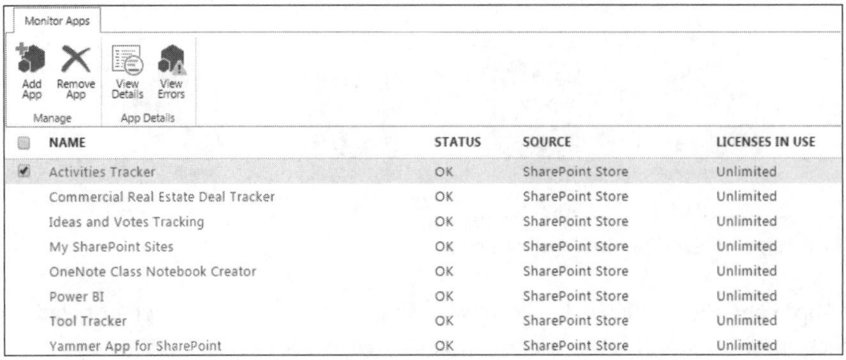

Monitor Apps

Add App | Remove App | View Details | View Errors

Manage | App Details

NAME	STATUS	SOURCE	LICENSES IN USE
Activities Tracker	OK	SharePoint Store	Unlimited
Commercial Real Estate Deal Tracker	OK	SharePoint Store	Unlimited
Ideas and Votes Tracking	OK	SharePoint Store	Unlimited
My SharePoint Sites	OK	SharePoint Store	Unlimited
OneNote Class Notebook Creator	OK	SharePoint Store	Unlimited
Power BI	OK	SharePoint Store	Unlimited
Tool Tracker	OK	SharePoint Store	Unlimited
Yammer App for SharePoint	OK	SharePoint Store	Unlimited

FIGURE 8-12 Monitor Apps administration page

When an app is selected by clicking the check box immediately to its left, the ribbon options will light up. At this point, you can remove an app, view its details, and view any errors associated with the app. If you click the View Details button to view the apps' details, you'll be presented with a popup box with information pertaining to the app itself, including the following:

- The number of licenses purchased and the number used
- Any errors in the past four days, including Failed Installs, Failed Upgrades, and Runtime Errors
- Installation information, including the number of Installed Locations, the number of Install Events, and the number of Uninstall Events
- A chart that outlines the number of launches of the app in the last 14 days and the number of unique users who launched the app

The information on the details page (not illustrated) can be rather helpful when deciding if the app is genuinely helpful to your organization. For example, if you see a high number of install and uninstall actions on a particular app, you know your users are trying out the app and not finding it helpful or useful. A high number of uninstall actions should concern you—especially if you spent a large sum of money to purchase the app in the first place.

However, if you see a large number of uninstall actions in a small number of sites, your users are repeatedly installing and then uninstalling the app in their site collection. This should be an indication to you to contact your users and find out more about why the app is being installed and uninstalled so many times.

Finally—and generally speaking—the higher the number of unique users who consume and app plus the higher the number of launches of an app in a given time frame, the more important that app is to your organization. (Note you can select to view the usage charge for a 12-month period, for the last three years, or for the last 14 days.) Now, I'll contradict myself just a bit by saying that for some types of apps (such as weather apps) that launch automatically when a site is visited, you need to consider whether or not these passive launches really are important to your organization. But for sure, you need to understand why a large number of launches across a wide range of users is occurring so that you can ensure you're providing as much value as possible to your users.

If you click the View Errors button, a popup box (not illustrated) is displayed that lists the errors associated with the app. Use these errors for further investigation as you strive to ensure your tenant is operating at optimal levels.

Manage app permissions

Every app that installs into SharePoint Online will need a set of permissions given to it in order to operate without error. The permission requests specify both the rights that an app needs and the scope at which it needs the rights. These permissions are requested as part of the app manifest during its installation. Permissions are granted on an all-or-nothing basis. There's no sense in trying to give an app a partial set of permissions it needs to operate as advertised.

The permissions that the app has been granted are also stored in the content database of the tenant. They are not stored with a secure token service, such as Microsoft Azure Access Control Service (ACS). When a user first grants an app permissions, SharePoint obtains information about the app from ACS. SharePoint then stores the basic information about the app in the app management service and the content database along with the app's permissions.

If an app is granted permission to an object after the app is installed and then the object is deleted, the corresponding grants are deleted also. When an app is removed, all the permissions granted to that app at the scope from which it was removed are revoked. This is to ensure that the app can't use its credentials to continue accessing protected SharePoint resources remotely after a user removes the app from SharePoint.

SharePoint apps can request the following scopes in their permission assignments:

- Entire tenant
- Site collection
- Site
- List

Regardless of the scope, permissions are applied automatically to all child objects within the given scope. For example, if the scope granted is Site, all the lists within the site are automatically included within the Site scope.

To avoid confusion between user roles (such as Contributor, Site Owner, and so forth) and app rights (such as Read, Write, Delete, or Full Control), names do not match. This is by design. Microsoft wanted to maintain a distinction between SharePoint rights names for user roles and rights names for apps. Because customizing the permissions associated with SharePoint user roles does not affect app permission request levels, the app rights names do not match the corresponding SharePoint user roles, except Full Control, which can't be customized through the permissions-management user interface.

> ***TIP*** **If you want to dive into the back end of app permissions, consider installing the Napa Office 365 development tool. For more information, consult this MSDN article:** ***https://msdn.microsoft.com/en-us/library/office/jj220038.aspx.***

When you (or your users) install an app in your site collection for the first time, you will need to trust the app. Before the app is added to the site collection from the organization's SharePoint store, a dialog box is displayed that lists what the app needs to run properly. As shown in Figure 8-13, the app will populate the popup box with information about itself and then require you to click the Trust It button before it installs. To stop the installation, click the Cancel button.

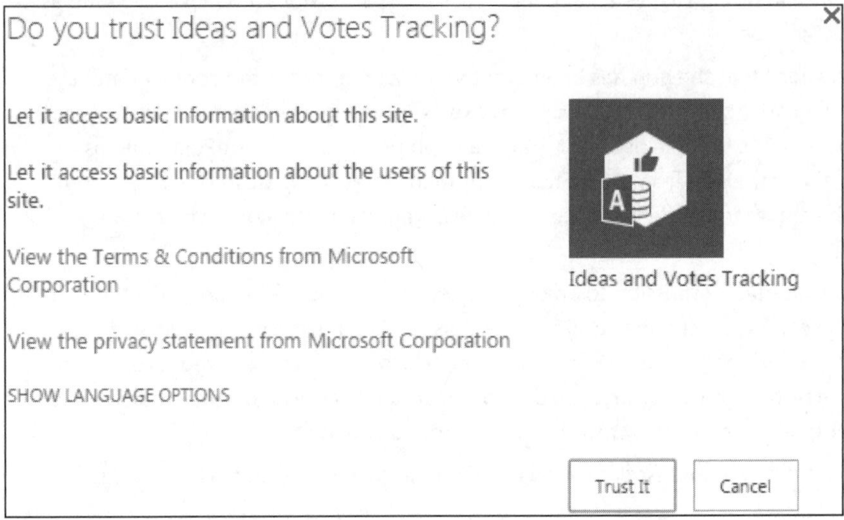

FIGURE 8-13 The app permissions informational box

After you choose to trust the app and install it, your users might want to display the app on one or more pages within their site. If they want to add the app to a page, they will need to enter the Edit mode on their page and then find the app under the Add An App Part portion of the ribbon.

Once the app is installed into a site, if it was given tenant-wide permissions, it will appear in the App Permissions page of the SharePoint admin area. It is on this page (not illustrated) that you can remove its tenant-wide permissions. If the app was given permissions at the site-collection layer, you'll need to work within the site collection's app administration area to remove its permissions within the site collection.

TIP At the time of this writing, there is an app that I want to highlight for your consideration. Even though this book is focused on SharePoint Online administration, the reality is that most who are charged with administrating SharePoint Online will also be charged with administrating the Office 365 tenant as well. To this end, you might want to be aware of the Office 365 Admin app. You can use this app to perform basic tenant administration from your iPad, Android, or iOS portable device. Check out the Office 365 Admin app at this Office blog post: *http://blogs.office.com/2015/03/13/administer-on-the-go-with-the-updated-office-365-admin-app/.*

Summary

In this chapter, you learned the basics of how to perform app management within the SharePoint Online administration interface. Apps are the way you add functionality to a site or site collection, and they are intended to replace other development methods for deploying new functionality.

In the next chapter, we'll look at the Settings area for SharePoint Online administration.

CHAPTER 9

Administrating general settings

For most of the platforms I've taught and written about, there usually is an area of administration where all the disconnected or single-decision configurations are hosted. In Microsoft SharePoint 2013, those configurations are in the General Settings area. In SharePoint Online, these configurations are in the Settings area. So I borrowed the SharePoint On-Premises wording to make it more clear that we're dealing with configurations that are not connected to each other or a larger set of configurations or processes. I think of these areas as the potpourri of the platform's administration. This is not to say the configurations are unimportant—on the contrary, often these single-decision configurations have significant impact on your deployment.

In SharePoint 2013, General Application Settings covers the areas shown in Figure 9-1.

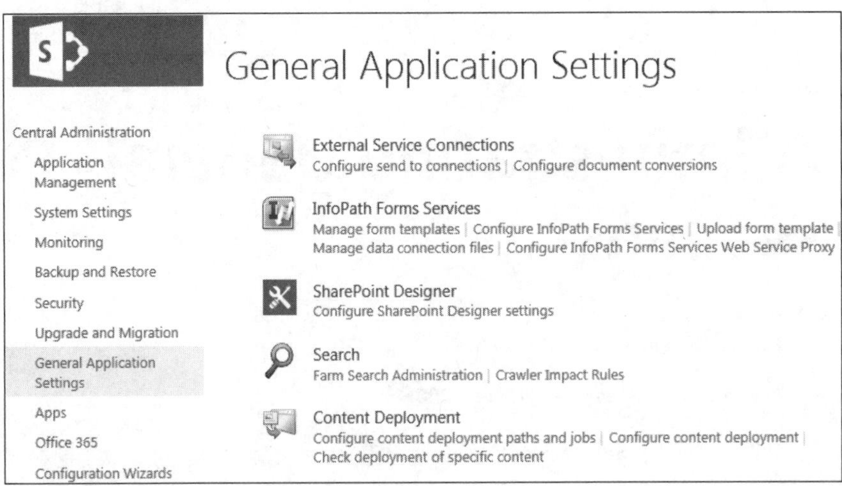

FIGURE 9-1 General Application Settings in SharePoint 2013

Notice that many of the General Application Settings now are managed by Microsoft in SharePoint Online or not available in SharePoint Online. For example, the entire Content Deployment technology (which has its pedigree in Microsoft Content Management Server 2002) is not available in SharePoint Online. Hence, document conversions aren't needed either, because document conversions are part of the larger content-deployment process.

In SharePoint Online, the Settings area covers a smaller set of administration tasks, which are partially illustrated in Figure 9-2. Note that these settings are displayed on a single webpage, whereas the SharePoint 2013 General Application Settings require multiple webpages in the SharePoint On-Premises platform. Here is the list of the settings for SharePoint Online:

- Top Navigation Bar User Experience
- Admin Center Experience
- Office Graph
- Enterprise Social Collaboration
- Streaming Video Service
- External Sharing
- Global Experience Version Settings
- Information Rights Management (IRM)
- Start A Site
- Custom Script
- Preview Features
- Access Apps

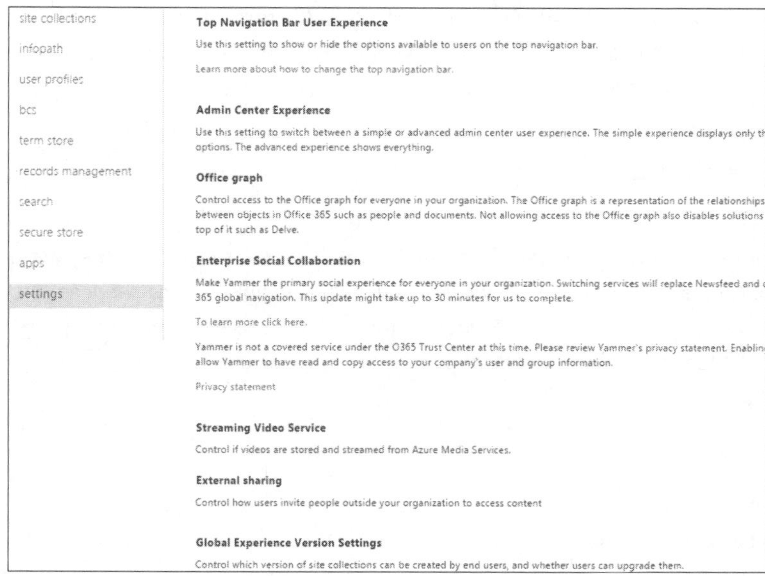

FIGURE 9-2 Settings area in SharePoint Online Admin Center

Let's dive into each of these settings and see what we can learn.

Top Navigation Bar User Experience settings

In a SharePoint site, the top navigation bar is the area of the webpage that extends from the logo image in the upper-left corner to the right margin across the top of the page. When the Publishing feature is deactivated, this navigation bar is called the *Top Link Bar*. When the Publishing feature is activated, it is called the *Global Navigation Bar*. In this setting, I am talking about neither state. Instead, I'm talking about the menu bar that appears above the site itself, as shown in Figure 9-3. It is called the *Top Navigation Bar* or the *SharePoint Online Navigation Bar*, depending on which article you're reading.

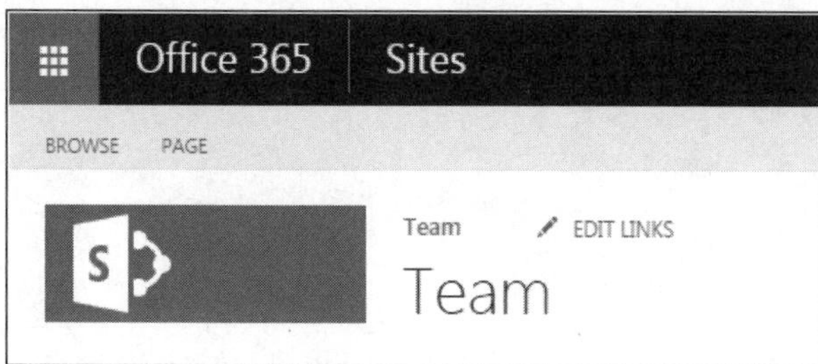

FIGURE 9-3 The SharePoint Online Navigation Bar

By default, the SharePoint Online Navigation Bar has links to Microsoft OneDrive, Yammer, or Newsfeed and Sites. You can customize the navigation bar by choosing which options you'll show to users and which options you'll hide. Here are your options:

- OneDrive
- Yammer or Newsfeed
- Sites

Hiding the options does not remove them from the tenant. It simply means that they are hidden, not exposed. And let me state the obvious: only turn on the links for the services you have purchased. For example, if you have the OneDrive for Business services, you turn on the OneDrive link, and not the other links—unless, of course, you purchased those services as well. This setting is illustrated in Figure 9-4.

Top Navigation Bar User Experience			
Use this setting to show or hide the options available to users on the top navigation bar.	OneDrive for Business	Show	Hide
	Yammer/Newsfeed	Show	Hide
Learn more about how to change the top navigation bar.	Sites	Show	Hide

FIGURE 9-4 Top Navigation Bar User Experience settings

Admin Center Experience settings

You can simplify the SharePoint Online administration interface such that only the Site Collections, User Profiles, and Settings areas are displayed in the left pane. The other areas of administration—InfoPath, BCS, Term Store, Records Management, Search, Secure Store, and Apps—are not displayed. You do this if you don't want to see those options in the interface because you're not using them or because you want to have a cleaner administration interface experience.

Figures 9-5 and 9-6 illustrate the difference between the two settings. The default is to have the full administration interface experience. Figure 9-7 illustrates the configuration option itself.

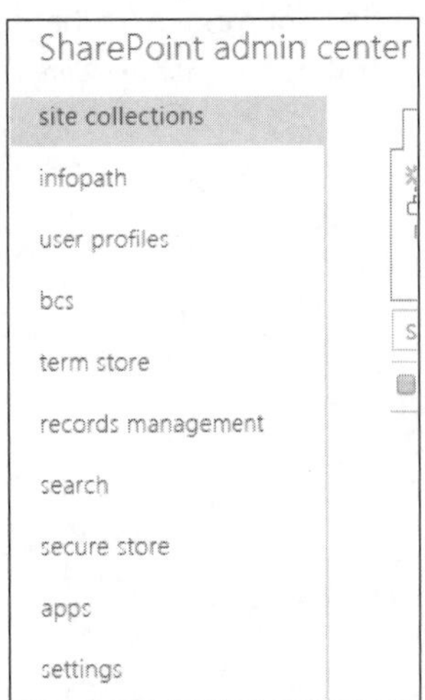

FIGURE 9-5 Full SharePoint Online administration interface experience

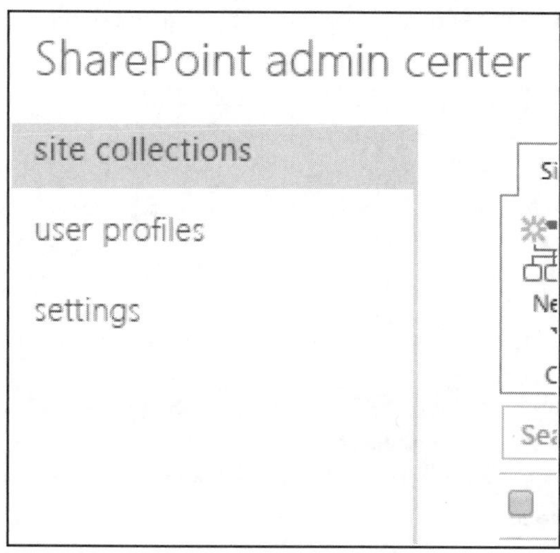

FIGURE 9-6 Simplified SharePoint Online administration interface

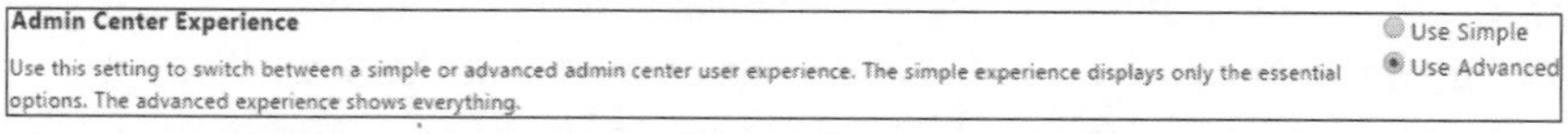

Admin Center Experience

Use this setting to switch between a simple or advanced admin center user experience. The simple experience displays only the essential options. The advanced experience shows everything.

Use Simple
Use Advanced

FIGURE 9-7 Admin Center Experience settings

Enterprise Social Collaboration settings

The heading for this section is a fancy way of referring to either Yammer or the SharePoint Newsfeed (sometimes called *microblogging*). Microsoft Office 365 includes two options for social communications: Yammer and the SharePoint Newsfeed. The Yammer tile appears on the Office 365 portal page and the app launcher, making it easy for Office 365 users to reach Yammer. Also, if your network is eligible, users can sign in to Yammer using their Office 365 account.

> **NOTE** If you choose Yammer to be your social experience platform, you'll need to follow the enterprise activation process. You can find that process here: *https://support.office.com/en-us/article/Yammer-activation-guide-4f924c74-87d2-49d0-a4f6-cba3ce2b0e7c*.

You can enable Yammer integration within SharePoint by picking Yammer.com as your social experience in SharePoint. You'll do this because you want to deploy a secure, yet private network that allows your users to collaborate across normal organizational hierarchies. Yammer will help capture tacit knowledge, something many organizations are concerned about as their older workers near the age of retirement.

You'll choose between Yammer and the default SharePoint Newsfeed by selecting either option, as shown in Figure 9-8.

Enterprise Social Collaboration
Make Yammer the primary social experience for everyone in your organization. Switching services will replace Newsfeed and change the Office 365 global navigation. This update might take up to 30 minutes for us to complete.
To learn more click here.
Yammer is not a covered service under the O365 Trust Center at this time. Please review Yammer's privacy statement. Enabling this feature will allow Yammer to have read and copy access to your company's user and group information.
Privacy statement
Use Yammer.com service
Use SharePoint Newsfeed

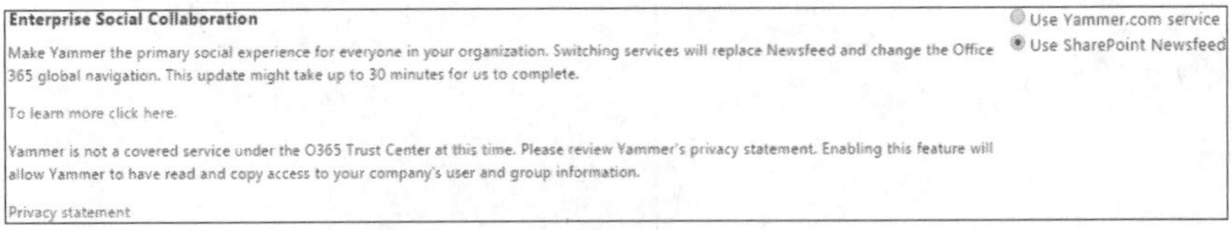

FIGURE 9-8 Enterprise Social Collaboration settings

> ***NOTE*** **If your organization switches to Yammer, SharePoint Newsfeed functionality doesn't go away. People can still access Newsfeed from their Sites page, and they can continue to follow SharePoint sites, documents, and tags there. However, they no longer have the option to send a message to everyone.**

Referring back to Figure 9-8, you might have noticed that Yammer is not a covered service under the Office 365 Trust Center. You'll want to familiarize yourself with what this means to your organization. You can start by reading up on the Office 365 Trust Center at *https://products.office.com/en/business/office-365-trust-center-cloud-computing-security.*

Streaming Video Service settings

Using Azure Media Services, you can choose to stream video within your SharePoint Online environment. When you make this selection, a video portal is created in the same site collection as your Managed Metadata Service hub. You use the video portal to create video channels for your users, such as a new employee orientation or a new product channel. With video being an integral part of our information services, it makes sense to dedicate a site with the appropriate services that can deliver video to your users. By default, your Managed Metadata Service hub is located at *https://*<tenant_name>*.sharepoint.com/portals/hub.*

A new site collection will be created for each new video channel, though it won't appear that way within the interface. If you stay within the video portal, it will appear as a new channel and the URL will contain a channel ID. But if you look at the list of site collections, you'll notice that a new site collection has been created for each new channel. Navigating to the root site collection will show a site collection with only two site-collection features activated: Document Sets and Video And Rich Media. At the site layer, only three features will be activated: Workflow Task Content Type, Following Content, and Access App. This means that you need to enable Access Apps (discussed later on in this chapter) for these video channels to work properly.

By default, this service is enabled, as shown in Figure 9-9.

Streaming Video Service
Control if videos are stored and streamed from Azure Media Services.
Enable streaming video through Azure Media Services and enable the Video Portal.
Disable streaming video through Azure Media Services and disable the Video Portal.

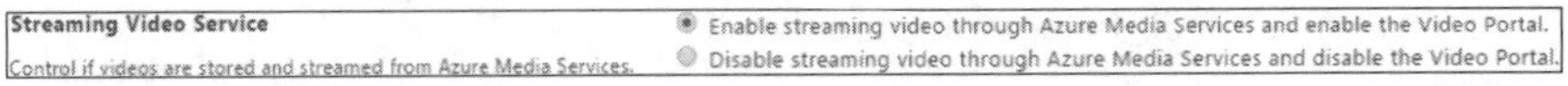

FIGURE 9-9 Steaming Video Service settings

Global Experience Version settings

As Office 365 upgrades become available, you, the SharePoint Online administrator will be the first point of contact for Microsoft. As the upgrade happens, it is delivered in a top-down method, starting with the tenant level of the hierarchy and then flowing down to site collections and sites below. You will determine who is allowed to upgrade their site collection and who will wait. You can restrict upgrade permissions to a select group, or you can delegate upgrade responsibilities to site-collection admins.

If you want to have a planned rollout of the new features or if you have customizations that need testing before the site or sites are upgraded, limiting the upgrade capabilities within the various site collections will make sense. However, if you have numerous site collections, enabling others to upgrade their sites will load balance the administrative effort required to get all the sites upgraded. In many upgrade scenarios, you'll find yourself limiting the upgrade capabilities for some of your sites while allowing others to upgrade when they feel they are ready. In either event, you'll want to ensure you have adequate initial and ongoing training and support for your users so that they can take advantage of the upgraded features and functionalities.

Within SharePoint Online is the concept of *site versions*. With site versions, you can update your subscription to the new environment but allow your users to continue creating sites that look and feel like the old version. This accommodates common scenarios in which users or teams are not personally ready to move all of their work to a new template. With site versions, they can continue to work in the previous version even though the underlying platform has been upgraded to the new version.

There are three options when configuring this setting, as illustrated in Figure 9-10. The options are as follows:

- **Allow creation of old version site collections, but prevent creation of new version site collections. Prevent opt-in upgrade to the new version of site collections** You'll select this options when you want to prevent users from using the new features until a later time. The most common reason for this is that your organization has not secured training for the new platform, so everyone decides to stay in the old experience until the training is available.
- **Allow creation of old version site collections, and creation of new version site collections. Allow opt-in upgrade to the new version site collections** You'll select this option when you want to give your users the power and authority to upgrade when they feel they are ready.
- **Prevent creation of old version site collections, but allow creation of new version site collections. Allow opt-in upgrade to the new version site collections** You'll select this option when you want to limit the number of old-version site collections to those that already exist.

Allow creation of old version site collections, but prevent creation of new version site collections. Prevent opt-in upgrade to the new version site collections.

Allow creation of old version site collections, and creation of new version site collections. Allow opt-in upgrade to the new version site collections.

Prevent creation of old version site collections, but allow creation of new version site collections. Allow opt-in upgrade to the new version site collections.

FIGURE 9-10 Global Experience Version settings

Information Rights Management (IRM) settings

Information rights management is a way to further protect documents through privacy settings that become embedded within the document. Privacy settings differ from permissions in that the latter is concerned with whether or not a given user can access the document, whereas the former is concerned with what the user can *do* with the document after she has accessed it. In addition, privacy and permissions differ in how they are applied: permissions are applied on the document, and if the document is moved, it will inherit the permission structure of the new location to which it is moved. Privacy settings are nested in the document such that if it is moved, its privacy settings will not change, regardless of the location to which it is moved.

From a governance perspective, information rights management is an excellent way to ensure that certain actions are not completed on specified documents, such as not printing the document or not forwarding the document to those outside the organization. For mission-critical documents or for documents that contain highly sensitive information that, if revealed, could cause significant damage to the organization, adding privacy to a strict permission structure is a prudent risk-mitigation method, especially when you consider that most data leaks are caused by careless human actions.

Not all Office 365 plans contain information rights management. SharePoint Online IRM relies on the Microsoft Azure Active Directory Rights Management service to encrypt and assign usage restrictions. You might need to set up the Azure Active Directory Rights Management service before using the IRM service in SharePoint Online. Microsoft has a good rights management roadmap that can help you set up rights management within your tenant. You can find that article at this location: *https://technet.microsoft.com/library/en-us/jj585005.*

This setting in SharePoint Online, as shown in Figure 9-11, does not set up information rights management. You merely use it to specify whether or not information rights management will be used within your SharePoint Online deployment. The Refresh IRM Settings button is used to update SharePoint Online with changes made to your underlying Azure Rights Management service.

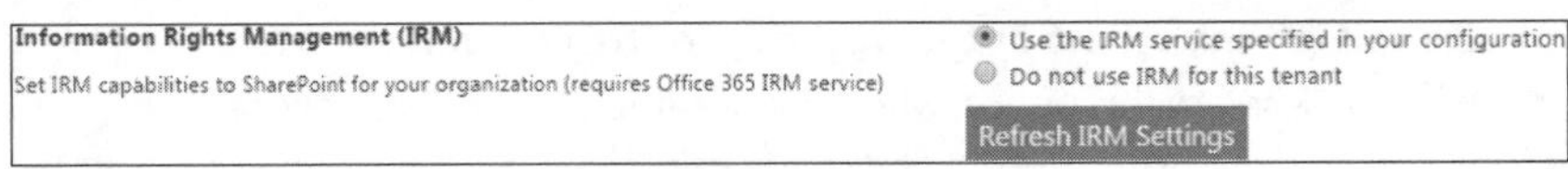

FIGURE 9-11 Information Rights Management (IRM) settings

If you want to see if information rights management has been set up in your tenant, just open an Office document in Edit mode and click on the Info link in the left pane. From there, click the Protect button (in Word, it is the Protect Document button) and then highlight the Restrict Access option in the shortcut menu that appears. If you receive the options shown in Figure 9-12, your information rights management is working. If it's not working, start with the TechNet article I mentioned earlier and work through those steps to ensure the information rights management service is set up correctly.

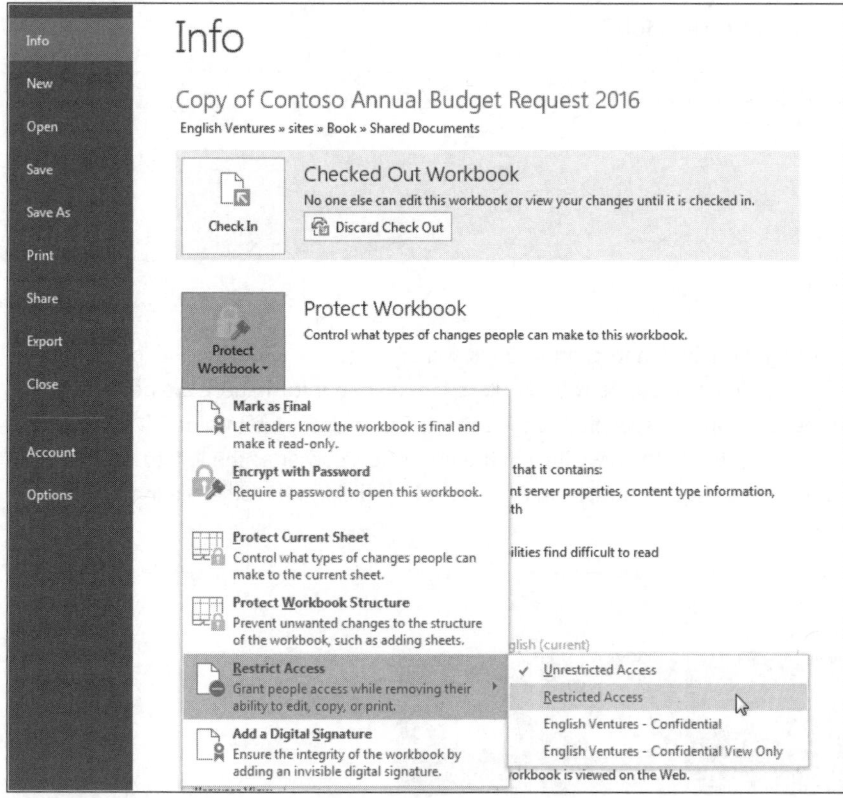

FIGURE 9-12 Verifying the information rights management service is working

Start A Site settings

The Start A Site settings make up the self-service site creation feature for SharePoint Online. But this feature differs from the SharePoint 2013 feature in that the SharePoint Online version allows users to create new sites within an established site collection, whereas in the SharePoint 2013 platform, users are allowed to create new site collections.

When you enable this function, the screen will update to offer you several configuration choices, as illustrated in Figure 9-13. You'll be able to specify the location at which you want new sites created, whether or not the site classification taxonomy will be available for users to tag their sites with, and whether a secondary contact will be required on the site's ownership. Moreover, if you want to use a custom form that has additional instructions or covenants with which the user must first agree before creating the new site, select the Use The Form At This URL check box and enter the appropriate URL. Remember, the default form allows only the input of a site name, so if you want any additional information input into SharePoint Online, you'll need to create a custom form.

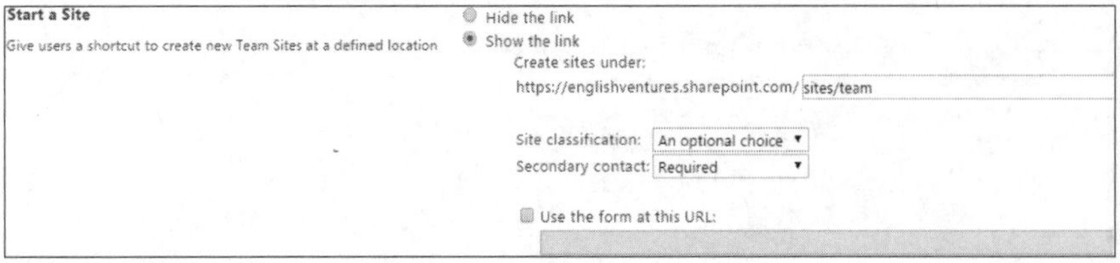

Start a Site
Give users a shortcut to create new Team Sites at a defined location
Hide the link
Show the link
Create sites under:
https://englishventures.sharepoint.com/ sites/team
Site classification: An optional choice
Secondary contact: Required
Use the form at this URL:

FIGURE 9-13 Start A Site settings

After this setting is enabled and configured, it will apply to the New sites link on the Sites page such that when a user clicks New and enters the needed information, the new site will be created in the location you specified in the setting. This page is a bit unintuitive in that you're clicking New (rather than New Sites) in the upper-left corner as the link to create a new site. You'll find the Sites page illustrated in Figure 9-14 by clicking the Sites tile in the Office 365 tile selection screen.

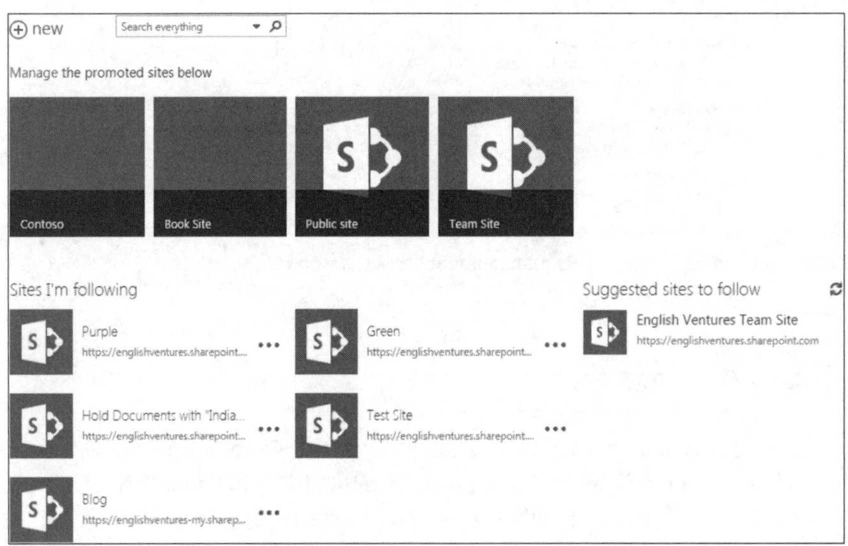

FIGURE 9-14 New sites link on the Sites page

A couple of final notes. First, the site will always be based on the team site template. There is no option to change this. Second, users need to create site permissions at the root site of the site collection. To minimize the security risk involved with this, you'll want to create a custom site permission. To do this, follow these instructions:

1. Go to the root of the site collection under which the new sites will be created.
2. Navigate to the permission levels within the site collection. (Site Settings, Site Permissions, Permission Levels).
3. Click Add A Permission Level.
4. Enter **Create Subsites** as the Name for the permission level.
5. Select Create Subsites from the Site Permissions list. Because of certain site-permission-level dependencies, other permissions will automatically be selected. This should not be a concern for you.
6. Click Create at the bottom of the screen.
7. Navigate back to the Site Permissions page.
8. Click Create Group in the ribbon.
9. Enter **Create Subsites** as the name for the New Group.
10. Select the Create Subsites As Permission Level check box at the bottom of the screen. If you want everyone to be able to create subsites, set the Allow Requests To Join/Leave This Group to Yes and set Auto-Accept Requests to Yes as well.
11. Click the Create button at the bottom of the screen. Your new group is created with the Create Subsites permission level.
12. Add Everyone Except External Users to your new group to give everyone within your tenant permissions to create new sites. Be sure to deselect the option to email everyone an invitation to the group.

Everyone should now have permissions to create a site within the specified location. As a general rule, I suggest creating a separate site collection under which new sites will be created. All things being equal, I don't recommend creating a plethora of new sites under a site collection that has an existing purpose, such as the Managed Metadata Service hub or a portal of some type.

Custom Script settings

The next section in the SharePoint Online settings is the Custom Script section. In this section, you can decide to deny users the ability to run custom scripts within their site collections in SharePoint Online. Some customizations are easily committed with the in-browser tools provided by Microsoft, such as changing a heading style or page layout. However, other customizations are more complex and require the use of custom script or markup language inserted into web parts or run with Microsoft Windows PowerShell.

The ability to add a custom script to sites and pages is given through the Add And Customize Pages permission at the site level. As the SharePoint Online administrator, you can turn this ability off or on globally here in the Settings area. However, bear in mind that anyone who creates personal sites and team sites is, by default, a site owner and, thus, can add any script they want to the pages on that site.

In addition, when users create new sites via the Start A Site method (as discussed in the previous section), they too become the site owner for that site and thus have the ability to run scripts in their site or sites. I strongly suggest that you limit the amount of scripting allowed in order to maintain the security and integrity of the sites in your tenancy.

Bear in mind that when you turn off scripting, this does not remove the Add And Customize Pages check box from appearing in the permission levels at the site-collection and site levels. The check box will be selectable, but its selection will be overridden by the global settings you select here.

Your selections are illustrated in Figure 9-15. The defaults are to turn off all scripting, so you'll need to manually and intentionally open up scripting as described in your two choices for users to be able to run scripts within the SharePoint Online environment. Essentially, your two choices are to open scripting to the user's personal sites or to the sites the users have created on their own.

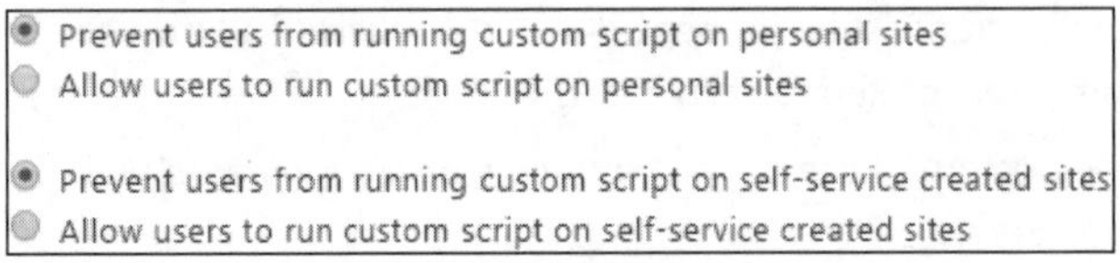

FIGURE 9-15 Custom script settings

Preview Features settings

You use the Preview Features setting to preview new features that Microsoft is building for SharePoint Online and Office 365. This differs from the First Release program in that you're *previewing* these features without necessarily *using* the feature in preview. If you like to see cutting-edge code, leave this setting enabled, which is its default setting (not illustrated).

Access Apps

By default, the Access Apps feature is enabled in SharePoint Online. It allows users to create databases in the cloud and present them as apps within their own sites and site collections. Creating an Access App is easy enough—it's a default app that can be added to your site by clicking the Add An App link from the cog in the upper-right corner of your site.

Once the app is created, you'll design your tables for the database using Microsoft Access 2013. In my example, because I continue to teach topics other than SharePoint, I thought it would be fun to create a simple course-registration system as an Access App. So I opened Access 2013 and selected several prebuilt tables to help me build my registration system. Fortunately, Access 2013 has all the templates I needed to create this system. So after adding several table templates, I clicked the Launch An App button in the Access 2013 ribbon (not illustrated) and my Access App was created, as shown in Figure 9-16. The tables are listed in the left pane, and the detail of the table in focus is displayed in the right pane.

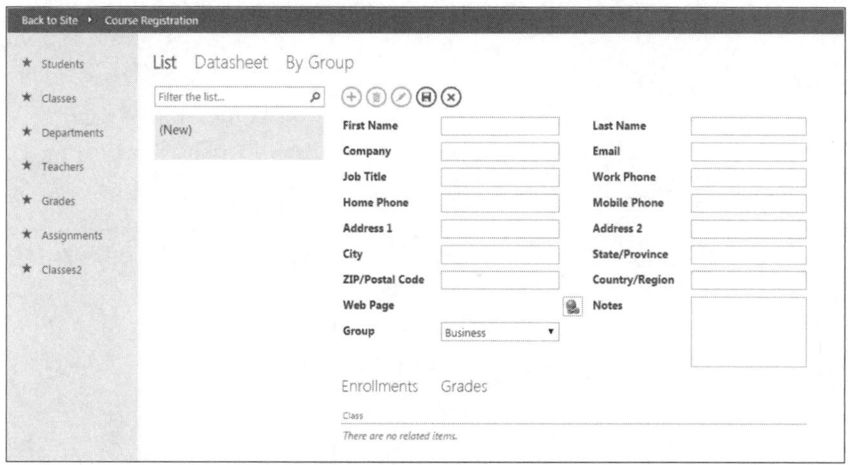

FIGURE 9-16 Access App for a sample course-registration system

Access Apps is one of the key features of SharePoint Online that can add real value to your organization. I recommend that you consider leaving this setting at the enabled default and teach your users how to work with Access 2013.

Summary

In this chapter, I covered a number of disconnected, single-decision configuration options that you, the SharePoint Online administrator, will need to consider as part of your administration activities. In the next and final chapter, I'll spend some time at the site-collection level discussing administrative activities in which you're likely to engage as the SharePoint Online administrator.

CHAPTER 10

Site-collection administration

In the old days of Microsoft SharePoint Portal Server 2001 and Microsoft Office SharePoint Server 2003, the ability to administrate the portal was the paramount administration skill in the SharePoint world. Well, we live in a different world now. Beginning with SharePoint Server 2007 and the advent of Central Administration plus the concept of a *site collection*, the core administrative tasks that have high visibility and end-user impact have been divided between these two areas. With SharePoint Server 2013, the importance of good site-collection administration has grown to the point where the site-collection administrator now has more prominence and is at least as important as the back-end Central Administration administrator.

Site-collection administration can be a complex area if you make it out to be that way. In my estimation, it is more diverse than complex—in part, because of the diverse ways the site collection can be built through the activation and deactivation of features. The ability to manage a wide range of features is no small feat, but it need not be overwhelming either. Because there is more than ample content on the topics of site collections and site administration currently available on the web, I'll focus on site-collection administration from a business and IT pro's viewpoint. Instead of going through the same old "Click here, then here and see this" type of instruction, I decided to venture (perhaps) where I shouldn't: I'm going to discuss the governance and shared administrative tasks that result from working within a highly connected system, where the administration activities are found based on the level of SharePoint at which you're working.

As the product has matured through its versions, I've noticed that more and more site-collection administration tasks have been assigned to the system administrator in many organizations. At minimum, there is a shared administrative effort where the end-user, site-collection administrator and the system administrator have informal agreements on which administration tasks will be performed by whom. This is a common scenario.

It might be helpful at this juncture to point out that as more features are activated in a site collection, more administrative effort is required to successfully manage that site collection. It's no small thing to go in and activate, for example, the Cross-Site Publishing, Content Organizer, Publishing, or In-Place Records Management features. Each of these—as well as others not mentioned here—can substantially change how the site collection behaves and have (potentially) wide-ranging ramifications for your organization.

In addition, with some features, governance issues must be addressed before they are activated. With other features, process issues should be addressed to leverage the feature to its fullest. All these considerations can become overwhelming to many on the business side of SharePoint, so the business folks leave much of the site-collection administration to the IT pro community. These people don't want to take the time to learn site-collection administration and, frankly, they don't find these activities to be within their scope of work. So the job of the IT pro shifts to include much of what happens at the site-collection area.

Many IT pros are fine with this. Given their tendency toward high control of their servers and networking environments, most would rather do the work themselves than to clean up after an unwise or careless user who screwed things up. It's easier to do it right the first time than it is to fix something that went wrong—especially when the diagnosis of the problem consumes hours, not minutes. Management tends to prefer this as well, for obvious reasons. Ironically, what started as a self-service platform (think back to the Windows SharePoint Services 1.0 platform and even earlier with the Digital Dashboard in the Microsoft Exchange 5.5 public folder tree) has evolved to be an administratively heavy program that requires significant skill and training to properly manage. This observation is given with the acknowledgement of the great value that SharePoint has brought to Microsoft customers.

Some have correctly observed that many IT pros are not sufficiently trained or experienced with the business side of what their organizations do. Many are not trained in process management, taxonomy development, eDiscovery, strategic organizational leadership, and so forth. As a result, they have a primarily technical view of what SharePoint is and what it can do for their organizations. Rather than seeing SharePoint living within a family of processes that support key organizational strategies and goals, some IT pros see SharePoint as an end in itself: they equate the feature set with a requirements set. Their attitude can be summed up as follows: "If SharePoint can do it, then it must benefit my organization." As I've said elsewhere in this book, just because SharePoint can do it (regardless of what *it* is) that doesn't mean that it should. The technically focused IT pro doesn't understand this—at least not entirely—because she doesn't fully appreciate that process efficiency and culture considerations usually trump technical elegance. And as processes change, their underlying information systems must adapt to those changes. Businesses don't implement processes for the fun of it; they implement them because the organization's survival depends on them running at a high level of efficiency.

Ultimately, organizations will find they need people who are cross-trained, if not cross-experienced, in both business and technology. This means they are looking for people who have a deep understanding of what it means to use a software package to support core business processes while, at the same time, understanding when the process must be adjusted to leverage the full value of the SharePoint Online platform. These people not only read white papers and KnowledgeBase articles about SharePoint, they also read publications like the *Harvard Business Review*, *Wall Street Journal*, or *Financial Times*. They are people with degrees, certifications, or both in business as well as computer science. These people are out there, but they are few and far between.

Governance honeycomb

You can think of *features* as a way of adding functionality to the SharePoint environment, whereas *apps* add functionality at a layer above the platform. Feature functionality is exposed through the SharePoint interface, whereas app functionality is exposed through the app itself. Without features, SharePoint would do nothing, literally. So, as new features are activated, SharePoint is thought to become more complex to administrate.

For these reasons, I've taken the liberty to list some of the features, describe what they do, and offer some thinking around the governance, training, risk, and process considerations for that feature. My only goal in this area is to help you gain a more business-oriented context because you probably will find yourself administrating SharePoint Online in that context.

For lack of a better framework, I'm going to borrow from the honeycomb concept to talk about the interactivity of the following elements that I feel should be considered before features are activated. Some features won't require this type of forethought or scrutiny, such as activating the Disposition Approval Workflow, but as we move forward with SharePoint's maturity through platform updates and new feature development, I suspect more and more features will have an impact on process, risk, compliance, training, and taxonomy. I suggest that when you look at features you see processes, risk, taxonomies, and training as part of the matrix. For the feature to have maximum benefit in your organization, the following considerations need to be thought through (in no particular order):

- **Configuration** The feature needs to be properly set up and configured in SharePoint.
- **Process** The feature needs to enhance or make leaner the process or processes it is supporting.
- **Taxonomy** The information managed by the feature needs to be adapted into the larger information organization taxonomies.
- **Training** Users need to know how to use the feature *within* the processes they are currently using.
- **Risk** A risk assessment needs to be completed before the feature is activated.

- **Compliance** The risk assessment should inform the organization of the compliance actions that will need to be undertaken to lower or mitigate the risks.
- **Administration** The more complex the feature, the more administration effort that will be required. And more than likely, new administrative roles and responsibilities will need to be established.

This honeycomb is illustrated for you in Figure 10-1.

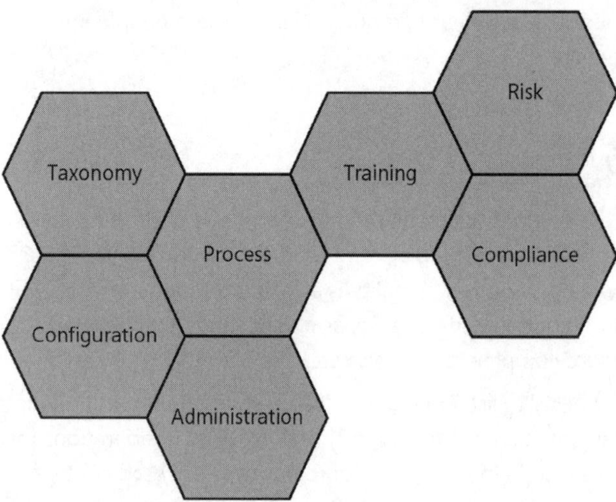

FIGURE 10-1 Governance honeycomb

When it comes to implementing a new feature that has some inherent complexity, you will do yourself a world of good if you take the time to go through a process that considers these various areas before the feature is activated. You'll find that changing one cell of this honeycomb will likely result in changes to other cells within the honeycomb.

As part of writing this chapter, I put together an elementary process for your consideration that you can use as a starting point for understanding the ramifications of activating a feature in SharePoint Online. The process I offer in this chapter is not meant to be set in stone, but rather to be a discussion starter within your organization to come up with a process that fits your culture and adds real value when you select new features to use within SharePoint Online. I don't believe you'll use this process for every feature activation, but I do think some of the features—such as those I discuss later in this chapter—are good candidates for this proposed process before they are activated for the first time in your tenant.

I know there will be some pushback to using a process for feature activation in SharePoint Online. Many readers, if not most, will say that this process is overkill. They will say that it adds unnecessary work without adding a commensurate amount of value to the organization. Many will say it simply isn't needed or that an organization will not go through all this drama simply to activate a feature.

Well, I offer this process because I believe it will save you support and training headaches in the future. I have repeatedly observed over the years that SharePoint has a unique way of surfacing culture and business dysfunction to a level that no other platform from Microsoft has been able to achieve. When the dysfunction is surfaced by SharePoint, the organization tends to view that dysfunction as a technology problem rather than as a process or cultural problem. So more money, time, and effort are spent on resolving a technology problem rather than solving the core culture or process problems. In my estimation, the pushback is a tacit admission that the organization is not in a position to admit the real value that a feature-selection process can bring to it. It's like the fisherman who is fishing for a 30-pound fish, hoping to catch that fish with a five-pound test line, all the while defining their real problem as the boat in which they are fishing is the wrong boat.

In highly dysfunctional organizations, people simply find it easier to blame the technology than to fix the culture or processes. These organizations don't even bother putting together a set of business or technical requirements before they decide to use their software platforms. If they do attempt to codify a set of business requirements, they down-step the feature set of the platform into their requirements documents and then say that they need those features with little consideration given to how their processes, training regimen, taxonomies, and potential risks might be negatively or positively affected by their feature-to-requirements equation. This happens, quite frankly, because most organizations don't document their processes. They don't have a formal structure for organizing their information, and they don't consider the risk of opportunity costs associated with a new or upgraded platform deployment. Nor do they consider how training might enhance the use of the software platform to achieve greater returns on their software investment. Removing soft opportunity costs is amazingly difficult in many organizations.

Figure 10-2 illustrates a sample feature-selection process an organization should implement.

So let's go over this process in a little bit of detail. First, a suggestion is made that the feature is needed to help solve a particular problem within your organization. Assuming that the suggestion concerns a feature with enough complexity to have an impact on processes in your organization, you might want to consider engaging in this feature-selection process. Because engaging in a process like this will consume time and resources, your organization will need to develop a set of criteria to decide whether or not to engage in the process.

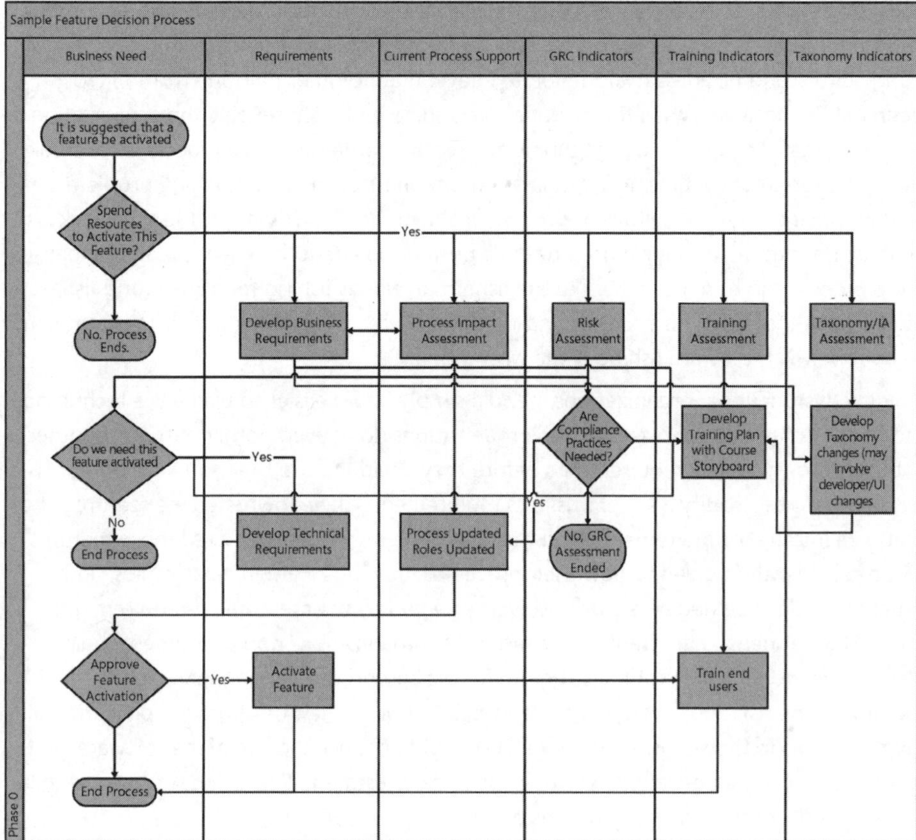

FIGURE 10-2 Sample feature-selection process

Once the decision to go forward is made, the first part is to perform four basic assessments while building the business requirements. The questions you're trying to answer in this first part are these: if we turn on this feature, what will the impact be in these four areas and what are the requirements we need this feature to fulfill? The four assessment areas are as follows:

- Process impact
- Risk assessment
- Training assessment
- Taxonomy assessment

The level of detail and depth of these assessments will differ from company to company. Some companies will look for highly detailed reports, while others will simply want a one- or two-paragraph summary assessment from somebody who understands what the feature can do and how it will impact that area of assessment. Note that these are not technical assessments of the feature. Instead, they are business-based and process-based assessments that account for how activating the feature will affect these four core areas of a governance honeycomb.

In terms of the process assessment, the reality is that any time you change a software package—which is what a feature activation is (essentially)—more than likely you'll change the process within which the user is working. Sometimes those process changes are quite small; other times, they are quite extensive. Even small changes can cause considerable consternation in some environments.

A common example of a process change is when users stop using their file shares and begin using SharePoint Online to host and manage their documents. Some might suggest that this is a software platform change, not analogous to a feature activation. But it is still a good example to use to discuss process change. If users had to open a browser each time to save a document to a SharePoint library, file servers would still reign in most environments, even though they have fewer document-management features than a SharePoint document library. But Microsoft knew this, so it built into SharePoint Online the old Groove technology, now called *OneDrive for Business*, where document libraries can appear in the File Save As dialog box and the Windows Explorer interface as shared drives into which users can save documents directly from their office clients, such as Microsoft Word, Excel, or PowerPoint. By minimizing the user-interface changes, even though it is a platform change, Microsoft increased its chances of a positive user adoption of SharePoint Online.

Believe it or not, I've met users who felt the real change came not when they moved from using a file server to document libraries, but when some of the taxonomy features—such as the Document Information Panel—were introduced. One might think this is a small thing—a simple panel that exposes the metadata fields on a document that allows the user to tag the document with correct metadata. But I'll attest that such an introduction is a huge deal in some environments. So even simple interface and process changes can be something that launches multiple discussions and perhaps some pushback.

The risk assessment for a feature activation has to do with what people might do wrong with the new technology, either nefariously or inadvertently. The risk assessment is meant to help inform the organization of the potential governance and compliance issues that should be considered before the feature has been activated and rolled out. In addition, once the compliance and governance issues have been articulated, they can be added to the end-user training materials to teach users what not to do with the technology.

The training assessment should consider how best to disseminate both the new technical information as well as process changes and compliance behaviors. Remember that governance is merely the enforcement of compliance behaviors, so helping your end users understand how the organization intends to enforce compliance should also be part of end-user training. If an enforcement mechanism cannot be developed that can be reasonably used, you simply need to create a guideline for the actions you're discussing with your end users in the training and ask them to comply by appealing to their goodwill.

Most features in SharePoint Online deal in one way or another with the organization of information. So looking at how information is organized, how the feature activation will change how information is organized, or how it might enlarge the quantity of information (such as when the publishing feature is activated and publishing pages then can be tagged) should also be part of your assessment. And the results of that assessment should be included in the end-user training materials.

Once the assessments have been completed, the organization should have enough information to decide whether or not to activate the feature. The organization might decide to not activate the feature and instead purchase a third-party product that has enhancements in those areas that the built-in feature simply doesn't have. Or the organization might decide to stay with the current processes and technologies and not activate the feature. Often organizations select less efficient methods of managing information if they feel the pain of change is too high for their user base. I have seen this on multiple occasions when working with customers. However, if the organization decides to move forward with the feature activation, a set of technical requirements will need to be developed to inform IT professionals and (potentially) the developers how the feature should be configured once it is activated.

In addition, the outputs from the assessment process should focus on updating the process in your Process Center of Excellence, the training materials, any taxonomy changes that are needed, and any governance and compliance requirements. The more open and direct your communication is with your end users, the more likely it is that they will adopt these changes. Explaining the relative advantages of why this change is needed and how it will benefit your users in their day-to-day work is essential to helping them adopt change.

What is not shown in the process in Figure 10-2 is any kind of feedback loop that helps inform the organization how the feature implementation can be improved. This process also does not include a feedback loop for users to inform the organization how the feature might be used in other ways that will benefit the organization. We call this *reinvention*: Users utilize an existing technology in new, unforeseen ways to benefit other processes or other parts of the organization. You will definitely want to have a reinvention feedback loop that is outside of your feature-selection process.

You might be thinking to yourself, "Hey, this process could be used in a number of ways other than just selecting features." You would be right. This process can be used to select a platform or new hardware. Or it can be used in any situation where organization-wide assessments need to be done to decide if the organization will move forward with some type of significant change. There's really nothing amazingly insightful about this process, other than it has been applied specifically to the selection of features. I presented here as a feature-selection process because I have seen many times how organizations go into SharePoint, turn on a bunch of features, and then wonder why people are confused as to how SharePoint actually operates. Subsequently, these organizations decide to avoid using SharePoint at all. If you want to ensure that you have a low return on your SharePoint investment, just activate all the features and don't explain anything to anyone. That's really a great prescription to ensure that people stay with their current, less efficient processes.

User-adoption principles

When we talk about user adoption of a new technology, which is what a feature activation is at the micro level, we're wading into the area of *diffusion theory.* In his seminal book, *Diffusion of Innovations*, Everett Rogers outlined the innovation adoption process that is directly applicable to how users adopt new software platforms and technologies. Although Rogers was working with Iowa farmers in the 1950s, his ideas and research should not be discounted when it comes to user adoption of new technologies in SharePoint Online. Let's review his work as it relates to new features and technologies in SharePoint Online.

Adoption occurs through a process in which a new idea (innovation) is communicated through certain channels over time among members of a social system. If it's perceived as a new idea, it's an innovation. The innovation decision process is illustrated in Figure 10-3.

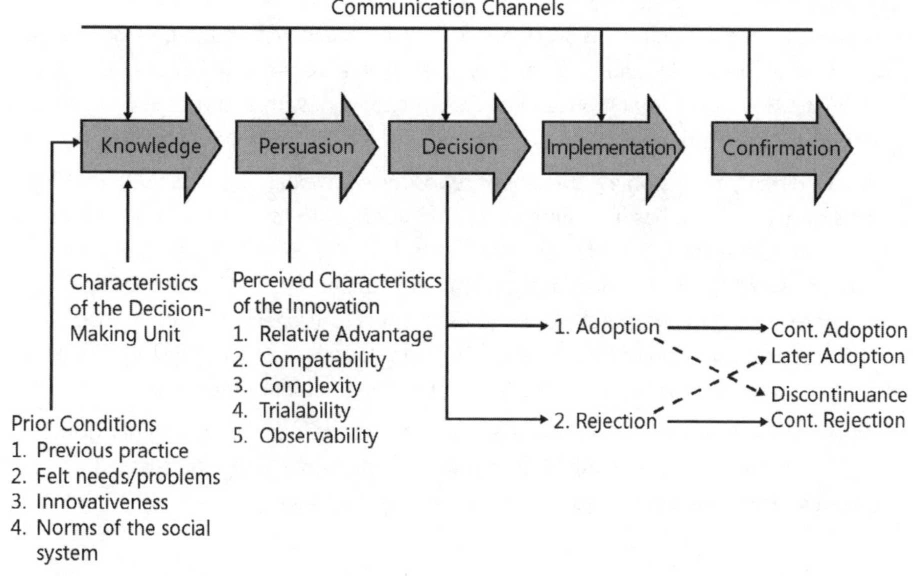

FIGURE 10-3 Innovation adoption process

Notice in the figure that there are five perceived characteristics of the innovation that people consider as they are being asked to adopt the new technology or idea. Understanding these characteristics is highly important in understanding how to develop an adoption program that will enable your organization to drive adoption of new technologies that support emerging process, taxonomy, and governance changes.

Relative advantage

Relative advantage is the degree to which an innovation is perceived as better than the idea it supersedes or is replacing. It does not matter if SharePoint has an "objective" advantage in your opinion or even in the opinion of many leaders in the organization. What does matter is if the user perceives the new feature as advantageous. If it is not seen as advantageous, the user will not adopt the technology. If adoption is forced on the user (which is really assimilation, not adoption), the user will use the new feature when paying attention to compliance issues. When given the opportunity—however small it is—the user will jettison the use of that technology in favor of whatever she feels is better for herself, personally. The way to demonstrate relative advantage is through training and seminars that show a comparison such as this: "Here's how you do it today—here's how you can do it tomorrow in a more efficient process with SharePoint Online."

For example, suppose an executive assistant is given a new SharePoint site in which to host the documents and calendars she works on for several executives. In the past, she saved her documents to an online document repository. She's now asked to save her documents to SharePoint Online. She has several thousand documents to work with and creates roughly 100 new documents each month.

She can save directly to this online document repository as well as SharePoint Online. But because she's busy and often has little time to think about how to manage her documents, she developed a folder system that fits her work habits, how she conceptualizes document organization, and so forth. So she tries saving documents to SharePoint Online only to discover that she's forced to enter metadata and use a check-out/check-in process. Also, sometimes, the synchronization of OneDrive for Business doesn't work as expected. She never had to deal with these things when using her present online document repository.

What do you think she'll do? She'll conclude that SharePoint Online is slowing her down and is more hassle than it's worth, so she'll stop using it. Remember, with cloud-based technologies, it's easier than ever to go around IT and just do it yourself.

Compatibility

Compatibility is the degree to which an innovation is perceived as being consistent with the existing values, past experiences, and needs of potential adopters. Their needs are probably the most important part: SharePoint might be perceived to be incompatible with the following:

- Existing Enterprise Content Management (ECM) systems
- Existing intranet systems
- Existing information flow processes

For example, suppose the same executive assistant also needs to save records in an existing records library hosted in an existing records-management system. If a new Records Center is set up in SharePoint Online, but no one tells her why she should save records in

SharePoint Online vs. the existing platform, she's likely to continue using the current platform because it is compatible with how she already works. If users are presented with two platforms that do (essentially) the same thing, the users will select the platform with which they are most familiar and have worked with the longest.

Complexity

Complexity is the degree to which an innovation is perceived as difficult to understand and use. This is probably the highest hurdle to overcome when introducing a new feature or platform, because any interface change will likely be perceived as an increase in complexity.

Because updates to software platforms tend to increase the number of features, they necessarily increase in complexity too. Seldom will you see feature enhancements to any software platform where the complexity is reduced simultaneously. Users might like the new functionality, but they'll not like the new complexity. It's human nature.

When you ask a user to adopt a new feature, you're asking him to like a new way of doing things while, in all likelihood, increasing the complexity of what it takes to manage his information. This is why including a training assessment is essential in your pre-activation phase: training can reduce complexity by introducing familiarity.

In addition, the quality of relationships and opinions within the social system are foundational to this characteristic. Remember that when you're asking users to adopt a new feature, there will be opinions discussed among the users outside of your earshot. What they say about the new feature can be strong enough to either kill or ensure the adoption of the new feature. Moreover, you'll need to remember that new ideas that are simple to understand are more readily adopted. This is why "closing" out SharePoint features is such a good idea. It gives your users time to adopt a discrete set of functionalities and find they are not as complex as originally thought. That gives them time to settle in to the use of that feature before another one is introduced.

Trialability

Trialability is the degree to which an innovation can be experimented with on a limited basis. New ideas that can be tried on the "installment plan" will generally be adopted more quickly. Learning by doing overcomes risk and uncertainty, which is why training is so important to a SharePoint platform and to feature adoptions. If you can, figure out a way for users to view and work with the new feature in a safe environment that mimics their real-world environment.

Observability

Observability is the degree to which the results of an adoption of a new idea are visible to others. The easier it is for individuals to see the results of an adoption of the new feature or idea, the more likely they are to adopt it—especially if the person they are observing is a well-respected opinion leader within their social group. Remember that social groups (and collaboration groups for that matter) almost never mirror the organization chart of who reports to who. So look for your opinion leaders and look for the core social groups in your organization. Then get the opinion leaders within those groups to adopt the new feature, if not a new platform.

User-adoption groups

You'll need to become content with the notion that not everyone will adopt a new feature (let alone a new platform) at the same rate or for the same reason. Rogers showed in his work that there were five distinct adoption groups. Ignoring them is an excellent way to ensure you have a very low return on investment for your SharePoint rollout. Figure 10-4 illustrates these groups when applied to a bell curve. The following sections describe each group.

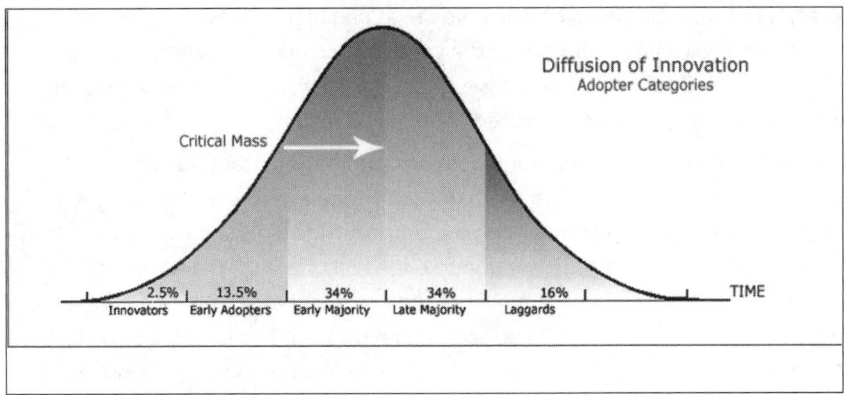

FIGURE 10-4 Adoption groups in diffusion theory

Innovators: Venturesome

Innovators are about 2.5 percent of your user base and should be the employees who work in your early-adopters program—if you have one. These folks enjoy a high degree of mass media exposure, and they like new stuff simply because it is new. They seek out new ideas and tend to have wide interpersonal networks. They are willing to cope with higher levels of uncertainty to learn new technologies. They are willing to accept setbacks to some extent to move forward with a new technology. Get them on board—they will help you understand early on where the problems are in your feature or platform relative to how they work and how they think. They can be an invaluable part of any rollout in your organization. They are the gatekeepers to new ideas in the organization, so be sure you're working with them early on.

Early Adopters: Respect

Early adopters are the next group that naturally adopts new technologies. They have the highest degree of opinion leadership within the organization and often serve as a role model (Observability) for others in the later adopting groups. They will help trigger critical mass when they adopt a technology because the next group (Early Majority) will be watching what they do and the results they get. This group will also decrease the level of uncertainty about the new technology. They are respected by their peers and embody successful, discrete use of new ideas. They are not willing to accept setbacks like the Innovators are, but if the technology works, they are willing to adopt it relatively quickly.

Early Majority: Deliberate

This group represents roughly one-third of the population. They seldom hold opinion-leadership positions and are connected to both Early Adopters and Late Majority members. This makes them an important link in the adoption process. People in this group will take their time—sometimes an extended amount of time—to adopt a new technology. In spite of their ability to observe the successes of a new technology for the Innovators and Early Adopters, they will still deliberate over adoption, sometimes to the frustration of others involved in the process. They are willing to adopt, but they will never lead in that process.

Late Majority: Skeptical

This group is also roughly one-third of the population. They tend to adopt a new technology because of peer pressure, economic necessities, or both. Before they adopt a new technology, they will require most uncertainty to be removed. Trialability and observability are important components that will help them adopt a new technology.

Laggards: Traditional

Many in the Laggards group are considered isolated in one way or another from the social system of the organization. They represent a small group. Their point of reference is the past, and they are suspicious of new ideas. Their rate of adoption lags far behind the other groups. They must be certain the new ideas will succeed before they will even consider adopting. They are fairly impervious to peer pressure. You'll find that it's usually economic forces that drive them to adopt a new technology.

Other notes on adoption

Bear in mind that the rate of adoption of a new technology will result in different groups using the new technology at different times with different levels of maturity. Also, bear in mind that as adoption moves through the groups, the ease of use must increase, not stay the same. The later groups will not adopt a complex technology, so you'll need to ensure that, over time, the new technology becomes more pragmatic and simpler to use, if possible.

Finally, because user-adoption ideas move through the social systems within your organization, you need to understand that adoption is as much about the quality of the relationships within the social systems. So paying attention to the "soft" factors is much more important than doing seminars that show some cool tips and tricks in SharePoint Online.

When you ask users to adopt a new feature or software platform, use this information to evaluate your adoption plans to make sure you're not violating one or more of the principles discussed in this section.

Feature discussions

Let's shift our attention to a discussion of the more commonly used features in a site collection and see what we can learn about them from a business standpoint.

AGGREGATED BUSINESS CALENDAR

This feature displays multiple calendars in an overlay format alongside Exchange and SharePoint calendars. From a training perspective, there are three groups to train: those who populate the calendars, those who configure the calendars in SharePoint, and those who consume them. From a governance perspective, you'll need to ensure that all three groups have a reason to see all the information on all calendars, both from a permissions standpoint and a process standpoint. Users who need to see only a subset of the information—even if they are not restricted from seeing it—will likely ask for a different overlay matrix to be developed or to be given the permissions to change the matrix for themselves. You'll also have to look at the process for how the calendars are populated. Presumably, this shouldn't be an extended discussion, but in some organizations where the calendar represents clash points, you might find that who gets to decide what activities and appointments go into a given calendar can be an important decision.

CONTENT TYPE SYNDICATION HUB

This feature turns on the *content type syndication* part of the Managed Metadata Service. From a training standpoint, the main group to train are those charged with creating the content types that will be consumed in the enterprise. In addition, you should train your taxonomists and librarians—really, anyone charged with managing the upper layer, enterprise taxonomy of the larger federated taxonomy. From downstream standpoint, you'll need to train users who create and use content types at the site-collection and site levels how to extend a syndicated content type with additional metadata fields (site columns) for their own purposes. From a governance perspective, you'll likely need to have a site-column naming convention so that global site columns that are syndicated with the content types do not conflict with local site columns created in the site collection. Moreover, you'll need to ensure that you have limited permissions to the content type hub, so that only those with certain roles and permissions are allowed to go into the site-collection content type gallery and make changes to the syndicated content types.

CROSS-SITE PUBLISHING

Cross-site publishing enables a site collection to designate lists and libraries as catalog sources. Building a robust cross-site publishing solution can be a rather large project to perform in SharePoint Online. I suggest that you do not activate this feature until you fully understand why you're activating it and you thoroughly document how the catalogs are going to be consumed by the consuming sites. Once you document the process, you want to have training for everyone who touches the process in regard to cross-site publishing. From a governance perspective, you're not harmed if cross-site publishing is activated and then not used. However, simply for the reason of reducing user-interface confusion, you should leave this feature turned off, or deactivated, until you know that you need it.

CUSTOM SITE-COLLECTION HELP

Custom site-collection help is a library that can store custom help files for your end users. Over the years, I've been surprised at how many companies do not take advantage of this feature and do not partner with vendors to write custom help files for the organization. For example, it would not take much effort for a company to grab stock training materials from a SharePoint training company, and then have those materials customized with their own internal screenshots and nomenclatures to produce a custom help experience that is genuinely helpful to their end users.

From a training perspective, you'll want to work with your support and documentation teams to help them understand how to create custom help files. You'll also want to train your site-collection administrators how to implement custom help files. From a governance perspective, you can link to all types of governance information regarding SharePoint, taxonomies, a center of process excellence, and so forth to give your users easy traversal between SharePoint and other systems that will help them do their jobs more efficiently.

> ***NOTE*** **Many organizations create Process Centers of Excellence that allow them to bank and organize their processes while also improving them on an as-needed basis. Process centers also give the organization a way of describing their capabilities.**

DOCUMENT ID SERVICE

The document ID service assigns unique IDs to each document in the site collection. In theory, the IDs can then be used to retrieve the documents, regardless of their physical location. Because the document ID service is not configurable, you're at the mercy of the code in terms of how it assigns the numerical portion of the ID. You can purchase third-party applications that will turn the document ID service into more of a configurable, true document numbering service. But if left by itself, the document ID service will give you marginal benefit. From a training perspective, you'll need to train users how to search for documents using the document IDs that are generated by the system. From a governance perspective, you'll need to have a site-collection document ID naming convention, and ensure that this naming convention is made known to all your users as part of their training.

DOCUMENT SETS

Document sets provide the content type necessary to treat a group of documents as a single unit for permission and workflow purposes. A taxonomy can be applied to document sets as well as to the individual documents within the sets. Under the hood, document sets are really SharePoint folders with additional capabilities. From a training perspective, users will need to be trained how to add the content type to the library in which they want to create document sets, use the document set to group one or more documents into a single unit, and then how to apply metadata and permissions both to the set and to the documents within the set. From a process standpoint, you should have a process that clearly requires a document set. For example, if you have a group of documents that needs to be routed through a workflow approval as a single unit, this is an excellent example of when a document set is needed. From a governance perspective, I see no additional governance required on document sets other than the normal assigning of metadata and ensuring the correct permissions are signed as well.

IN-PLACE RECORDS MANAGEMENT

The concept of what a record is means different things to different organizations. In most cases, a *record* is thought to be a truthful and honest representation of the topics and content discussed within the document. And in most cases, the concept of a record has legal implications. Activating in-place records management is an easy thing to do, but from a governance perspective, I caution you not to do it without first talking with your legal advisers as to the ramifications of maintaining records. In some organizations, the maintenance of records is expected and required both by governmental and industry standards. In other organizations, such as small service or consulting companies, the maintenance of records is optional. This is especially true in privately held businesses. Inconsistently creating records in your organization could result in legal, negative ramifications down the road if you ever find yourself in litigation where the opposing counsel has the right to look into your SharePoint environment as part of their E-discovery process.

The in-place records-management feature is there to ensure that users do not have to send artifacts to a record center to have them declared as records. Once this feature is turned on, you'll need to make sure that users fully understand which artifacts and at what stage in their life-cycle process they will be declared as records. Furthermore, consistently applying the process will be important when it comes to undergoing a compliance audit or an E-discovery process. Few things will hurt your organization more than having some users adhere strictly to the records-declaration process while other users are careless in applying the same process.

This is why I tend to recommend that companies have either third-party or custom code that walks the SharePoint database and surfaces all the artifacts that have been declared as records. Performing spot-checks on the application of an in-place records process will help your organization ensure that it is fully compliant either with a regulatory standard or with an E-discovery process.

Finally, from a training perspective, this is not a once-and-done training effort. Presumably, your organization has implemented a records-declaration process for significant and legal reasons. If the process rarely touches the majority of your users, they will need to be regularly trained on the process, under the assumption that the old saying is true: "If you don't use it, you'll lose it." It is also good to remind your users of the importance of following an in-place records-declaration process. As the process is updated, of course, your users should be retrained.

OPEN DOCUMENTS AND CLIENT APPLICATIONS BY DEFAULT

This feature configures links to documents so that they open in client applications instead of web applications, by default. Essentially, by activating this feature, you're telling SharePoint Online to open up Word, Excel, or PowerPoint documents (and other office application documents) in the native application instead of in the browser.

I don't see a huge training issue related to this feature. Frankly, this seems more a matter of preference and how your users prefer to work with documents than it is a training, security, or governance issue. If your users like to work with documents in the native application because they are more robust, activate this feature. This doesn't preclude documents from being opened in the browser; it just means that, by default, SharePoint Online will attempt to open them within the client applications rather than the browser.

SHAREPOINT SERVER ENTERPRISE SITE-COLLECTION FEATURES

Activating this feature is more of an issue in a SharePoint 2013 environment than it is in a SharePoint Online environment. You'll find that in most SharePoint Online site-collection templates, this feature is activated. The reason for this is because the features that come with this feature—such as InfoPath Forms Services, Visio Services, Access Services, and Excel Services Application—are the more heavily demanded functionalities that users want in SharePoint Online. So it makes sense for Microsoft to turn this feature on in your tenant.

From a training perspective, each of these areas will require end-user training. For example, if users want to use Visio Services within one of their site collections, it makes sense to show them the advantages of displaying Visio drawings within the site and be sure they understand the functional limitations between the Visio 2013 client and Visio Services interface. From a governance perspective, I don't see a lot of risk associated with using any of these functionalities, as long as the information is properly secured and, if you're using information rights management, properly privatized. From a process standpoint, it seems to me that the services make some processes a bit leaner, enabling users to view information without having to open the client application.

SHAREPOINT SERVER PUBLISHING INFRASTRUCTURE

The publishing infrastructure makes so many changes to a site collection that it would take literally two to three pages simply to list all of them. These changes take a typical site collection and turn it into one that can be used within a content-management system. The publishing infrastructure of a regular document library—and here, I'm referring to the major minor versioning of a document library—is augmented with a pages library, but it also has major minor versioning within it. Whereas wiki pages will have the navigation embedded within them to traverse from one page to the next, publishing pages that are created in the pages library have the navigation pulled from their metadata fields, which are populated presumably by the values you find in a term set in the Managed Metadata Service.

Over the years, I've observed that there is not much available instructor-led training focused on the publishing model at the site-collection level. If you're going to turn on publishing at the site-collection and site layers, you're doing so for particular reasons. More than likely, you're doing it to try to support content-management processes you want in place when using SharePoint. To that end, users who are charged with creating and publishing pages, administrating the navigation, creating local term sets, pending terms from global term sets, scheduling pages to appear on certain dates and go away on the other dates, and embedding graphics and video content into these pages should be well trained in both the entire publishing process as well as the technical details on how they accomplished each part of the publishing process within the SharePoint Online interface.

As a follow-on to this, note that the cross-site publishing feature is complementary to, not redundant of or mutually exclusive to, this publishing-infrastructure feature.

From a governance perspective, I don't see an elevated risk associated with the activation of the SharePoint Server publishing infrastructure. However, I do see risk associated with inadvertent or careless mistakes made while managing and working within the publishing infrastructure. Your greatest risk mitigation when it comes to this feature is training. The other core risk is that the process of content management is not well defined within the organization, and this leads to confusion among users about how to use the technology given to them to fulfill the content-management process. Remember, any time there is confusion at the desktop in any process, users will naturally fill in the gap. They will make assumptions about what they think is true as a way to fill that gap, and then they will proceed to work as if their assumption is the correct one that fills in that gap. While a minority of your users will be paralyzed by not having a clear process, the majority of users will simply modify what they know about the process to meet their own needs and to fit their own work habits.

When you turn on the SharePoint publishing infrastructure and enable publishing at the site layer, you will create the opportunity for users within the site collection to create their own local term sets in the Managed Metadata Service. How this is done is discussed more fully in Chapter 4, "Managing a term store in SharePoint Online." From a governance and training perspective, the users who work with that local term store will need training in your organization's taxonomy as well as in how to create content types and use those term sets as navigation elements in your site and as refiners in your search results. Frankly, because the learning curve can be rather steep in this area, those who spend a consistent amount of time working within the publishing infrastructure to manage content in SharePoint should have that reflected in their job descriptions.

SITE POLICIES

Site policies allow site-collection administrators to define retention schedules that apply to the site and all of its content. Although these are relatively easily to implement, site policies always represent an information-management, training, governance, and process set of issues. I say this is because the retention of information and its eventual disposition is an issue that organizations wrestle with on a regular basis. This is why the disposition of information should have a very clear process associated with it that includes several evaluation stages. These stages include evaluating information for the legal and risk ramifications if the information is no longer available, loss of intellectual capital if the information is not retained, lack of regulatory compliance (if needed), and loss of goodwill if customers, partners, or vendors need that information in an unforeseen way in the future.

In rare circumstances, some might need a process that calls for information hosted within the site to be printed in hard copy before a site policy is applied to the site. But the larger point is that your process to wind down a site should specify who makes these decisions, how the approval of the disposition of the information is committed, what your organization will do with backups of such information, and whether to have any rollback windows if the need arises to recover this information after the disposition workflow process has been completed.

As regulations, case law, industry standards, and the needs of your customers and internal teams change, so will your disposition process for old information. Users should have regular training to ensure that they understand what the process is, and spot-checks or other methods should be used to ensure that users are strictly following the process.

CONTENT ORGANIZER

You use this feature to create metadata-based rules that move content submitted to this site to the correct library or folder. To the extent that your information-management processes are clearly articulated, the content organizer can have enormous value when you're moving content in your organization. But the content organizer can also add value when those processes are not clearly articulated, as you'll learn in just a moment.

From a training standpoint, the groups that need to be trained include your content creators, those who manage content types, as well as people who are responsible for making sure the content is moved correctly from one location to another. Many organizations don't have a role that is responsible for content movement and velocity. They generally rely on workflows or the content creators to move the content as needed.

From a staffing standpoint, I've seen an emerging role in several organizations for people who act as an extension of a librarian role, in that they manage the deliverability of artifacts to the correct location when users don't know where to send them. Users can send documents to the content organizer's drop-off library, which is basically a holding library for documents that still need to be routed to their final location, when they know a document should be moved out of their SharePoint site but don't know where it should be moved to. After consulting with users about where the users think the artifacts should be hosted, the person in this role moves the artifacts for users and builds more organizer rules to accommodate those specific situations. Over time, the rules become robust enough that most users can move most artifacts without manual intervention.

The better way to accomplish this is to have a well-thought-out file plan that informs the content organizer administrator of the routing rule or rules that need to be created before they are needed. But because most organizations don't do file plans, they fall back to less efficient processes like the one I described in the previous paragraph.

From a governance perspective, the loss of information is a real cost to the organization. Several studies have shown that users spend an average of three to five hours a week trying to find information that they know exists but don't know the location of. Cycles spent toward finding information are cycles lost on being productive for the organization. And the truth is that you can't use what you can't find. Moreover, information that is hard to find is hardly used. And information that is considered lost, from a process viewpoint, need not be information that is unfindable by anyone at any time. Instead, I suggest you define the phrase "lost information" to be missing information that is needed at a point in time during a process that forces the user who needs to use that information to scurry around hunting for it instead of using it to get their job done. The content organizer can be used to help lower the amount of lost information in your organization, but it will take persistent administration and training, as well as process and document life-cycle improvement, to realize a significant gain from using the content organizer.

FOLLOWING CONTENT

When you turn on this feature, you allow users to click Follow on a document so that they can be informed through their social media technologies of changes to that document. They also can follow sites and people within SharePoint Online. In a very real sense, there is little difference between the Follow feature and alerts. It's just that the Follow feature has a social aspect to it, whereas alerts seem to be outdated and rather impersonal.

The value of this feature to your organization will directly depend on the value that the social technologies bring to your organization. From a training standpoint, there is little to train on other than to show users how to click the Follow button and then find a list of those artifacts and people that they are following within the SharePoint user interface. From a governance perspective, I don't see much risk in activating or deactivating this feature. From a process standpoint, I find it hard to fathom that the Follow button could be a significant aspect to any of your core processes.

Shared administrative configurations

A few administrative activities at various levels within the site collection involve a shared responsibility of configuration and management between you, the information technology professional, and the site-collection administrator. I call these *shared administration activities* for lack of a better phrase.

The connection between managed properties and Query Builder

The first area of shared administration that I'll discuss will be the connection between managed properties and Query Builder. Query Builder can be found by clicking on the Launch Query Builder button (shown in Figure 10-5) in the Query Transforms section of building a new result source. (You'll need to select either the Local or Remote SharePoint protocol for the button to be active.) When you click it, Query Builder launches (shown in Figure 10-6), and you're able to build a unique but persistent query of the index that will return the exact results you're after.

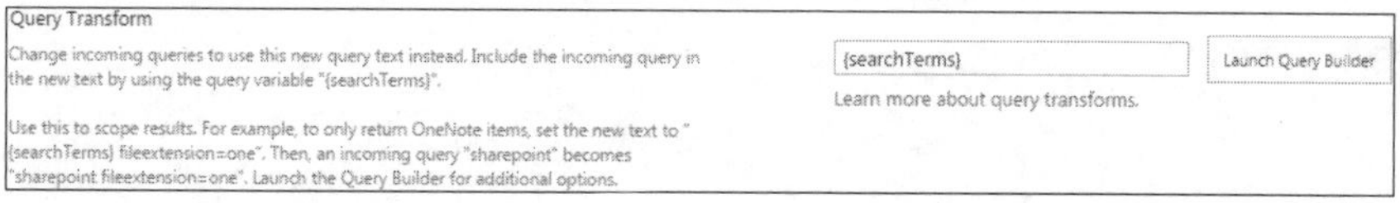

Query Transform
Change incoming queries to use this new query text instead. Include the incoming query in the new text by using the query variable "{searchTerms}".
Use this to scope results. For example, to only return OneNote items, set the new text to "{searchTerms} fileextension=one". Then, an incoming query "sharepoint" becomes "sharepoint fileextension=one". Launch the Query Builder for additional options.
{searchTerms}
Launch Query Builder
Learn more about query transforms.

FIGURE 10-5 Launch Query Builder button

FIGURE 10-6 Property Filter list in Query Builder

Notice that on the Basics tab of Query Builder, the properties you will use to filter the query are managed properties that have been set as queryable in the properties of the managed property. (See Figure 10-7.) Your site-collection administrators cannot configure a managed property as queryable—only you can do that within the SharePoint admin center. So what you do at your end directly effects the managed properties your users can use when building their queries.

Main characteristics	
Searchable: Enables querying against the content of the managed property. The content of this managed property is included in the full-text index. For example, if the property is "author", a simple query for "Smith" returns items containing the word "Smith" and items whose author property contains "Smith".	☐ Searchable
Advanced Searchable Settings: Enables viewing and changing the full-text index and weight of the managed property.	Advanced Searchable Settings
Queryable: Enables querying against the specific managed property. The managed property field name must be included in the query, either specified in the query itself or included in the query programmatically. If the managed property is "author", the query must contain "author:Smith".	☑ Queryable

FIGURE 10-7 Queryable setting in the properties of a managed property

> ***MORE INFO*** **You can learn more about managed properties in Chapter 6, "Configuring search."**

The connection between the query rule builder and the term store

When you're building a new query rule on the Add Query Rule page, you can specify a context in which the rule will fire. The architecture is such that if the context rules are met, the rule will fire. But the interface is a bit confusing because it talks about *categories*, not *term sets*. On this page, the categories are populated with term sets from the term store. Not specifying a term set will not keep you from building a new query rule, but using them can specify when they fire. For example, you can specify a context in which the rule doesn't fire unless the title of the user who is executing the query is equal to a certain position title.

Figure 10-8 shows the Context section of the Add Query Rule page, and Figure 10-9 shows that when you click the Add Category link, a selection dialog box from your term store appears. This means you'll need to ensure you have term sets that can help your users receive more relevant result sets when they are building query rules.

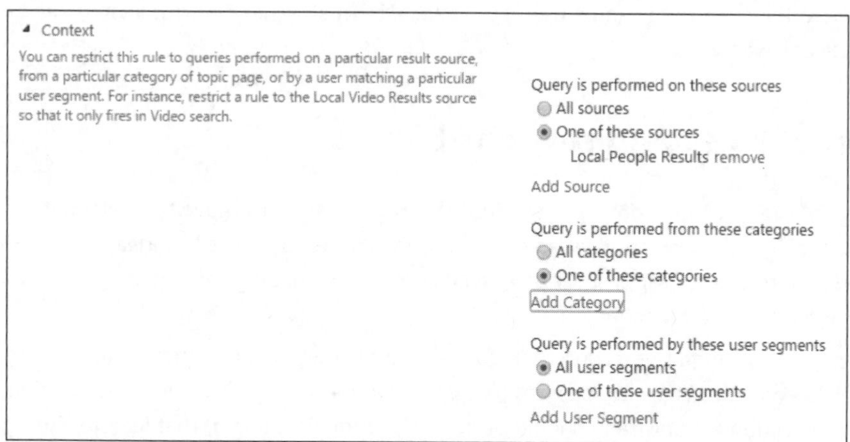

FIGURE 10-8 Context section of the Add Query Rule page with the Add Category link

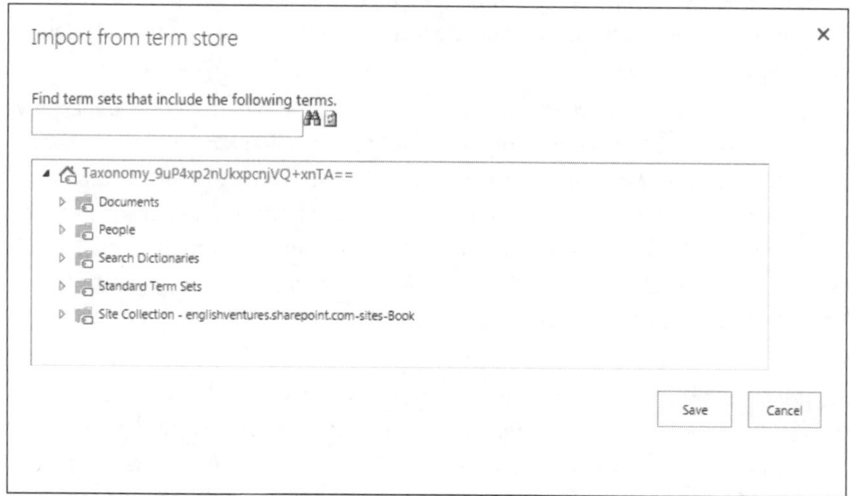

FIGURE 10-9 Term sets from the term store that are offered as category selections after clicking the Add Category link

The connection between the global and local term stores

As discussed in Chapter 6, after the publishing features are activated at both the site and site-collection level, you're given the ability to create a local term set from the navigation configuration page under the Look And Feel section of Site Settings. When you create a local term set, it is available only to the term-store administrators in your local site collection. However, you can pin terms from global term sets that were created in the term store. This ability to pin terms is a shared administrative activity where the terms that you or your tenant librarian build in the term store can be used by the local term-store administrators in their respective site collections.

Division of roles and responsibilities

Sometimes confusion exists as to who is responsible for which administrative tasks when it comes to managing a site collection vs. an individual site. I'd like to offer a few ideas that might help define roles and responsibilities when it comes to managing these items in SharePoint.

The first principle I suggest you consider is connecting the role of administration to the feature that was enabled. What this means is this: if the feature is enabled at the site-collection level, the site collection administrator should perform the administration of that feature. For example, if the Document ID feature is activated, which is a site-collection-level feature, the document ID administrative effort should fall to the site-collection administrator. By the same token, the Content Organizer feature is a site-level feature, so the owner of the site in which the Content Organizer feature is activated should be responsible for managing the settings and the rules for the Content Organizer.

Some features require a cooperative effort because they create a shared set of administrative activities. The feature that comes to mind in this regard is the Publishing feature. To experience the full "goodness" of publishing in a SharePoint site collection, you need to activate publishing at both the site-collection and site levels. In this situation, a level of cooperation needs to exist between the individuals in the Site Collection Administrator and Site Owner roles. In many organizations, both roles will be assigned to the same individual; but in other organizations, two or more people perform these two roles, leading to a need for ongoing cooperation and collaboration.

The second principle is this: when you're assigning roles, those who are interested in performing these roles should be given preference. I realize that what I'm writing here will not work in some organizations, but I've observed these administrative roles (both site-collection administration and site administration) being given to people who couldn't care less about performing these tasks and then finding the tasks are rarely completed. There needs to be some genuine interest on the part of the person who is being assigned either administrative role.

The third principle is this: as more sites are created within a site collection, the need to divide the site-collection-administration and site-administration roles between two or more individuals increases. By way of contrast, if a site collection has a few sites—say, less than five—both the site-administration and site-collection-administration roles probably can be performed by the same individual. However, if a site collection has numerous sites—say, more than 50—it seems improbable that the same individual can perform both the site-collection-administration and site-administration tasks in an effective manner. This principle assumes that as the number of sites increases in a site collection, user interaction and demand for services also steadily increases and that this demand will be sustained over the long haul. I know this might not be the case in a minority of situations, but in general, I think this assumption is reasonable.

The last principle I'll offer is this: the closer you can connect the functions within the site collection to one or more processes, the more you should allow the processes to inform your thinking about who should be performing individual administrative tasks, whether those are site or site-collection administrative tasks. Usually, in a lean process, certain roles perform certain business tasks that involve the use and, sometimes, the transformation of information. Those who need the information in a certain form at a certain time within the process should be consulted when SharePoint administrative tasks have a direct impact on their ability to work effectively and efficiently within their processes.

Summary

In this chapter, I tried to shift the discussion about site-collection administration into a business and governance context, rather than presenting a technical and "how to" discussion. Most likely, you'll be asked to administrate one or more site collections. When or if this happens, keep in mind the connection to process, taxonomy, risk, and training your work has within your organization.

Index

A

B

C

M

N

O

P

Q

R

S

T

U

V

W

Y

About the author

Bill English works as a Solutions Architect with Summit 7 Systems, specializing in Enterprise Content Management, Taxonomy, and Process development with customers who work within the SharePoint technologies.

Bill also works as an Associate with the Platinum Group in Minneapolis,
working with small business owners in turnaround situations, growth strategies, and buy/sell engagements. He consults with new businesses and nonprofits to help them establish their long-term vision and organizational core values.

Bill is an Adjunct Faculty member at the University of Northwestern in Minneapolis, where he teaches ethics and other business courses in the university's adult and undergraduate programs and is a Licensed Psychologist in Minnesota as well as an NRA and Minnesota and Utah Carry instructor.

Bill holds two masters—one in theology and the other in psychology—and recently completed the requisite studies to earn the Certified Professional in Business Process Management (CPBPM) from Villanova University.

Bill can be heard Wednesday mornings on the Faith Radio network (*myfaithradio.com*). Faith Radio is a network of eight radio stations in the upper Midwest, including the major markets of Minneapolis/St. Paul and Kansas City. Appearing as a regular guest on *Austin Hill in the Morning*, Bill discusses the integration of faith with small business ownership and writes about the same at his blog at the *bibleandbusiness.com.*

You can reach Bill in one of two ways. If your inquiry has to do with SharePoint consulting or training, you can reach him at *bill.english@summit7systems.com.* For all other inquiries, please contact Bill at *bill.english@theplatinumgrp.com.*

Free ebooks